CONTRIBUTORS

Theodor W. Adorno

Peggy Kamuf

Friedrich Kittler

Philippe Lacoue-Labarthe

David J. Levin

Jean Starobinski

Klaus Theweleit

Samuel Weber

Slavoj Žižek

1993

Opera Through Other Eyes

Edited by David J. Levin

STANFORD UNIVERSITY PRESS   STANFORD, CALIFORNIA

Stanford University Press
Stanford, California
© 1994 by the Board of Trustees of the
Leland Stanford Junior University
Printed in the United States of America
CIP data appear at the end of the book

Photographs in "The Replay's the Thing"
by Peggy Kamuf are reproduced
courtesy of the Bettmann Archive.
Photographs in "Taking Place" by Samuel Weber
are reproduced courtesy of Mara Eggert.
Excerpts from Alice Goodman's libretto
Nixon in China appear by permission of the author
and Hendon Music, Inc., a Boosey & Hawkes Company.
Libretto © 1987 by Alice Goodman.

Acknowledgments

■ Many people and institutions have helped to make this volume possible.
The German Academic Exchange Service (Deutscher Akademischer Aus-
tauschdienst) in New York and its director Dr. Wedigo de Vivanco provided
key financial assistance at various stages: I was able to spend a year and a
half working at the Frankfurt Opera under the auspices of a DAAD grant,
and the DAAD sponsored a panel session on Opera, Technology, and Representation at the fifteenth annual meeting of the International Association
for Philosophy and Literature at Irvine in 1990, where some of the work
presented here was read. A generous grant from the Columbia University
Council for Research in the Humanities enabled me to complete work on
the manuscript. My greatest debt is to the contributors, who were willing
to venture beyond familiar disciplinary territory. And a number of friends
and colleagues offered essential critical commentary and assistance: Adam
Bresnick prepared stellar translations and, as always, offered particularly
astute criticism; additional (and significant) help came from Anthony Bar-

one, Michel Chaouli, Marie Deer, Edward Dimendberg, J. Courtney Federle, Ehren Fordyce, Joseph Kerman, Winfried Kudszus, Evi Levin, Thomas Y. Levin, Walter Levin, Michael Macrone, Veronika Rall, Diana Reese, Hinrich Seeba, and Kerry Walk; my thanks to all of them. My thanks as well to a number of people at or associated with Stanford University Press: Helen Tartar, whose editorial expertise was suffused with enthusiasm for the book; Peter Kahn, who shepherded the text through production with an exemplary combination of patience and determination; Cope Cumpston, who designed the book with imaginative zeal; and the two anonymous readers for the Press, who offered especially helpful commentary: incisive, insightful, even humorous. Finally, a note of appreciation to a number of people at the Frankfurt Opera, including Ruth Berghaus, Michael Gielen, Pamela Rosenberg, and Klaus Zehelein, each of whom provoked me into rethinking my sense of opera and paying closer and better attention to it.

D. J. L.

Contents

Contents

Contributors

■ Theodor W. Adorno is the author of a prestigious array of major literary-critical, musicological, philosophical, and sociological works. His publications available in English include *In Search of Wagner* (1981), *Against Epistemology* (1982), *Negative Dialectics* (1983), *Kierkegaard* (1989), *Alban Berg: Master of the Smallest Link* (1991), *The Culture Industry: Selected Essays on Mass Culture* (1991), and *Notes to Literature* (1991–92).

■ Peggy Kamuf is Chair of the Department of Comparative Literature and Professor of French at the University of Southern California. The author of *Signature Pieces: On the Institution of Authorship* (1988) and *Fictions of Feminine Desire: Disclosures of Heloise* (1982), she has also edited *Between the Blinds: A Derrida Reader* (1991).

■ Friedrich Kittler is Professor of German Studies & Media Theory at the University of Bochum in Germany. His *Discourse Networks: 1800/1900* was published in English in 1990; his other publications include *Grammophon, Film, Typewriter* (1986), and *Dichter, Mutter, Kind* (1991).

■ Philippe Lacoue-Labarthe is Professor of Philosophy at the University of Strasbourg, France. His books include *Heidegger, Art, and Politics: The Fiction of the Political* (1990), *Typography: Mimesis, Philosophy, Politics* (1989), and (with Jean-Luc Nancy) *The Title of the Letter: A Reading of Lacan* (1992) as well as *The Literary Absolute* (1988).

■ David J. Levin is Assistant Professor of German at Columbia University. His publications include essays on literature, ballet, opera, and psychoanalysis. In addition to his academic pursuits, Professor Levin has also worked extensively in German theater, serving as dramaturg at the Bremen Opera, the Frankfurt Opera, and, most recently, for William Forsythe and the Frankfurt Ballet.

■ Jean Starobinski is Professor of Literature and Intellectual History at the University of Geneva. Professor Starobinski is an Honorary Member of the American Academy of the Arts and Sciences; he has twice been awarded the Schiller Prize and has also received the Grand Prix de Littérature française. His extensive publications include *Montaigne in Motion* (1985), *The Living Eye* (1989), and *Jean-Jacques Rousseau: Transparency and Obstruction* (1988).

■ Klaus Theweleit is a cultural and literary theorist. His work has appeared in English translation in the two-volume *Male Fantasies* (1987–89). The first volume of a projected four-volume work entitled *Buch der Könige* was published under the title *Orpheus und Eurydike* in 1988; in 1990, he published *Objektwahl: (All you need is love—)*.

■ Samuel Weber is Professor of Comparative Literature at the University of California, Los Angeles, and Director of the University of California's Paris Program in Critical Theory. Professor Weber is known for his writings on Freud and Lacan, including *The Legend of Freud* (1982) and *Return to*

Freud: Jacques Lacan's Dislocation of Psychoanalysis (1991); a collection of his essays entitled *Institution and Interpretation* was published in 1987. Professor Weber is also active in theater production: he has served as a dramaturgical consultant for theater and opera productions throughout Europe.

■ Slavoj Žižek holds doctorates in philosophy and psychoanalysis and conducts research at the Institute for Sociology, Ljubljana. His most recent publications include *The Sublime Object of Ideology* (1989), *For They Know Not What They Do: Enjoyment as a Political Factor* (1991), *Looking Awry: An Introduction to Jacques Lacan Through Popular Culture* (1991), and *Enjoy Your Symptom! Jacques Lacan in Hollywood and Out* (1992).

A Note to the Reader

■ An unnumbered footnote at the base of the first page of each paper provides details about publication history and, where relevant, the translator. Additional notes are numbered one-up for each essay and are grouped at the end of the book. They are of two kinds: original and translator's notes. All notes are by the author unless they are enclosed in brackets and end with —*Trans.* or —*Ed.*

■ Paragraphs are signaled by ■ throughout; section breaks are marked by blank lines.

Introduction

David J. Levin

■ In his essay "Bourgeois Opera," Theodor W. Adorno refers to opera's odd historical function as "a bourgeois vacation spot." Like many vacation spots, opera is one where not much critical reading gets done. For the most part, literary and cultural theorists have shied away from any sort of sustained consideration of the form. No doubt their reticence has something to do with the sort of mastery that operatic analysis would seem to require: a familiarity with the operatic literature and, perhaps more daunting, with musical analysis as well. But I suspect that there are other reasons why theorists have kept their distance from opera—among them, taste. Writing in 1930, Bertolt Brecht described opera as a "culinary" art; today, opera, as both art form and social institution, has become more saccharine, more overdone, even more of an acquired taste than it was in Brecht's time.¹ Some of the qualities that may well have kept theorists away—the tackiness, the datedness, the bulk and bombast—have attracted critical interest, but mainly as they occur in other genres.[2] If North American and English literary theorists have pointed to opera at all, then they have usually done so in passing, along the course of an argument that is headed elsewhere. And opera criticism by musicologists and literary theorists alike has largely kept it that way.[3] But why would opera be off-limits to contemporary literary theory? The answer has to do with opera's place in cultural criticism and cultural criticism's place in opera.

■ This book responds to two related phenomena: a history of opera criticism that places music at the center, and the suppression or banalization of the libretto that has enabled that criticism. It is no coincidence that opera is no place for contemporary literary theory, for the introduction of certain practices and presuppositions of reading would challenge some of the most entrenched and jealously guarded notions of how and what opera communicates. That communication is usually conceived as necessarily auditory and musical: opera, in this conception, is a musical genre, a genre to be heard and enjoyed. The introduction of literary criticism into opera criticism does not necessarily threaten the primacy of hearing in the experience of opera, but it does challenge the claims that can be made for that hearing. The notion that operatic meaning resides principally if not exclusively in the music has reinforced two tenets of traditional opera criticism: first, opera is accorded the epistemological claims made for music (specifically, its status as nonlinguistic); second, it is exempted from the epistemological claims made against words (claims issued in structuralist and post-structuralist literary theory concerning the necessary heterogeneity and instability of linguistic signification). Insisting that opera be thought of as music has meant steering clear of critiques of language in opera and, beyond this, critiques of opera as language. By insisting that words contribute to the production of operatic meaning, we undermine opera's ability to mean what it says and complicate our own ability to say what it means.

■ Traditional opera criticism has effectively repressed this problem by disregarding the libretto, concentrating instead on the adjudication of musical meaning. And precisely because music cannot be said to refer to any one thing, it is made to refer to any number of things. Thus, contemporary operatic productions are regularly criticized for violating "the musical meaning" while that meaning is inevitably and necessarily left undefined. References to purported violations of musical meaning are usually smoke screens for a much more personal claim, namely, that a given production violates one's own jealously guarded sense of how a production ought to look and what a work ought to mean. Because these preferences are deeply personal, relying as they do on amorphous things like nostalgia and individual experience, it makes sense that they would be ascribed to the music, whose meaning likewise is understood to be personal and vaguely inarticulable. But this move to seek (un-)critical refuge in the music is a defensive move, a move that would avoid a contestation of meaning, instead seeking its sanctification.

■ The banishment of literary theory from the opera house has actually attracted some literary critics to opera, especially those seeking relief from their work as well as those frustrated by or hostile to recent developments in the discipline. Perhaps, then, we ought to amend Adorno's claim and think of opera as a vacation spot for the bourgeoisie's textual criticism, a spot where textual criticism goes on vacation.

■ If opera has traditionally been seen as a musical genre, and thus as an inappropriate place for literary-critical analysis, *Opera Through Other Eyes* seeks to recast opera criticism by redirecting it, not just to the words, but also to the difficulties that attend them. This book features a variety of critical perspectives, including deconstruction, discourse analysis, feminism, post-structuralism, and psychoanalysis. The authors are drawn from a variety of fields (comparative literature, literary theory, media studies, and philosophy); each is renowned for having staked out a prominent position in contemporary debates about the forms and structures of textual meaning; most have not previously written on opera. The book includes considerations of a variety of works (including German, Italian, and American operas) spanning operatic history, from Claudio Monteverdi and Alessandro Striggio's *L'Orfeo* (1607) to Alice Goodman and John Adams' *Nixon in China* (1987).

■ That is not to say that the volume covers either the full range of contemporary critical perspectives or the entirety of the operatic literature—far from it. But given the scope of this project—namely, to engage a number of leading literary theorists in a discussion of operatic texts—and the relatively modest forum provided by a single volume, it was inevitable that important works and composers from the operatic literature as well as important thinkers and trends in literary theory would be missing. The point of this volume, however, is not to provide a comprehensive survey of literary-theoretical approaches to opera but to suggest the richness of the material, a richness that may preclude comprehensiveness.

■ The essays presented here question the presumed stability of what we might warily term the operatic "text," suggesting that operatic meaning is hardly as unambiguous and unproblematic as is often assumed. My wariness of the term operatic "text" derives from its lack of specificity, for it encompasses first and foremost the libretto, but also—and less concretely—

those aspects of opera that can be read: for example, the music, the stage directions, and the preparation, presentation, and reception of the work (which encompasses the social deployment of a specific work or of the form in general). Despite the highly charged, expansive nature of the term, the primary focus of the essays presented here is on the libretto.

■ In a self-proclaimed polemic against the project of reading opera, Paul Robinson counsels fervently against employing the word "text" with reference to opera. While I share Robinson's unease with a term that is imprecise and overused, I do not share his conviction that students of opera should avoid the practice of textual analysis (which he refers to, with ironic imprecision, as "textual talk") because such analysis supposedly "disfigures the object of their love."[4] This is the old claim that understanding is inimical to pleasure, a claim that is especially familiar in opera criticism and one that this book is intended to contest. My argument with Robinson is extensive, and I will have more to say about his essay below; for now, let us focus on the prefix "dis-" in "disfigures." Surely the knowledge gained by demystifying a love-object (which in this case involves critically reading the libretto and, by extension, the operatic "text") allows us to figure that love-object, and figure it better. Thus, far from *dis*figuring an object of love, the process of textual analysis undoes the damage done by the disfiguring operations of an undifferentiated and uninformed rapture. To paraphrase Stephen Booth, any reader superstitiously fearful that the magic of an opera will vanish with a critical understanding of its sources need not worry any more than a student of zoology need worry that gazelles will slow down if he investigates the reasons why they can run so fast.[5] Put more directly: libretto bashing disfigures opera; libretto analysis does not.[6]

■ Of course, the libretto is not only bashed; more frequently, it is simply dismissed or ignored. Traditionally, the libretto has served a somewhat complicated aesthetic role. As the embodiment of poetic banality, the libretto has begged its own dismissal, staging the ostensible (and ostensibly singular) badness of the poetic goods that it delivers. Thus the libretto has served to direct attention away from itself and toward the music or spectacle or both. In short, the libretto has been made to create the listener. I mean this in a double sense, for the libretto has often been made (in the sense of created) so as not to attract attention to itself, in order to facilitate musical expression or at least not distract from it. In addition, opera criticism has made it fulfill this function, has, in effect, constrained it to do so. It is this latter phenomenon that I would like to consider here.

■ Let us return to Robinson's "Reading Libretti and Misreading Opera," where we encounter the familiar claim that opera is "in its essence not a textual but a musical phenomenon, and interpreters of opera should proceed with great delicacy when they come to discuss its textual component" (330). In issuing this call for critical decorum, Robinson is actually calling criticism off the text: "The important point," he announces a bit later in his essay, "is that an operatic text *really has no meaning worth talking about* except as it is transformed into music" (341–42; emphasis added). But why should this be so? Perhaps because the very notion that an operatic text has meaning is undesirable. For if an operatic text has meaning, then we might enter into discussions, even arguments, about that meaning. We can avoid this interpretive instability by disavowing the libretto and restricting our attentions to music and its nonreferential transcendent "unknowability." The practical implications of this disavowal are clear: the libretto must be disavowed *so as to forestall the introduction of reading into opera.*

■ Of course, one way to avoid the problems posed by the words is to ignore them. Having sworn off "textual talk," Robinson resorts to something we could term "pre-textual talk" in order to sing the praises of listening without a libretto. Thus he reminisces about a first hearing of Gounod's *Romeo and Juliet*. "The singing is so wonderful that I found myself listening to the performance over and over. I listened without a libretto; nor did I consult a synopsis of the opera. I simply indulged myself in the thing itself" (344). For Robinson, as for many other critics, opera's meaning *cannot* be textual and linguistic; instead, it is incontestably personal, inextricably bound to a nostalgic desire for an art form that is wholly absorptive, enveloping, and transcendental. To speak of the operatic text is to complicate that experience, since that discussion could easily strand us in the murky waters of discursive and referential instability. Robinson's indulgence in "the thing itself" is simple because its complications have been repressed, for as critiques of the notion of the thing itself have shown repeatedly, that thing is riven with the instabilities produced by its linguistic mediation. To experience "the thing itself" (and to indulge in it simply) is to deny this mediation, and this denial has to be directed at the words, at the most evident traces of language's entrance into opera. Robinson performs this very denial: in erasing those traces, in listening without a libretto, he stages a double escape— from the "prison house of language" and the perils of the symbolic into (or, to the extent that this is a regressive move, back to) the immediacy of music and the bliss of the imaginary.[7] As long as the words are repressed, the traces of this mediation remain remote, and opera can be enjoyed not for what it is, but for what it has become—a pure meta- or prelinguistic form of expression, a nostalgic trip to the imaginary, a vacation from language and the insights of contemporary language-based accounts of textual meaning.

■ Although musicologists have certainly participated in this disavowal, they are not its sole or even its principal practitioners. In fact, a number of recent publications have placed musicologists at the forefront of a movement to think critically and seriously about the role of words in the creation of operatic meaning. The recent publication of *Analyzing Opera: Verdi and Wagner* (edited by Carolyn Abbate and Roger Parker) suggests that musicologists are increasingly prepared to account for the heterogeneity of operatic expression: "'Analyzing opera,'" the editors write, "should mean not only 'analyzing music' but simultaneously engaging, with equal sophistication, the poetry and the drama." That simultaneous engagement challenges musicology on two related fronts: first, it uproots an entrenched aesthetic position, common but not exclusive to musicology, that regards the work of art as inherently homogeneous and unified; second, it dispenses with the convenient but inadequate conviction that opera is music alone.[8] In conceiving of opera as an "interplay of systems,"[9] *Analyzing Opera* outlines what amounts to a revisionist program for musicological studies of opera, a program that has great promise, even if, as the editors tacitly admit, it has yet to gain widespread acceptance.

■ But there are predictable disciplinary limits to the willingness of even the most progressive musicologists to engage in a serious discussion of the libretto's function in opera. Almost every statement of that willingness is accompanied by an assurance—presumably directed at wary musicologists— that the excursion into textual analysis is undertaken in the service of *musicological* understanding. Thus, in their Introduction to *Analyzing Opera*, Abbate and Parker subordinate their interest in poetry to the larger project of musical interpretation: "What of opera's 'interplay of systems'? . . . Reading libretti as poetry may well generate an interpretation at odds with the reading imposed by the music. Music can misread words; it can ignore them; its view is not always literate. If we are insensitive to the literary text, we are not in a position to know when music corresponds to words, or responds to words, and when it does not" (22).

■ This glowing and welcome endorsement of a new attentiveness to the words is fine as far as it goes, but it does not go far enough. For although Abbate and Parker are prepared to present work that offers heterogeneous readings of the music, they do not—nor do any of the essays in their collection—suggest that this heterogeneity extends to the text as well. Thus, in their conception (and not in theirs alone),[10] the words remain implicitly homogeneous and univalent, providing a presumably stable ground upon which music is seen (or heard) to rest, from which it takes off and to which it may return. But language's referential ground is hardly so stable: if we look (or listen) a bit more closely, we can perceive the shifting, restless quality of the words, how they take off and respond not necessarily just to the music, but by, from, and to themselves. Thus we might rephrase Abbate and Parker's observation: if we are insensitive to literary theory, we are not in a position to know—or at least to speculate about—when words correspond to words, or respond to words, and when they do not.

■ This is an important point, because it complicates a traditional and tidy juxtaposition of opera's signifying systems. For if words are recognized as an erratic player in the interplay of systems, we can no longer simply juxtapose music's ability to emote with language's ability to concretize and refer. If we take into account any number of recent critiques of that referentiality, our picture of a harmonious division of aesthetic labor between opera's referential and nonreferential systems (that is, between words and music) begins to dissipate. (This, then, is also a reason for *not* taking those critiques into account, since they undermine opera's status as an island of peaceful discursive harmony, a place where all the discourses get together and coexist happily.) Instead, the split between words and music presents us with competing modes of complicated referentiality. To those for whom such complication is undesirable and unattractive, the best and simplest option has been to repress the text, thereby eliminating the critique by rendering it inappropriate; to those for whom that complication is attractive and interesting, the best route has been to concentrate on the role of words in the production of operatic meaning. So in addition to serving as a vacation spot *from* textual analysis, opera can also serve as a largely unexplored and inviting spot for it.

■ It can serve as such a spot, but until recently it has not done so. For when they have turned to opera, literary and cultural theorists have tended to endorse rather than critique the primacy of music, if not its singular authority in the production of operatic meaning.[11] Why? As I suggested above, the argument for the primacy of music is an attempt to save opera from a threat to the presumed homogeneity of its discursive systems. The need to defend opera is all the greater because it is so susceptible to the critique: as an explicitly heterogeneous medium, opera is the logical vehicle for a critique of discursive homogeneity and stability.

■ The vacation spot is always an indicative spot, marking the need for escape and the cultural response to that need. In the United States, some of the most successful vacation spots are places (or, more precisely, stand-ins for places) that produce the artworks that temporarily forestall the very need for a vacation: Disneyland, Universal Studios. Thus we escape to the place where escapes are supposedly concocted, a place which is itself of course concocted as an escape. In turning our attention to opera, we end up attending—or, in the case of this book, attending to—an outdated spot, one that, while it bears affinities to today's vacation spots, also bears the traces of past scenarios of escape.

■ For Jean Starobinski, that escape was (and, upon reflection, is once again) an escape to someplace illicit: opera "leads us astray to chimerical shores where we become the toys of a powerful bewitchment." Over time, these shores have become familiar, and the stray course is by now well charted. But this familiarity does not make opera any less bewitching or chimerical. Opera does not lead us astray because we do not know the way, nor does it bewitch us because we are gullible; we do not become opera's toys out of some unwitting manipulation. Instead, opera's assigned and socially sanctioned function is precisely to bewitch and seduce. In this sense we can think of opera as a sort of Halloween for those who have outgrown trick-or-treating, where seduction and bewitchment are essential to the rhetoric of the event, but are hardly experienced except insofar as one consciously *chooses* to be seduced and bewitched. This is in part because opera is so evidently anachronistic. Today, the form and its peculiar grandiloquence function as a doubled escape: an escape to the escape from back then.

■ In fact, the determination to go back to an earlier (and lost) form of escape is integral to the very development of the form: opera was invented in late sixteenth-century Florence as part of a programmatic determination to re-create Greek tragedy. As such, it was born of nostalgia and marked from its inception by a determination to regain a lost anteriority. Not surprisingly, various scenes of loss and attempted retrieval became central to the genre, variations of what we might consider to be opera's primal scene. In the course of staging and restaging that scene, another scene evolved, the scene, that is, of the loss that characterizes subjectivity itself. In his essay "'The Wound Is Healed Only by the Spear That Smote You,'" Slavoj Žižek examines the history of opera and discovers "the contours of a certain vicious circle which defines the dimension of subjectivity." Responding to the famous line from *Parsifal* in his title, Žižek discovers in Wagner's last work a fundamentally paradoxical notion of subjectivity first articulated by Kant, in which "what we call 'subjectivization' (recognizing oneself in interpellation, assuming an imposed symbolic mandate) is a kind of defense mechanism against an abyss, a gap, which 'is' the subject."

∎ In a sense, opera has come to function as a sort of "fort/da" game played by and for the bourgeoisie, where its—opera's as well as the bourgeoisie's—origins are cast off in order to be recovered, but where the recovery masks (as it marks) the sense of absence that produces the diversion. The determination to regain that anteriority has continued to characterize the form, which often takes its audiences back to lost cultures and remote epochs (from Hades to ancient Egypt to prehistoric China, among others). Thus, like Greek tragedy itself, these lost cultures and epochs are simply (which is also to say lavishly) regained. What happens, however, when opera resorts to the recent past for its subject matter, when the historical trajectory of the "fort" is quite short, is, indeed, virtually "da"? In this case, opera would appear to be doubly out of its element: neither its composition nor its subject matter takes place "way back then." As Peggy Kamuf observes in her essay on Alice Goodman and John Adams' *Nixon in China*, the proximity of the historical "source" does *not* stabilize the relationship between the original ("historical") event and its ("contemporary") reproduction. "What falls due in the age of television, of teleopera, and of teleoperations in general is the long-deferred necessity to take into account the irreducible interval or deviation [we might add: the already lost anteriority] *within* the same event and the event of the same." Kamuf's essay raises a thorny question, namely, whether opera, itself marked by a loss of anteriority, also necessarily marks its subject matter as lacking a stable anterior referent, even when, as in the case of *Nixon in China*, that referent is a proximate, available historical event.

■ Perhaps the best analogy for opera in the age of television is professional wrestling, which, as Roland Barthes noted, issues its own claim to the inheritance of Greek drama. According to Barthes, "The virtue of professional wrestling is that it is the spectacle of excess. Here we find a grandiloquence that must have been that of ancient theaters."[12] Like wrestling, opera packs a peculiarly hyperbolized and highly stylized punch: it is the artifice that hits you. In his book *In Search of Wagner*, Theodor W. Adorno observes that "many of Wagner's heroes perish without physical pain, and indeed without any other justification than the mere idea that they should die."[13] Adorno's point does not just apply to Wagner: in opera, as in wrestling, the killer punch signifies immense pain and suffering although it hardly hurts. But that is not to say that it does no harm. For even if the specific punch does little physical damage, its address is indicative, as is our pleasure in viewing this spectacle of (feigned) humiliation.

■ The opera libretto is one place where we can locate the stylization and hyperbole of wrestling, what Barthes terms its "rhetorical amplification."[14] From the very beginning, the libretto has been subjected to a process of revision in which the oppositions that it presents become more strident, and the (usually Manichaean) terms become clearer. And yet, in the case of the libretto, this inflation is subject to an imperative of condensation, abbreviating the expression (but not inhibiting the terms) of hyperbole. As a document of the tension between the rush of bravura and the requirement of brevity, the libretto is often characterized by a radically cropped grandiloquence. In the libretto, the body of the text often appears to consist of its margins. In telling so much of so little, the operatic text represents a special form of overdetermination. The sort of lurid overstatement of understated narrative material that we generally, if also vaguely, associate with opera as a genre is, then, an important quality of the operatic text.

■ Hyperbole enters into opera's political and social registers as well. Here, the hyperbole of opera's subject matter bleeds into the appearance of its audience, such that both are often remarkably lavish. This shared penchant for lavishness has found its way into the thematics of operatic plots, which are often bound up with certain anxieties about consolidating aesthetic and social wealth. Since its inception, opera has seen and raised its audience's bid on the trappings of power, marshaling huge aesthetic resources in a massive display of aesthetic wealth—a massive display of massive display. In his essay on *L'Orfeo*, Klaus Theweleit points out that there is more at stake in that piece than the mere reproduction of social wealth in aesthetic terms. According to Theweleit, *L'Orfeo*—which Adorno labels "the first authentic opera"[15]—specifically stages the desire for a reproducibility of sound: the hero (Orpheus, the man) searches for someone (Euridice, the woman) to record and reproduce his tones. This need could be said to apply to opera in general, whose patrons need something (in this case, the opera *L'Orfeo*) to record and reproduce (in aesthetic terms) their claims to mammoth, imposing political power. Opera serves as one of the privileged media for the expression of this need.

■ As a cultural hand-me-down of the elite, opera has also served as one of the privileged cultural institutions (and an institution for the culturally privileged) effecting the orderly transfer of the cultural trappings of power from one generation of the "entitled" to the next. The violence that underlies this transferal is often displaced onto the stage, where it forms the explicit stuff of operas, which thus feature a struggle for accession to political and social power, a struggle that is complicated by the unstable (read: potentially illegitimate) grounds of the claim to inheritance.

■ As I suggested above, the critical literature on opera has recently become more ambitious, lively, and interesting. The publication in 1988 of *Reading Opera* did much to introduce literary critics and criticism to opera. The book's goals were modest: to present intelligent, insightful essays on individual libretti, most of which were produced in the latter half of the nineteenth century. But in setting such a modest goal, the editors did not elicit any larger discussion of the nature of operatic textuality per se. Thus, while they noted the symptomatic resistance to the study of libretti and traced its history, they and their contributors hardly analyzed the aesthetic implications. In fact, the editors seemed intent on defusing a potential (and potentially fruitful) confrontation between libretto and music when they wrote that "we certainly do not deny the primacy of music in the performance of opera and in opera scholarship, and would scarcely be interested in opera were it not for the music" (1).

■ Jeremy Tambling's *Opera, Ideology, and Film* has not received the attention it deserves, perhaps because its vocabulary is a bit daunting for those not versed in contemporary theory or because its tone is a tad arrogant, but more likely because the audience for the project of thinking opera and film together has not yet been assembled.[16] The widespread attention accorded the publication in 1988 of the English translation of Catherine Clément's

Opera, or the Undoing of Women introduced an unexpectedly large number of English-speaking readers to the dramaturgical analysis of opera. Clément's book not only directed attention to the fate of women on the operatic stage, but implicitly argued for a more general practice of what it preached: attentiveness to the thematics and machinations of operatic plots.[17]

■ Joseph Kerman's *Opera as Drama*, originally published in 1956 and reprinted in a revised edition in 1988, is still the best-known and the most successful general inquiry into the form. The book is cogent, polemical, and insightful; it is elegantly written and forcefully argued. Because Kerman is a musicologist, it is not surprising to find him arguing for the primacy of music in the production of operatic meaning: "Opera is a type of drama whose integral existence is determined from point to point and in the whole by musical articulation. *Dramma per musica.* Not only operatic theory, but also operatic achievement bears this out."[18]

■ This argument is less clear-cut than it appears to be. There is no doubt that operatic drama is in *some sense* determined by musical articulation (although, in his essay on Wagner in this volume, Friedrich Kittler argues forcefully that the reverse is true).[19] But it is not clear why that determination should be "integral" to the existence of the form. Is it not far more integral to Kerman's conception of the form than to its existence? Kerman's statement seems more readily applicable to musicology, to the mode of analysis, than to opera, the object of analysis. An examination of how operatic meaning is articulated would do well to take into account what Kerman terms "musical articulation," but it does not have to stop (nor does it have to start) there. Even if we grant a claim to the temporal or, for that matter, the conceptual primacy of the music, a primacy often ascribed to the notion of *prima la musica, dopo le parole*[20] (which is not necessarily a valid claim, nor one worth granting),[21] we still need to account for that second term of the phrase, for the (ostensibly subsequent, secondary) appearance and operation of the words.

■ Theodor W. Adorno has certainly produced some of the richest and most rigorous writing on opera, and yet most of his reflections on the form remain unavailable to an English-speaking audience. This volume includes the first English translation of Adorno's 1959 essay "Bourgeois Opera," one of his most polemical and comprehensive statements on the ideological, historical, and aesthetic status of the form.[22] In *Introduction to the Sociology of Music*, Adorno refers to "Bourgeois Opera" as an attempt to reconceptualize opera. The broad terms of Adorno's essay—he considers, for example, the aesthetic similarities between opera and film, the ideological character of operatic form, the paradoxical status of opera as the sole guardian of "the magical" in art—set the interdisciplinary tone for the various considerations of opera presented here.

■ Of course, scholars are not the only ones rethinking the role of words in opera. Since the late 1970's, a number of stage directors have produced radical rereadings of the traditional operatic repertoire, reviving a tradition of modernist interpretation which had its heyday in Weimar Germany.[23] These directors—Ruth Berghaus, Patrice Chéreau, Hans Neuenfels, and Peter Sellars, among them—have repositioned the listener as a figurative if not an actual reader, provoking an awareness that opera's synaesthesia also involves a significant textual dimension. Their productions—including Chéreau's 1976 *Ring* at Bayreuth, televised throughout Europe and North America[24]—have foregrounded some of the characteristics of the libretto that are normally repressed: thus they often offer a clear account of what is at stake in operatic dramaturgy, including the condensation of dramatic materials, the bald juxtapositions of situation, the Manichaean terms of character, and the strained willfulness of plot construction and resolution. In the first section of his essay in this volume, Samuel Weber considers one such production in some detail—Hans Neuenfels' staging of *Aida* in Frankfurt—focusing on the symptomatic antagonisms that it aroused.

■ The essays collected here follow the lead of these directors, seeking to rethink operatic textuality and to account for some of the bizarre meaning produced by the form. In doing so, they present an argument about the value of the words in destabilizing or at least displacing a sense of the homogeneity of meaning in opera.

Opera and Enchantresses

Jean Starobinski

■ Supported by princes, denounced by priests, opera was from the beginning of the game an ambiguous pleasure. Produced at first for the glory and
entertainment of the great, opera could not escape the reproach of those
who were alarmed by the spiritual risk run by fascinated souls. As the
triumph of high poetic language—exalted by the music, supported by
the orchestra, thrown back as an echo by the *tromp-l'oeil* architectures
of the sets—did it not carry the illusion of "the world" to its extreme? In the
view of religious censors, the peril of the theater and its "impurities" was
aggravated in opera by the effect of even more insidious seductions: voice,
dance, harmonies. . . . It was the trap where the Tempter lay in wait for souls
in order to take possession of them. One must not smile at these accusations
that were dictated by a fear of perdition. Later, Rousseau will renew them,
no longer to oppose the celestial vocation to the temptations of the world,
but to give preeminence to social and civic values: like the priests of the
preceding period, he will incriminate the diversion of consciousness by the

"Opera and Enchantresses" appears here for the first time in English. The translation is by Adam Bresnick.
The essay was originally published under the title "L'Opéra et les Enchanteresses," in *1879–1979. Le
Grand Théâtre de Genève: Reflets d'aujourd'hui* (Geneva: Fondation de Théâtre Genève, 1979).

bedazzlement of the spectacle, the evil spell which alienates individuals from their real lives and tasks. More recent grievances—according to which opera would be the quintessence of an elitist and "bourgeois" culture—only resume Rousseau's theses and, through him, those of the religious moralists. . . . Even if these attacks have lost their force of conviction, we must not be insensitive to their sting: we restore to opera a little bit of its original quality when we admit that there is no innocent pleasure, that opera leads us astray to chimerical shores where we become the toys of a powerful bewitchment. And perhaps our pleasure, if one recalls just how forgetful it is of the demands of reality, will be accentuated by the deficiency that it perceives in itself, a deficiency that renders pleasure even sharper and more exquisitely painful.

■ "The proper quality of this spectacle is to hold minds, eyes and ears in an equal enchantment," writes La Bruyère, who maintains that all means of wonder, including *machines*, are necessary to opera. We must give the word "enchantment" its strongest meaning: magic, sorcery, the illicit operation that mobilizes the forces of nature and the supernatural. It is for this reason that so many enchanters and enchantresses have reigned on the operatic stage from the moment of its inception, as if the authors had wished to represent and to personify the very prestige of the art they practiced among the figures they invented and among the situations they imagined. When the beautiful magicians of chivalric poems—Alcina, Armida—become operatic figures and display their irresistible powers onstage, when they attract warriors and hold them sighing and troubled in the delights of idleness and love, it is opera that reveals to us its own magical essence, its own perilous sovereignty. The gardens that open to an endless view, the enchanted palaces that take leave of the earth, the caves that offer a secret retreat are the marvels that respond to the call of the enchantresses and are at the same time the fictions necessary for the set designers, for the musicians, for the engineers of machines, for the actors to be able to demonstrate the full breadth of their resources. It is thus the art of the spectacle itself, with its power of illusion, that embodies and allegorizes itself, as in a mirror or *en abîme*, in those characters whose voice, gestures, and presence draw from mysterious sources the power of making desire's injunction triumph. That enchantresses should be susceptible to love, to jealousy, or to spite, that they should feel their power threatened in the end—it is this which intensifies their seduction: tears and groans in such beautiful people are formidable love potions. Through their mouths, the music redirects its power of harmony, its faculty of commanding stars, stones, and living creatures, in favor of profane and sensual ends. "Here is a harbor from the world," sings the voice of a nymph in the gardens of Armida, but this harbor only offers repose in the form of ephemeral delights immediately traversed by melancholy, delights that will soon vanish at the moment of awakening and of exorcism, when the consciousness of heroic tasks is reborn along with the image of the future and of the paths prescribed by Duty and Goodness. Magicians are vanquished in the fable which opera itself tells us: by delivering them to defeat, by making intervene some principle of disillusionment and thus dissipating the false immortality promised by the seducers, art conjures up its own danger and accedes to a new legitimation. Surely it is itself illusion, but it bears its own remedy within itself, it knows just as well how to represent the undoing of magic spells and how to celebrate a power of light that is stronger than the ruses of sensual delight. After having deployed its demonic magic, the music demonstrates that it can redeem itself—and gives itself a series of salutary representatives in the form of heroes and gods whose imperious voices dissipate the mirages devised by the enchantresses. These voices are generally heard *ex machina*, at the end of works, in the major chords of the denouement—and are, by consequence, less tied to the deployment of musical enchantment than to its glorious end, to the moments of resolution and dissolution soon covered up by the final curtain.

■ I dream of a history of opera that would retrace the long genealogy of seducer characters, through whom music and fable give a human (or superhuman) figure to their specific powers of gratifying the senses, of inebriating the imagination, of multiplying illusion. Characters whose excess of passion permits art to carry itself to its paroxysm and, in so doing, to exert all its influence: Poppea and Salome, Medea and Dido, the Queen of the Night and Turandot, Carmen and Lulu. This role does not apply exclusively to feminine voices: let's not forget Don Giovanni (the singer of serenades and the organizer of spectacles) or Klingsor.... One would never finish evoking those characters whose total *meaning* does not stop at the role they are assigned—themselves heroes or obstacles interposed on the heroes' route—in the dramatic intrigue. Their mission is to embody opera's power of bewitchment. And the singers who play them must have the gift of appearing, if only for a brief moment, as the very geniuses of theatrical song, the presence *in person* of lyrical art in all its falsity and all its éclat. A moving presence because, being linked to the untruth of the spectacle, it is associated at the same time with a negative power that will express itself openly at the level of the intrigue by death or disappearance. The swallowing up of Alcina's fleet, the trapdoor which opens under the feet of Don Giovanni or the Queen of the Night, the knife which stabs Carmen and Lulu, the little morning of regained faith that dissipates the vapors of the Venusberg are the multiple emblems of this *putting to death* which guilty magic secretly called for from the moment of its first flight.

■ The last variation on this theme, and not the least touching, replaces death by the conscious refusal of the supernatural and of magic. In *Die Frau ohne Schatten*, the Empress renounces her sterile perfection as a daughter of the spirit world: she wishes to accede to the mortal condition, to have a shadow like all fleshly creatures. In this heroine, one of the last descendants of the line of enchantresses, Hofmannsthal offers us the gesture of a voluntary abdication. He makes us understand in a new way that art must not entrench itself in the inhuman purity of enchanted palaces and separate worlds. As opera has done since its inception, it is up to art to put us on our guard against the traps of a too perfect fairytale world.

■ Perhaps one day opera will die, like everything else that has been born over the course of time. Opera has not always existed; it was born at a precise moment in the history of the West, on the uncertain frontier between the end of the Renaissance and the beginning of the Baroque. Let us recognize, however, that it will have lived to sing its own death superbly in the death that is always begun again, the death of its enchantresses.

Bourgeois Opera

Theodor W. Adorno

■ To focus one's thoughts about the contemporary theater upon opera surely is not justifiable in terms of opera's immediate relevance. Not only has the crisis of opera been well known and persistent in Germany for thirty years (that is, since the time of the great economic crisis),[1] not only have opera's place and function become questionable in today's society, but, beyond this, opera in and of itself [*an sich*] has, without considering its reception, come to seem peripheral and indifferent, an impression which is forcefully combated to a limited extent by attempts at innovation. Indeed, it is hardly by accident that these attempts at innovation, especially in the musical medium itself, usually come to a standstill. It is far more appropriate to speak of opera because it marks in more than one respect a prototype of the theatrical—indeed, a prototype of precisely that which today is deeply shaken. Instances arise in opera's collapse which belong to the most basic level of the stage. One experiences these instances perhaps most drastically in opera's relation to costume. Costume is essential to opera: in

"Bourgeois Opera" was originally delivered as a lecture entitled "Theater-Oper-Bürgertum" at the Darmstädter Gespräche on 23 April 1955. The proceedings of the conference were published in a volume entitled *Theater*, edited by Egon Vietta (Darmstadt: Neue Darmstädter Verlagsanstalt, 1955). Adorno's lecture appears on pp. 119–34, and a transcript of the lengthy discussion that followed it is included on pp. 135–52. The lecture was republished (without the discussion) in *Der Monat* 7, no. 84 (Sept. 1955):

contrast to a play, an opera without costume would be a paradox. If the gestures of singers—which they often bring along as if straight from the prop room—are themselves already part costume, then their voices—which natural people, as it were, don as soon as they step upon the operatic stage—are entirely put on. The American expression "cloak and dagger,"[2] the idea of the scene in which two lovers sing to each other while murderers lurk left and right behind pillars, eccentrically expresses something of the matter itself: that aura of disguise, of miming, which attracts the child to the theater, not because the child wants to see a work of art, but because it wants to confirm its own pleasure in dissimulation. The closer opera gets to a parody of itself, the closer it is to its own most particular element.[3]

■ This may explain why some of the most authentic operas, like *Der Freischütz*, but also *The Magic Flute* and *Il Trovatore*,[4] have their true place in the children's matinee and embarrass the adult, who imagines himself too sensible for them, simply because he no longer understands their pictorial language. Traces of this element of opera stick to every great drama, and the act of theater performance becomes imbalanced when those traces fall victim to intellectualization, like the last memory of the green wagon.[5] (However, the imperative of intellectualization cannot be suspended by calling for naivety.) The "Prelude in the Theater" was already such a call, and that is why Goethe subjects it to irony.[6] *Faust* balances on the narrow ridge traversing the naive and the spiritual and articulates its consciousness thereof. In the most powerful and most exalted [*geistig*] entities that have been bequeathed to the theater, like *Hamlet*, one can perceive that operatic quality—like a trace of *Simon Boccanegra*[7]—and were it erased, then the truth content of the tragedy of individuation and alienation would remain impotent.

532–38. A slightly revised version with the new title "Bürgerliche Oper" appeared in Adorno's *Klangfiguren* (Frankfurt am Main: Suhrkamp, 1959). This first English translation is by David J. Levin; it is based on the *Klangfiguren* version as reprinted in volume 16 of Adorno's *Gesammelte Schriften*, ed. Rolf Tiedemann (Frankfurt am Main: Suhrkamp, 1978), 24–39. Significant variations in the text of the published versions of the essay are described in the notes, all of which are by the translator.

■ Opera is governed by the element of appearance [*Schein*], in the sense of Benjamin's aesthetics, which has positioned it in contrast to the element of play [*Spiel*]. The term *Spieloper*[8] for a special genre attests precisely to the primacy of appearance, in that it brings forth as a characteristic that which otherwise recedes. Opera reaches the state of crisis because the genre cannot dispense with its appearance without surrendering itself, and yet it must want to do so. Opera runs head on into the aesthetic barrier of reification. For instance, if one—made wise or weary by innumerable backstage jokes—were to offer a *Lohengrin* in which the swan is replaced by a beam of light, then the presupposition of the whole would be attacked to such an extent as to be rendered pointless.[9] If the fabulous animal no longer can be tolerated, then one rebels against the plot's horizon of imagination, and the abstract swan only serves to underscore this. A child who attends a *Freischütz* and finds the wolf's glen reduced to natural symbolism is right to feel cheated out of the best part.[10] Unavoidably, reified opera threatens to become a kind of arts and crafts, where stylization threatens to substitute for the crumbled style. Modernity, which does not really intervene in the matter, becomes a mere getup, becomes modernism—and yet, the operatic stage director finds himself repeatedly forced into all sorts of desperate interventions.

■ The borders of reification reveal themselves even more drastically in the production than in the *mise en scène*.[11] When the reification of opera began more than sixty years ago, the "cloak and dagger" principle was, in all innocence, fervently maintained in the name of realism: *Cavalleria* and *Pagliacci* offer a thing or two in this regard.[12] But even new music, in which opera is self-reflexive, has not cleared that hurdle. Not only has Schönberg as an operatic composer remained in the arena of expressive opera and thus of *musica ficta*, of appearance, both in aesthetic terms and in terms of his relationship to the text;[13] but with artistic finesse and the subtlest touch, Alban Berg—to this day, the only first-rate opera composer in the new century—has sustained the illusionary as an operatic essence removed from empirical reality. In *Wozzeck* the monologic isolation of the half-crazed hero affords a medium of dreamlike displacement in which the drama of the setting sun and the imaginary conspiracy of the Freemasons play into one another.[14] *Lulu* is modeled on the circus, in accordance with Wedekind's sense that something of opera resided there, namely, a consciousness of the muteness of the spoken word, and Lulu's coloratura soprano voice has to perform a vocal ballet which prevents any identification of the events with the everyday and thus of course makes the performance eminently more difficult.[15] Incidentally, in his most productive scenic works, *Le Renard* and *L'Histoire du Soldat*,[16] Stravinsky—who with good reason avoided opera and finally sought to master it through simple stylistic imitation—also resorted to the circus, probably under the influence of the Cubist painters. According to Wedekind, the circus was "corporeal"—that is, an art form withdrawn from the spell of expression—and yet entirely removed from empirical reality. Precisely where opera seeks an identification with that reality, where it seeks a solid representation of some so-called social problem—as in Max Brand's *Maschinist Hopkins*[17]—it falls victim to helpless and corny symbolizing.

■ The limit of the reification of opera revealed itself perhaps most drastically when an arch-enemy of romanticism like Brecht—who in his day pronounced the following judgment concerning a concert performance of Hindemith's *Cardillac*:[18] "That is *Tannhäuser!*"—took an interest in opera. At the time, he and Kurt Weill used technical-dramaturgical means to inquire whether music was supposed to be "cold" toward the scene or whether it was supposed to "warm" stage events, and both decided in favor of the latter. In creations like *The Threepenny Opera*,[19] they left expression in its place, albeit as shredded and parodic expression—which was presumably the main reason for its broad popular success. This was one of the last successful works of musical theater which was avant-garde, at least in its dramaturgy.

■ But one would miss the essence of opera and the romantic were one thus to call opera an entirely romantic genre, especially since its history partook of all those differentiations of style subsumed under terms like "classical" and "romantic." Even Wagnerian music-drama, which music history ascribes to late romanticism, is full of anti-romantic strains, among which the technological perhaps assumes primacy. It would be appropriate to consider opera as the specifically bourgeois genre which, in the midst and with the means of a world bereft of magic, paradoxically endeavors to preserve the magical element of art. This thesis concerning the bourgeois nature of opera sounds provocative for more than one reason. For ever since Prospero laid down the magic wand, ever since Don Quixote encountered truths in windmills, the overall aesthetic tendency of the bourgeois era has of course been the opposite, that of disillusionment. But the positivist tendency of bourgeois art—if one can call it that—never ruled purely and uncontestedly. Just as aesthetic magic itself bears something of enlightenment within itself, in that it renounces the claim to unmediated truth and sanctions appearance as a special realm, so bourgeois art—in order to be at all possible as art—has once again brought magic to the fore while transforming it. Opera was all the more suitable for this process, since music itself elevates the very existence [*Dasein*] against which it strikes. There are also other genres that have arisen out of ostentation (the archetype of all operatic appearance) and in the context of the bourgeois-ification of art: according to recent theories even the cathedral arose thus. In his work "Egoism and the Freedom Movement," Horkheimer has demonstrated the significant role of pomp for all bourgeois ideology, in which one could perhaps see a secularization of or a substitute for cultic/ritualistic display.[20] Secular ostentation—the material representation as it were of the irrational power and greatness of the class which at the same time imposed the ban on irrationality itself—has been essential to opera from a very early stage of its development right up to Richard Strauss: in opera, costume can scarcely be separated from ostentation.

■ There are also historical grounds for ascribing opera to the bourgeoisie rather than to feudal or courtly culture, with which it arranges the *convenu*.[21] Sonorous fullness and choral masses alone point toward an incomparably greater circle than the aristocratic one, which laid claim to the privilege of the proscenium, but left the gallery, the actual viewing space of opera, to the bourgeoisie. One could indeed ask whether in a strict sense there has ever been a feudal or aristocratic art at all. Did not the feudal lords, who despised all menial work, always allow art to be created by members of the bourgeoisie? And has not the Hegelian master/slave dialectic always prevailed in art, such that whoever works on the object is also granted control over it, so that bourgeois artists working for the high and mighty prefer to address their equals rather than their patrons? The depiction of feudal relations, as they have been portrayed in works of art since Homeric times, already presupposes that these relations are no longer accepted in unmediated terms, but instead have in a certain sense become problematic unto themselves. Feudal lords rarely think in "restorationist" terms: instead, from Plato to de Maistre,[22] they always and only seek autonomous, rationally speculating subjects who look for explanations for an already past state of things. Feudal lords, in the form of kings and heroes, are the subject matter of older art; at the same time, they cannot shape that matter at a distance from themselves; Volker von Alzey is Hagen's friend, but he is not Hagen.[23]

■ In any case, the origins of opera have a rationally constructed—indeed, an abrupt—quality which would be extremely difficult to reconcile with the conceptions of feudal traditionalism. Like late technological genres such as film, opera owes its existence to a decision which invokes historical correspondence—the revivification of ancient tragedy—but which, apart from the very rudimentary madrigal-opera, fits into no historical continuity. According to the title of an essay written by Hanns Gutman some thirty years ago, literati invented opera, namely, a Florentine circle of connoisseurs, writers, and ascetic-reformist musicians toward the end of the sixteenth century.[24] The genre first blossomed in the republic of Venice, that is, under the social conditions of an evolved bourgeoisie, and the first great opera composers, Monteverdi, Cavalli, Cesti, belong there;[25] it is hardly coincidental that the German vogue for opera developed in the Hanseatic city of Hamburg, thanks to Reinhard Keiser.[26] The actual courtly phase of opera, the late seventeenth and the eighteenth centuries, the world of maestri, prima donnas, and castrati which grew out of the Neapolitan school,[27] already marks the late phase of absolutism in which the general emancipation of the bourgeoisie was so far advanced that opera hardly isolated itself from the bourgeoisie. It was around this time that the bourgeoisie also forced its way onto the musical stage, into the plot of the intermezzo.[28]

■ Opera shares with film not just the suddenness of its invention but also many of its functions: among them, the presentation of the body of common knowledge to the masses; as well as the massiveness of the means, employed teleologically in the material of opera as in film, which lent opera—at least opera since the middle of the nineteenth century, if not earlier—a similarity to the modern culture industry.[29] Meyerbeer had already done up religious wars and historical state events, personalized them and thereby neutralized them, in that nothing of the substance of the conflicts was left, and Catholics and Huguenots of the St. Bartholomew's Day massacre are admired side by side, as in a wax museum.[30] Out of this, film, at least color film, in turn shaped its canon. It is, by the way, astounding how early some of the most reprehensible qualities that one holds against today's culture industry announce themselves in opera, precisely where the naive person, in looking to the past, expects to find something like the pure autonomy of the genre. In this sense, the text of *Der Freischütz* is already an "adaptation" like those prepared in Hollywood, while the "script writer" Kind has rerouted the tragic conclusion of the novella of romantic destiny upon which the opera is based into a "happy ending," presumably in deference to the Biedermeier audience, which was already anxiously keeping watch to ensure that the heroes get married as well.[31] Even the Wagnerian Humperdinck[32]—stuffed full of the defamation of all things commercial by the Bayreuth founders—made the Brothers Grimm commercially viable, in that the parents of Hansel and Gretel no longer cast the children out as in the fairy tale, since respect for the devoted father in the late nineteenth century must not by any means be further affronted. Such examples demonstrate how deeply opera as a consumer product—in this sense related to film—is entangled in calculations regarding the public. One cannot allow oneself to disregard this as if it were a mere superficiality in the notion of aesthetic autonomy. According to its own logic, dramatic form implies the audience. The thought of a stage as such [*an sich*] is as absurd as the idea of poems as such, or music as such, is justified.

■ But the logic of opera has been bound to myth ever since the experiments of the Florentines, even throughout the course of its ongoing secularization. Only this relationship to myth does not simply imply the imitation of mythic connections through musical ones—to think of it thus was perhaps Wagner's undoing. Rather, in opera, music intervenes in and transforms fate's blind, inescapable ties to nature (as they are represented in Western myths)—and the audience is called upon as a witness, if not indeed as an appellate court. The intervention is itself anticipated in one of the great Greek myths, that of Orpheus, who with music softens the horrible reign of Pluto, to whom he lost Eurydice. As a result of his manically fascinated gaze at the realm, he once again falls prey to that very fate which he had escaped with Eurydice. The first authentic opera, Monteverdi's *L'Orfeo*, took just this as its subject matter, the Gluckian reform went back to Orpheus as the archetype of opera,[33] and it is hardly too much to claim that all opera is Orpheus—a claim which is denied only by Wagnerian music-drama.

■ The operas which fulfill the genre most purely almost always correct myth through music, and thus the statement that opera partakes of the Enlightenment as a total societal movement has an even greater claim to validity than that it partakes of myth. Nowhere is this more evident than with *The Magic Flute*—in which magic weds freemasonry, rendering the natural powers of fire and water powerless before the sounds of the flute, and in which the spell of the always-same dissolves itself.[34] Sarastro's sphere rises out of the land of mothers and its ambiguous interlocking of right and wrong.[35] He knows no revenge, the redemption from which the mythologist and enlightener Nietzsche declared to be his highest will.[36] The fanfare of *Fidelio* also consummates almost ritualistically the moment of protest that breaks open the eternal hell of the prison cell and puts an end to the rule of force.[37] This interlocking of myth and enlightenment defines the bourgeois essence of opera: namely, the interlocking of imprisonment in a blind and unselfconscious system and the idea of freedom, which arises in its midst. Opera's metaphysics is not to be simply separated from this sociality. Metaphysics is absolutely not a realm of invariance which one could grasp by looking out through the barred windows of the historical; it is the glimmer—albeit a powerless glimmer—of light which falls into the prison itself: the more powerful it becomes, the deeper its ideas embed themselves in history; the more ideological it becomes, the more abstractly it appears in the face of history. Opera, hardly touched by philosophy, has sustained itself on metaphysics more than drama, which contaminated its metaphysical content with conceptual contents [*Gedankenstoffe*]. For just that reason, drama lost its metaphysical content, and the philosophy which it objectively intended, to the philosophemes, which it itself simply meant.

■ The unity of truth content and historical content can be graphically demonstrated in those operas whose texts—or, as they are more properly called, *libretti*—have fallen into disrepute ever since Wagner's criticism: those of the nineteenth century. One can hardly deny the conventionality, the freakishness, and the manifold silliness of these booklets, nor can one deny their affinity to the marketplace, the commodity character which in fact made them into placeholders for the as-yet-unborn cinema. At the same time, one can also hardly fail to recognize that libretti—which are of course not literature but stimuli of music—contain an anti-mythological, Enlightenment element, namely, exactly in relation to that secularized mythical stratum. Libretti contain that element precisely by virtue of their subjection to the self-glorifying and already imperialistically greedy bourgeoisie. The anti-mythological, Enlightenment element is contained in the idea of the subjection to destiny [*Schicksalsverfallenheit*], which *Il Trovatore* and *La Forza del Destino*[38] take to the verge of farce. The form of the anti-mythological in the libretti of the nineteenth century is, however, exogamy, just as on the other hand, and quite logically, Wagner, who delivered opera as prey over to myth, shifted incest to the center of the opera ritual.[39] Already in Mozart's *Entführung* the voice of humanity—of course, at this point and for the moment, it is merely a *speaking* voice—is that of the exotic tyrant who holds the European couple in custody, in order, like Thoas, to release them, appeased.[40] Since then opera has shown an endless love for those who are of foreign blood or are otherwise "outside." Halévy's *La Juive*,[41] Meyerbeer's *L'Africaine*,[42] *La Dame aux Camélias* in Verdi's version[43] and the Egyptian princess Aida,[44] Delibes' Lakmé,[45] and in addition the slew of gypsies, culminating in *Il Trovatore* and *Carmen*:[46] all ostracized or outsiders, around whom passions explode and come into conflict with the established order.

■ In comparison with this ritual of attempted escape, Wagner, the enemy of convention, remained far more conventional than the librettists whom he despised: with Wotan's aboriginal wisdom that "everything is according to its kind,"[47] he strengthened the immanence of bourgeois society and blocked that escape; indeed, he propagated a biological stew at the very spot where sinning siblings apparently shock those in the audience seated in the expensive seats. The transfiguration of that which is simply according to its kind, which is simply there, into a mystery, that metaphysics, which he wrongly considered far superior to the state spectacles of grand opera, is precisely related to the fact that in Wagner, for the first time, the bourgeois imagination disavows the impulse toward escape and resigns itself to a situation which he himself conceived as worthy of death. In the nineteenth century, the bourgeois yearning for freedom had successfully escaped to the representative spectacle of opera, just as it had escaped to the great novel, whose complexion opera so frequently recalls. Wagner, in whose works[48] myth triumphs over freedom, was the first who on this point showed himself to be quite submissive in his unrealistic music-dramas to the demands of resigned and cold bourgeois realism. And only in the era of full-fledged imperialism, with Puccini's *Butterfly*, is the exogamy motif built back into the motif of the abandoned little girl, but without the Navy officer—whose marriage is racially pure—ever being seriously drawn to the Japanese lady.[49] It is precisely because opera, as a bourgeois vacation spot, allowed itself so little involvement in the social conflicts of the nineteenth century, that it was able to mirror so crassly the developing tendencies of bourgeois society itself. It is the seal of authenticity in Alban Berg's oeuvre that, in his second opera *Lulu*,[50] simply following the instinct for play and the operatic sense of costume, he once again selected exogamy and escape as operatic material; the girl without a father and mother is irresistible, everyone who steps into her circle wants to up and leave with her like Don José with the gypsy,[51] all are overtaken by the revenge of the extant, and in the end revenge engulfs the picture of beauty herself, who is different and who, in going under, celebrates the greatest victory. In opera, the bourgeois transcends into a mensch.

■ The opera texts offer merely a hint of all this. What is decisive is the relation of the music to the text, or rather—since the opera text has long been what the film script in Hollywood admits to being, a "vehicle"—the relation of the music to the scene and those performing onstage. The contradiction between real, live people who speak as in drama, and the medium of singing, which they make use of in the process, is well known.[52] Repeatedly—in the Florentine monody,[53] the Gluckian reform,[54] the Wagnerian *Sprechgesang*[55]—one has tried to get around that contradiction, or to alleviate it, and thus to promote the pure, unbroken, undialectical closure of operatic form. But the contradiction is far too deeply embedded in the form itself to be resolved through half measures like the recitative, which surely has its place in the form as a means to create contrast. If there is any meaning to opera at all, if it is more than a mere agglomerate—and surely one must be allowed to assume this, as far as the great examples of the genre are concerned—then that meaning is to be sought in contradiction itself, rather than in vainly seeking to do away with contradiction in the name of an all too seamless aesthetic unity, the kind that gloomily flourishes under the name "symbolic."

■ In the process one is reminded of the definition which Lukács offered forty years ago of a complementary art form—the novel.[56] According to that work, the novel asks, in the midst of a disenchanted world: how can life become essential?[57] But the answer is also sought whenever a live person on a stage is about to sing. The singer's voice seeks to catch something of the reflection of meaning for life itself. Indeed therein lies the specifically ideological element of opera, the affirmative element. The heroes of Attic tragedy, from which opera is separated by a historico-philosophical chasm, had no need to sing. In that which befell the ubiquitous myth during the course of the tragic process, the meaning—the emancipation of the subject from its mere place in nature—discharged itself without mediation. It would not have occurred to anyone to confuse the heroes of the tragic stage with empirical people, since of course that which takes place in them and through them is nothing other than the representation of the birth of Man himself.

■ Opera, on the other hand, shaped to an equal extent by Christianity and modern rationality, has from the very beginning had to do with empirical people, namely, with those who are reduced to their mere natural essence. This accounts for its peculiar costume-quality: mortals are disguised as heroes or gods, and this disguise is similar to their singing. Through song they are exalted and transfigured. The process becomes specifically ideological in that such a transfiguration precisely befalls everyday existence [*Dasein*]; that something which merely *is* presents itself as if its simple being were already greater, as if social orders—as mirrored in operatic convention— were identical with the orders of the absolute or the world of ideas. This original ideological essence [*Urwesen*] of opera, which is its dreadful condition [*Unwesen*], can be observed in extremities of decline, as in the comically meaningful affectations of a singer who fetishizes his voice as if it truly *were* the gift of God, as the cliché would have it. Surely, the true reason for the sense of disillusionment which one has labeled the "opera crisis" is that this ideological aspect became unbearable, that the presentation of the meaningless as meaningful has become a mockery in a world in which mere existence, the context of bedazzlement, threatens to swallow people up.

■ But opera exhausts itself in this ideological aspect as little as does aesthetic appearance. The latter is both: the gilding of what already exists and the reflection of that which would be otherwise; the surrogate of the happiness which is refused to people, and the promise of true happiness. The gesture of dramatic characters singing covers up the fact that, even though they are already stylized, they have as little reason to sing as they have op-

portunity. But in their song there resounds something of the hope for reconciliation with nature: singing, the utopia of prosaic existence [*Dasein*], is
at the same time also the memory of the prelinguistic, undivided state of
Creation, such as it sounds at the loveliest point in Wagner's Ring poem, in
the words of the forest bird.[58] Opera's song is the language of passion: not
just the exaggerating stylization of existence [*Dasein*] but also an expression that nature prevails in man against all convention and mediation, an
evocation of pure immediacy. Ever since the invention of figured bass and
opera, there has been a doctrine of musical affect, and opera is in its element wherever it gives itself over breathlessly to passion. In this "giving
itself over to nature" lies its elective affinity with both myth and the modern
successor to the epic, the novel. But passion, which finds expression, is appeased insofar as sung passion comes flooding back like an echo, and insofar as the sound of the immediate, rising above the mediations of the
hardened life, is reflected. And thus the constrained existence of those who
sing in the opera is appeased as well, so that they appear unconstrained.
That is why opera is no simple copy of myth but its rectification in the medium of music, which is both an element of nature and its reflection all the
way through the intellect [*Geist*]. In opera, song allows free rein to that
which, as passion, incorporates people into the context of nature. At the
same time, in song, people experience themselves as nature, which their
prejudice against nature resists, and as a result the mythic element, i.e.,
passion, is pacified. Their freedom does not lie in the intellect [*Geist*], which
high-handedly raises itself above creation. Instead, intellect as music becomes similar to nature and, on the strength of that similarity, discards its
lordly essence.

■ The genre celebrates this process in the singing of people, who as people are—and must be—ashamed to sing. Opera fulfills itself perhaps most completely where it sacrifices its claim to soul and expression and employs artificial language; the coloratura is no mere form of outward exaggeration, but precisely in it the idea of opera emerges most purely as an extreme. Nowhere did Wagner come closer to that extreme than in the role of the forest bird.[59] Berg was inspired by operatic genius when he wrote the role of Lulu, the destructive nature with which his opera reconciles, as a coloratura, without, however, in the least thereby committing himself to reproducing irretrievable phases of opera.

■ That Berg could not complete the instrumentation of the work says something about the genre.[60] Opera has been in a precarious situation since the moment when the high bourgeois society which supported it in its fully developed form ceased to exist. The inner convulsion of the genre and its lack of resonance correspond to one another, although the origins and consequences of this correspondence are not easily determined. Opera was founded on so many conventions that it resounds into a vast emptiness as soon as these conventions are no longer vouchsafed to the audience through tradition. The newcomer—at once barbaric and precocious—one who did not already as a child learn to be bowled over by opera and to respect its outrageous impositions, will feel contempt for it, while the intellectually advanced public is almost no longer capable of responding immediately or spontaneously to a limited store of works, which have long since sunk into the living-room treasure-chests of the petite bourgeoisie, like Raphael's paintings, abused through innumerable reproductions. However, the growing immanent difficulties of the genre—primarily the repression of inner tension which can be seen in the entirety of contemporary artistic practice—have thus far prevented opera from gaining new relevance through production. In fact, opera corresponds to a great extent to the museum, even in the sense of the latter's positive function, which is to help something threatened by muteness to survive. Taken together, what happens on the operatic stage is usually like a museum of bygone images and gestures, to which a retrospective need clings.

■ Accordingly, there is that type of operatic audience which always wants to hear the same thing and suffers the unfamiliar with hostility, or, even worse, with passive disinterest, since, alas, it is condemned to it by its sub-scription tickets. The state of opera is not to be envied amid an administered humanity, which, regardless of political system, no longer concerns itself with liberation, escape, and reconciliation, as in the opera of the early bourgeoisie, but instead desperately stops up its ears to the sound of humanity in order to be able to stand the hustle and bustle, happy, contented, and resigned. At one time, the bourgeoisie bore the critique of mythology and at the same time bore the concept of the ultimate reestablishment of nature; today that critique has become as foreign to it as the longed-for concept, and the bourgeoisie has reconciled itself as much to its own alienation as to the appearance of inevitability which envelops it—a second mythology. As long as this state of mind and the harsher conditions that dictate it continue, opera can expect little.

■ This would perhaps change if opera could succeed in freeing itself of its ideological essence which transfigures mere existence, and if it could instead give prominence to that other essence, reconciliatory and anti-mythological. But can one have the one, the so-called positive, without the other, the negative? The limit of any concretization of the theater through principles of construction is living people, to whom the scene still refers. If theater dispenses with private psychology or the fraud of human immediacy, then it is threatened by prefabricated slogans, by an overarching intention arbitrarily imposed upon empirical experience [*Dasein*], which would only become bearable were one to omit everything from empirical existence from which it, in turn, actually derives its certainty and force. The impasse is hardly resolved by simply dismissing what was disliked by labeling it romantic—an asceticism which then often leads to the path of least resistance, a regressive, simple, compositional practice. Consider, for example, the technique of demystifying opera by stringing together thinly motivic materials without development, and with stereotypical rhythmic displacements—borrowed from Stravinsky, and consistently lagging behind his superior ability; even today, the anti-dramatic music for musical drama exudes so much monotony and boredom that one wonders why the composers themselves, Stravinsky included, do not rebel. In the movement toward a non-ideological, unpretentious method of operatic composition, one can at least demand that the differentiation and complexity of the compositional process be preserved in its entirety and the superstitious belief in origins be abandoned.

■ One ought to compose with a hammer, just as Nietzsche wanted to philosophize with a hammer, but that means testing the soundness of the structure, listening with a critical ear for hollow points, not smashing it in two and confusing the jagged remains with avant-garde art on account of their similarity with bombed-out cities. Today, the worn-out notion of a musical economics of scarcity—a prosaism which exempts itself from taxing the imagination and credits its own self-satisfaction with overcoming that which one is not—has become as clichéd as the conventions of the court theater. This has not led to the unchallenged survival of the preserved magic of theater as a special sphere seeking to escape from film. But the richer, the more multifarious, the more contrasting, the more intricate the construction of theatrical works becomes, the sooner the works, through such artistic and, so to speak, windowless rectitude, will share in a meaning which they no longer want to proclaim of their own accord. Only when the entire fullness of musical means in the face of a complaint worthy of humanity awakens something of that tension between the musical and the scenic mediums—totally lacking in the theater today—only then could opera once more match the power of the historical image.

The Caesura of Religion

Philippe Lacoue-Labarthe

■ No doubt, it is not impossible to say that Wagner fundamentally *saturated* opera. A proof of this, which is nonetheless indirect, is that everything which followed without exempting itself from the exorbitant ambition he had imposed upon the form carries the stigmata of the end. This may be in the nostalgic and relatively comfortable mode to which the late Strauss resigned himself, a mode that in short ended his career with an adieu, more disenchanted than really melancholic, to the two genres in which, as he well recognized, a limit had been reached (this is why the so-called *Four Last Songs*, if only because they return to the "law of genre," that is, to a pre-Mahlerian state of the *Lied*, have a meaning analogous to the auto-reflection "in the manner of" which orders *Capriccio*). But it may also be in the mode of redundancy, and thus of oversaturation, for which the early Strauss was renowned (or the Schönberg of the *Gurrelieder*) and in which the Puccini of *Turandot* pathetically exhausted himself. But then again, it may be in the more equivocal and more subtle (more "French") mode of

"The Caesura of Religion" was written for this collection and was translated by Adam Bresnick. It was later included in *Musica Ficta*, which is forthcoming in translation from Stanford University Press.

destructuration à la Debussy. Or finally, it may be in the style of properly modern radicality, the style of violent rupture and incompleteness, of "failure": Berg's *Lulu*, Schönberg's *Moses and Aaron*. And here, it is incontestable, things are much more grave. One might say, not only because it raises the ante where the means of expression are concerned (a move that Nietzsche had already denounced as an art subordinated to the search for effects), but rather because of its *systematic* character, in the strict sense of the term, that Wagner's work left to its posterity a task every bit as impossible as the one left by German Idealism (Hegel) to its great followers in philosophy: to continue that which is finished. Thus, just as one may speak of the "Hegelian closure" of philosophy, one might speak of the Wagnerian closure of opera and even of art itself, or as they said at the time, of *great art*, for such was the "ambition" of art. As a result of their anti-Hegelianism, what Wagner's writings and *The Birth of Tragedy* most clearly show is that in wishing to overcome [*überwinden*] opera and all its "culture,"[1] Wagner devotes himself with the *Gesamtkunstwerk* to a totalizing sublation, to an *Aufhebung* of all the arts, and to a *restoration* of "great art" which is all the more powerful for being all the more modern (with other technical means, in effect): a restoration of Greek tragedy, of course. At the same time, if the other arts were able to take another direction, and allowed themselves to be guided from the outset by another concept of "great" and another intuition of "art," opera, itself a recent art though it would wish itself ancient, suffered severely from such a declaration of completion. In fact, it was unable to recover from it, or only did so poorly.

■ Here *saturate* means simply: too much music or, if one prefers, despite the paradox, too much "Italianism" and too much credit accorded the *prima la musica*. In short it is the belief in music's "sublational" capacity (or, as he would say, its "synthesizing" capacity) that destroys for Wagner any chance of acceding to "totality" and binds him to musical saturation, condemning him to choose sides in what is after all nothing but the classical dilemma of opera. Saturation is a false totalization, at least insofar as it testifies to the false character of any will to totalization, be it conceptual or not. On this point at least, though for entirely different reasons, Heidegger and Adorno agree with one another, and both of them attribute the responsibility for this unrestrained, "infinite" melocentrism to Schopenhauer, to the metaphysics of "feeling" and the "unconscious" (to the vague mysticism, Adorno says, of "thalassal regression"). Wagner definitively considered nothing but the problem of opera and did so to the nearly exclusive benefit of music and not to that of theater, where, in relation to the Italian apparatus, his innovations are rather slim. Or to put it otherwise: as a *Dichter-komponist* (a monstrous term, as Adorno remarks), Wagner confused language with "words" and music with the essence of language, its origin and its assumption. In the demonstration which he conducts in the "Music Drama" chapter of *In Search of Wagner*, Adorno cites some passages that are in this sense damning:

Science has laid bare to us the organism of language, but what she showed us was a dead organism, which only the poet's utmost can bring to life again, namely, by suturing the wounds with which the anatomic scalpel has gashed the body of language and by breathing into it the breath that may animate it with living motion. This breath, however, is—music.
. . .
The necessary bestowal from within oneself, the seed that can only in the most ardent transports of love condense itself from its noblest forces—which grows only in order to be released, i.e. to be released for the purposes of fertilization, indeed which is in and of

itself [*an sich*] this more or less materialized drive—this procreative seed is the poetic intention, which brings to the gloriously loving woman, Music, the stuff for bearing.[2]

■ Despite their erotico-dialectical pathos (the same pathos, though less rigorous, or, as Adorno would say, more "voluptuous" than that which governs the opening paragraphs of *The Birth of Tragedy*), texts of this genre have at least one merit: they reveal the reason why all operas that have seriously tried to resist Wagnerian saturation, leaving aside those that have deliberately renounced totalization (this is above all true of Berg), have taken the form of a sort of "performative" meditation on the essence of language (of speech) in its relation to music, and thus on the very nature of the opera form. In Strauss, who is the most belated and no doubt the most "informed," the protocol, under its slightly belabored eighteenth-century elegance, is relatively coarse, even if it gives ample evidence of a certain intelligence about what is at stake. But finally it is a bit disarming to take as one's subject the *Querelle des Bouffons* or that of the Piccinists and the Gluckists, for with an opera in opera or about opera (*Ariadne, Capriccio*) one remains in the simple register of the *mise en abîme* and citation. In the end, one does not choose at all; with an emphatic wink one leaves the generic conflict of opera in suspense. By contrast, in Berg (Wozzeck, the "poor creature," is the interdiction of eloquence and music, and consequently is interdiction itself) and above all in Schönberg, the problem is touched upon with an entirely different profundity, and with an entirely different acuity.

■ Above all in Schönberg: it is well known that this problem is the very subject of *Moses and Aaron* and, what is more essential, that it is constitutive of the opera's treatment. The opposition of speech and singing (or, more exactly, of *Sprechgesang* and *Gesang*) which, no matter what Adorno says, very rigorously transposes the biblical opposition of Moses' stammering and Aaron's eloquence into the register of the work—and here the very question of the prohibition of (re)presentation, which thus is *also* the subject of the opera, is condensed—leads the opera to put its own principle into question with great lucidity. And consequently it reopens the scar that Wagner, by musical saturation, had intended to suture definitively in a sort of hyperbolic assumption of opera itself. Now what Adorno, who is in fact one of the few who have confronted Schönberg's *oeuvre désoeuvrée*, "saves" from *Moses*, despite his vigilance with respect to Wagnerism, is precisely musical saturation. In the final pages of his great essay of 1963, "Sakrales Fragment: Über Schönberg's *Moses und Aron*,"[3] Adorno remarks that Schönberg, who evidently does not order his work according to a serialist dramaturgy of opera, also does not order his work according to a dramaturgy of the Wagnerian type (if a traditional model is still operative, it would be that of oratorio). This prevents nothing: when Adorno wants to justify what he calls the "success" of *Moses*, what he brings forward is the work's "power," and does so all the more because this power accords with the metaphysical (or religious) aims of the work. Now with what does this power or, and this amounts to the same thing, this "monumentality of tone" have to do? Not with simplicity, at least not immediately, but rather "with everything which is gathered together in this music and which occupies the musical space" (244). Adorno comments:

In no other work does Schönberg so consistently and with such facility follow the rule that the compositional effort—that is to say, in the first place the sheer quantity of simultaneous events—should correspond to the content of the music, of the events to be represented. In *Moses* he takes this to extremes. Nowhere else is there so much music, almost in the literal sense of so many notes, as here *ad majorem Dei gloriam*. The sheer density of the construction becomes the medium in which the ineffable can manifest itself without usurpation. For it is this that can be wholly and convincingly created in the material by Schönberg's own musical consciousness. (244–45)

Once again the style of this saturation is not Wagnerian, if only because the writing is too complex and because it no longer orders itself according to the imperative of a *melos*. But all the same, it is a saturation. And it is linked to a religious or metaphysical content as its most adequate mode of expression. It is as if in the end *Moses and Aaron* were nothing other than the negative (in the photographic sense) of *Parsifal*, thus accomplishing, in a paradoxical manner, the project of the total work. And in fact, this is virtually what we read in Adorno's final remarks:

By conceptualizing this we have probably arrived at the full measure of Schönberg's success in his biblical opera. It is intensified by what seems at first to stand in its way: the inordinate complexity of the music. This leads to the liberation of Schönberg's supreme talent, his gift for combination, his precise grasp of distinct but simultaneous events. The idea of unity in diversity becomes a sensuous musical reality in him. He was able not just to imagine, but actually to invent complexes of opposed extremes, which yet occur simultaneously. In this respect he represents the culmination of the tradition in which every detail is composed. This talent reveals his metaphysical ingenuity. The unity of what he had imagined truly does justice to the idea which forms the subject of the text. The striking effect and the unity of the disparate are one and the same. Hence the simplicity of the end result. The complexity is nowhere suppressed, but is so shaped as to become transparent. If everything in the score is clearly heard, its very clarity means that it is heard as a synthesis. (247–48)

In its near clarity (and yet . . .), one sees that this description could apply to Wagner. In any case, the possibility of a synthetic perception, the unified (and thus totalizing) character of music, the adequation of such a unity to the "idea" of the text (to its metaphysical significance), "obligation" itself, these are all incontestably principles which pertain to Wagnerian aesthetics. Thus we are confronted with a question, and one which is not without consequences: How is it that the shadow of Wagner can continue to cloud the hope, which was as much Schönberg's as Adorno's, to put an end—lucidly—to Wagnerism? Which is to say, to the worst (the most disastrous) conception of "great art"?

■ If there is any chance of making sense of this, we must reread "Sakrales Fragment."

■ At the end of his analysis, that is, just before the Benjaminian *Rettung* of the work which neatly finishes the essay on Schönberg, we find this statement (Adorno, who, without ever mentioning the word, has cataloged the reasons for the failure of *Moses*, has just indicated that in the end, Schönberg was the victim of the bourgeois illusion of the "immortality of art," of the belief in genius—that metaphysical transfiguration of bourgeois individualism—indeed, of the absence of doubt as to the reality of greatness; or to put it otherwise, that he was the victim of his own renunciation of "that extreme of the aesthetic, the sole legitimation of art" (242), and he continues):

In Schönberg's fragmentary main works—the term 'main work' is itself symptomatic—there is something of the spirit that Huxley castigated in one of his early novels. The greatness, universal validity, totality of the masters and masterpieces of yore—all this can be regained if only you are strong enough and have the genius. This has something of the outlook that plays off Michelangelo against Picasso. Such blindness about the philosophy of history has causes rooted in the philosophy of history itself. They are to be found in the feeling of an inadequate sense of authority, the shadow-side of modern individuation. To overcome this blindness would mean relativizing the idea of great art even though great art alone can provide the aesthetic seriousness in whose absence authentic works can no longer be written. Schönberg has actually rendered visible one of the antinomies of art itself. The most powerful argument in his favour is that he introduced this antinomy, which is anything but peculiar to him, into the innermost recesses of his own *oeuvre*. It is not to be overcome simply by an act of will or by virtue of the power of his own works. The fallacy that it is necessary to negotiate or depict the most rarefied contents in order to produce the greatest works of art—a fallacy which puts an end to the Hegelian aesthetics—derives from the same misconception. The elusive content is to be captured by chaining it to the subject matter which, according to tradition, it once inhabited. A futile endeavor. The prohibition on graven images which Schönberg heeded as few others have done, nevertheless extends further than even he imagined. To thematize great subjects directly today means projecting their image after the event. But this in turn inevitably means that, disguised as themselves, they fail to make contact with the work of art. (242–43; translation slightly modified)

Schönberg's merit, which all the same no longer permits one to "save" the work, is thus to have "rendered visible one of the antinomies of art itself" (and not just, as one might think, an antinomy of the art of the "bourgeois era" and of the epoch of individuation, even if it has devolved to properly modern art to manifest it). This antinomy is very simple, and is without resolution: "great art" *is* and *cannot be* (or can no longer be) the guarantee, indeed, the norm of authenticity in art. The notion of "great art," which alone provides "the aesthetic seriousness in whose absence authentic works can no longer be written," must be "relativized" (243). But one does not relativize the absolute. "Great art" remains the norm—just as, for reasons that are hardly different, it was for Hegel and Schelling, for Nietzsche, for Heidegger—but it is a ruinous norm for all art which would submit itself to this category. This is why "great art," the will to "great art" is the impossibility of art. This contradiction is at the very heart of Schönberg's work, and especially of *Moses*, and we will see that it is this which makes for its "greatness," beyond its "intention." In its *Wahrheitsgehalt*, as Benjamin said: in its truth content.

■ This is, at bottom, what defines the essence of art, at least of modern art: it is only itself in the impossibility of effecting that which founds its authenticity. It does not follow from this that one must renounce apprehending "the most rarefied contents" (the spiritual contents, as Hegel said, the metaphysical as such, for this is and has always been "the high"). But it does follow, on the other hand, that one must renounce "negotiating or depicting [*darstellen*] the most rarefied contents." If one credits Adorno, here, with the greatest lucidity (and the allusion to Hegel cannot but lead one to do so), what is seen as the "error" is exactly what Heidegger, in the first version of his lectures *The Origin of the Work of Art*, denounced as the "remarkable fatality" to which "all meditation about art and the work of art, every theory of art and all aesthetics" is submitted, from the Greeks at least to Hegel, which is to say, to us: the artwork "always allows itself *also* to be considered as a fabricated thing [*ein Zeugwerk*, an allusion to the Platonico-Aristotelian misinterpretation of *tekhnē*], presenting a 'spiritual content.' Thus art becomes the presentation of something supersensible in a palpable material submitted to a form" (52–53).⁴ Now because of Schönberg but also beyond him, Adorno refers this questioning of *Darstellung*—art is not *essentially* (re)presentation—to the biblical prohibition of representation—to the "iconoclastic prescription," as Jean-Joseph Goux says⁵—which "Schönberg heeded as few others have done," and which "extends further than even he imagined." It goes without saying that here all comparison with the Heideggerian procedure ends. If there is indeed something which Heidegger could not—or rather would not—recognize, even if his thought and the deconstruction of Hegelian aesthetics ought to have forced him to do so, it is that one might refer the problematic of *Darstellung* to such an origin. But Adorno had every reason to do just this. And so it is that he affirms, in a mode that Heidegger would probably have impugned, that all that is left is to "conceive" the "trace" of these "great contents" today, which brings us back all the same to modern art, to an art in which, by tradition, the content was attached to certain subjects. All of which amounts to saying that great contents "fail to make contact with the work of art."

■ Here it is clear that we have touched the problem of the "end of art." Since Hegel, the end of art signifies the birth of aesthetics (the philosophy or science of art, or even the simple "reflection" on art) no matter where one situates the event: in the decline of the Greek fifth century, as Heidegger above all would be tempted to think, or in the exhaustion of Christian art. (In the meantime, the question is relatively secondary: in both cases, the end of art means in reality the end of religion, and this is the essential point.) In his manner, Adorno remains faithful to this determination: no doubt there was once "great art," which is to say that "great contents" were once able to supply matter to artworks. But that all that remains is to conceive the trace of this—and this makes all the difference—in no way suffices to define the program of an aesthetics. The reason is simply that "great contents" do not belong *essentially* to the work of art. If one must maintain the project of an aesthetics—and it is well known that Adorno, perhaps against Heidegger, will resolutely devote himself to this—this will not reduce itself to end, as is the case in Hegel and also, though in a more complex fashion, in Heidegger, as a nostalgia for a religion, which is to say, a community.

■ This is why it is not at all a matter of indifference that this bundle of questions—at once very close to and very far from Heideggerian questions, but near at least in that it is the enclosing domination of Hegelian aesthetics that is abjured—should thus present all the marks of a philosophical reflection on the essence, the history, and the destination of art even as it proceeds both very rigorously and very loyally in its interpretation of *Moses*. This is an artwork, and not just any artwork, in its intentions, in what lies beyond its intentions, and in the failure or success of the two, which carries or at least allows one to assemble such a bundle of questions. All things being equal, Schönberg is for Adorno what Schiller, for example, is for Hegel, Wagner for the early Nietzsche, and Hölderlin for Heidegger: the offering of a work which explicitly thematizes the question of its own possibility as a work—this makes it modern—and which thereby carries in itself, as its most intimate subject, the question of the essence of art. Such works necessitate a philosophical decision as to the future of art or its chances today—which is to say, from now on. Schiller sanctions the end of art (its "death"), but Wagner is the hope of a rebirth. And Hölderlin, always on the condition that we do not envisage his final dereliction, is the hope of "another beginning."

■ Thus the question is to know exactly what *Moses and Aaron* offers to Adorno (to the continuing project of aesthetics).

■ The response to this question lies entirely in the title Adorno gives to his essay: "Sakrales Fragment."

■ Despite the peremptory (and perhaps uselessly romantic) declaration that virtually opens the essay, according to which "everything is in pieces, fragmentary, like the Tablets of the Law which Moses smashed" (225), this title is not justified solely by the fact that *Moses and Aaron* is unfinished. This would hardly explain the fact that, despite appearances, the simplest meaning of the word "fragment" is in the end not at all the meaning retained by Adorno. The reference here to the Tablets is in reality not formal; it is even less formalist, in the genre of a more or less subtle *mise en abîme*.

As it appears a bit further on, only the word "sacred" is able to explain the "fragment," and it is to the meta-romantic speculation of Benjamin that one must connect the following corrective:

Important works of art are the ones that aim for an extreme; they are destroyed in the process and their broken outlines survive as the ciphers of a supreme, unnameable truth. It is in this positive sense that *Moses und Aron* is a fragment and it would not be extravagant to attempt to explain why it was left incomplete by arguing that it could not be completed. (226)

No doubt there is still something of the *mise en abîme* in this final formula. But the *mise en abîme* is necessary here because it is nothing other than the effect of the *reflection* that structures *Moses and Aaron*. And it is difficult to see how an art that takes itself as its own object, being constrained to put its own possibility to the test, might escape from it.

■ The Benjaminian hermeneutic principle that Adorno obeys obliges him in effect to perform a double reading.

■ On the one hand he locates, as the very *intention* that presides over the work, what he calls the "fundamental experience" of *Moses*: that of properly *meta-physical* heroism (more so, it would seem, than that of "religious" heroism). In applying himself to the beginning of the *Pieces for Choir*, op. 27: "Heroic, those who accomplish acts for which they are lacking in courage," Adorno designates the subject of *Moses* as the pure contradiction of a (consequently impossible) task, the task of being "the mouthpiece of the Almighty." This task is defined in a strictly Hegelian manner if one remembers the *Lectures on the Philosophy of Religion* where Hegel says that Moses has nothing other than "the value of an organ" "over there" (in the Orient, I suppose). Moreover, "contradiction" is defined in the Hegelian lexicon as the contradiction of the finite and the infinite: the absolute—rather than

God, for what is at stake in Schönberg's libretto is "thought" and not faith—evades finite beings with which it is incommensurable.

[According to Moses,] to act as the mouthpiece of the Almighty is blasphemy for mortal man. Schönberg must have touched on this theme even before *Die Jakobsleiter*, when he composed a setting for Rilke's poem in the songs Opus 22: "All who attempt to find you, they tempt you / And they who thus find you, they bind you / to image and gesture." Thus God, the Absolute, eludes finite beings. Where they desire to name him, because they must, they betray him. But if they keep silent about him, they acquiesce in their own impotence and sin against the other, no less binding, commandment to name him. They lose heart because they are not up to the task which they are otherwise enjoined to attempt. (225–26; trans. slightly modified)[6]

And it is, moreover, to this contradiction that Adorno refers Moses' exclamation, at which point the music composed by Schönberg interrupts itself. For Adorno, this is the point where the work itself is condemned to fragmentation:

At the end of Act II of the biblical opera, in the final sentence which has become music, Moses breaks down and laments, 'O word, thou word that I lack.' The insoluble contradiction which Schönberg has taken as his project and which is attested by the entire tradition of tragedy, is also the contradiction of the actual work. If it is obvious that Schönberg felt himself to be a courageous man and that he invested much of himself in Moses, this implies that he advanced to the threshold of self-knowledge about his own project. He must have grasped the fact that its absolute metaphysical content would prevent it from becoming an aesthetic totality. But by the same token he refused to accept anything less. (226)[7]

Now this contradiction, which Adorno very strangely calls "tragic" (I will come back to this), is not simply the subject of the work. Adorno insists a great deal on this: it is indeed the contradiction of the work itself, that is, "the fact that its absolute metaphysical content would prevent it from becoming an aesthetic totality" (226). Thus the essential and not accidental incompleteness of *Moses*. This incompleteness is inscribed, at bottom, in Moses' very first words, which Adorno has no need to recall: "Unique, eternal, omnipresent, invisible, and unrepresentable God."

■ But, Adorno remarks, "tragic" is not an adequate adjective. And suddenly the structure of the *mise en abîme* (the impossibility that the "work reflects as properly its own") is insufficient to open an adequate access to the work, for it is too premeditated: "The impossibility which appears intrinsic to the work is, in reality, an impossibility which was not intended. It is well known that great works can be recognized by the gap between their aim and their actual achievement" (226).

■ This is why, on the other hand, with all due respect this time to the "truth content"—to that very thing, Benjamin would say, which constitutes the work as an "object of knowledge"—Adorno invokes a second, more essential reason for the incompleteness of *Moses*, for its impossibility. This reason is the end of art, that is, the end of the possibility of "great art":

The impossibility we have in mind is historical: that of sacred art today and the idea of the binding, canonical, all-inclusive work that Schönberg aspired to. The desire to outdo every form of subjectivity meant that he had subjectively to create a powerful, dominant self amidst all the feeble ones. An immense gulf opens up between the trans-subjective, the transcendentally valid that is linked to the Torah, on the one hand, and the free aesthetic act which created the work on the other. This contradiction becomes fused with the one which forms the theme of the work and directly constitutes its impossibility. Theologians have complained that the designation of monotheism as 'thought'—that is, something which is only subjectively intended—diminishes the idea of transcendence in the text, since every thought is in a sense transcendental. Nevertheless, a truth manifests itself in this, however clumsily it is expressed: the absolute was not present in the work other than as a subjective intention—or idea, as the philosophers would say. By conjuring up the Absolute, and hence making it dependent on the conjurer, Schönberg ensured that the work could not make it real. (226–27)

■ Whence Adorno's thesis, if I may drily summarize it: in its intention, *Moses* is a "sacred opera"; but because "cultic music cannot be willed" (228) and because "the problematic character of a religious art that single-handedly tears itself free from its epoch" cannot efface itself (227; trans. modified), *Moses* is in truth a "sacred fragment."

■ It is not my intention to critique this thesis. It is perfectly solid, and takes its authority from precise and reliable historical and sociological considerations. It is supported by extremely fine textual and musical analyses, and the whole thing has the weight of self-evidence. Nevertheless, I believe it is possible to put this thesis to the test of an "aesthetic" category to which Adorno, at least here,[8] does not make the slightest allusion although everything in his text calls for it, and does so constantly: the category of the *sublime*.

■ If I was astonished a moment ago that Adorno could describe as tragic the contradiction of the finite and the infinite, which according to him is the subject of *Moses*, this is because this contradiction in Hegel—and this contradiction as Adorno himself envisions it—is nothing other than that of "sublimity," which, as is well known, defines the properly Jewish moment of religion.[9] Moreover, at least since Kant,[10] the Mosaic utterance (the Law, but above all the prohibition of representation) has been presented as the paradigm of the sublime utterance. And it is probably the case that since Michelangelo, if we correctly interpret what Freud wished to say, the *figure* of Moses, as paradoxical as this might seem, has been taken as the emblematic figure of the sublime. The sublime, in the tradition of the sublime, is overdetermined by the biblical reference. And everything takes place as if Adorno did not want to hear a word of this.

■ Here things necessarily take a turn: though he manifests the will to exceed the Hegelian determination of "great art," and thus of the beautiful—of the sensual presentation that is adequate to a spiritual content, to an Idea, which is for Hegel the (Greek) truth of the (Jewish) sublime, that is, of the affirmation of the fundamental inadequation of the sensual and the Idea, or of the incommensurability of the finite and the infinite, whence the prohibition of representation precisely originates—and given that he sketches this gesture vis-à-vis Hegel and, behind him, vis-à-vis the whole philosophical tradition since Plato, insofar as it thinks the beautiful as the *eidetic* apprehension of being (and Adorno has a very clear consciousness, for example, of the "figurative character of all European art," including music, if only because of the invention of the *stilo rappresentativo* and of *musica ficta*), how is it that Adorno was unable to see or did not want to see that in reality Schönberg's endeavor expressly inscribes itself in the canonical tradition of the sublime? This would have in no way prevented him from producing the demonstration that he produces and which is incontestable because the contradiction of *Moses* is in fact incontestable. But this would have permitted him, perhaps, to reach another "truth" of *Moses* or to attempt a *Rettung* which would not be solely aesthetic, that is, imprisoned by the principle of adequation and judging the "failure" or "success" of the work solely from the viewpoint of the beautiful. That is, definitively, judging from the Hegelian point of view.

■ For, if there is no "critique" to be made, there is all the same a "reproach" to be offered. I will try briefly to explain myself.[11]

■ One can begin again with this: if Adorno were attentive to the problematic of the sublime—if only he had remembered that Kant offers the prohibition of representation itself as the privileged example of the sublime—he would have been able to maintain his analysis without any essential modifications.[12] In any case, it is the Hegel of the considerations on Judaism and sublimity which props up Adorno's procedure here, whether he knows this or not, and these considerations presuppose the "Analytic of the Sublime." Thus with one stroke he could have returned to all the analyses of purportedly sublime works or works recognized as sublime which, since Kant and Schiller, generally agree with one another in thinking that there is no possible sublime presentation—or, *a fortiori*, figuration—and thus that the question of the very possibility of a sublime art always arises, at least as long as we continue to define art by (re)presentation. To take an example which Adorno could not but be aware of, this is exactly the difficulty Freud encounters when, on the basis of Schillerian aesthetics (the essay "Grace and Dignity"), he tackles Michelangelo's figure of Moses: not only does he remain perplexed as to the meaning of the figure, but in fact he wonders whether in the end it is still art, that is, if it is "successful" (and it is a "limit," he thinks).

■ At the same time, one cannot forget that, as regards Kant, leaving out that which arises from nature's sublime (and which poses altogether different problems), the only examples of the sublime given by the *Third Critique* are examples of sublime *utterances* (as is traditional since Longinus), of which the most important are not poetic utterances but are, rather, prescriptive utterances and more specifically prohibitions, precisely like the Mosaic Law.[13] Thus Kant speaks of "abstract (or restrictive) representation," indeed, of "negative representation." And because it also bears on representation or figuration, the Mosaic utterance, in its sublime simplicity (it is a purely negative commandment), is evidently a meta-sublime utterance, if I may use this term: it tells the truth of the sublime in a sublime manner: that there is no possible presentation of the meta-physical or of the absolute. *Mutatis mutandis*, this is a bit like the exclamation "O word, thou word that I lack," which for Adorno completes Schönberg's *Moses*. But above all, and one must not forget this, Kant says that inasmuch as a "presentation of the sublime" can belong to the fine arts (and one can well imagine why he remains extremely circumspect on this point), the only three modes or genres that one can rigorously recognize as "sublime genres" are (sacred) oratorio, the didactic (that is, philosophical) poem, and verse tragedy (*Critique of Judgment*, §52).

■ Now it is precisely these three genres of the art of the sublime—if such a thing exists or can exist—that *Moses* works together jointly, for it is simultaneously oratorio ("sacred" as Adorno says), philosophical poem (whose subject is nothing less than the absolute itself), and, I will come to this, tragedy (in verse). It is, at least, *if we abstract from the opera form*. And this is why I ask the question whether Adorno, beyond his critique of the opera as such, might not have been able to accede to another "truth" of the work.

■ That *Moses* is an opera, this is particularly difficult to dispute. From the dramaturgical point of view, it has all the faults of the genre: among other things, I am thinking of the episode of worshipping the Golden Calf, which Adorno considers admirable from the viewpoint of musical composition, but which, in the style of an "obligatory ballet" (in the second act, of course), lacks nothing of the lascivious absurdity of the "flower maidens" in *Parsifal*. But it is already less difficult to dispute that the dramaturgical principles which he obeys are those of the Wagnerian music-drama. Even if *Moses* can be understood as an anti-*Parsifal* (which would thus retain all that is essential from that against which it protests), it does not seem to me that one might affirm without further consideration, as does Adorno, that Schönberg has the same attitude toward the biblical text that Wagner has toward the myths that he reelaborates, even if Adorno's argumentation appears from the outset unimpeachable and is difficult to resume. Adorno conducts his demonstration in the following manner:

With the vestiges of a naivety which is perhaps indispensible [Schönberg] puts his trust in proven methods. Not that he is tempted to resort to formulae in order to revive or renew sacred music. But he does strive for a balance between the pure musical development and the desire for monumentality, much as Wagner had done. He too extended his critique of the musical theatre to the bounds of what was possible in his day. But at the same time he wanted the larger-than-life as evidence of the sacred. He deluded himself into believing that he would find it in myths. They are inaccessible to the subjective imagination that aspires to the monumental while suspending the traditional canon of forms which alone would create it. *Moses und Aron* is traditional in the sense that it follows the methods of Wagnerian dramaturgy without a hiatus. It relates to the biblical narrative in just the same way as the music of the *Ring* or *Parsifal* relate to their underlying texts. The central problem is to find musical and dramatic methods whereby to represent the idea of the sacred—that is to say, not a mythical but an anti-mythical event. (239–40)

There is no doubt that *Moses* represents a compromise, nor is it doubtful that, as Adorno insists a bit further on, the musical language that Schönberg wanted to enlist in the service of monumentality, subject to dramaturgical constraints that are contrary to him, ruins itself as such: "The new language of music, entirely renovated to its innermost core, speaks as if it were still the old one" (240). And it is true that the "unified pathos" of the work, a pathos which hardly suits "the specifically Jewish inflection" (240) of Moses, causes the musical elaboration, because of this exterior fact, to disavow "the over-specific idea of the work as a whole": "The aesthetic drive towards sensuous expression works to the detriment of what that drive brings into being" (241). Is the dramaturgical model on which Schönberg bases his work that of Wagner?

■ Adorno points out this contradiction: a mythical dramaturgy with antimythical aims is only in effect a contradiction under two conditions: on the one hand the dramatic action must be of a mythical type, which is not to say that the myth must supply the material for the libretto, but—this at least is the solution Wagner found—that the scenic acts, indeed all the signifiers and mythical cells, must be constantly musically overdetermined (hence, the *Leitmotiv*). This is not at all the case in Schönberg. (To put it otherwise, Schönberg no doubt aims for a "music-drama," in the broad sense of the term, yet all the same he does not respect Wagnerian dramaturgy.) And on the other hand, it is necessary that opera should wish itself, as Adorno says, a "sacred opera," which *Parsifal* manifestly wanted to be.

■ Now it is exactly on this point that Schönberg's lucidity is greatest. His religious intentions, his search for a "great sacred art" are undeniable. Equally undeniable is his determination to write an anti-*Parsifal* (at bottom, this imposed itself). At the time when *Moses* was in the works, this determination is indissolubly artistic, philosophical, and political. All the same, he renounced this determination, and not just at any time, but in 1933 precisely. On this point Adorno says what must be said, and not just in any way, though his remarks appear a bit short.

■ Perhaps it is the case that in all of his argumentation—and this would be at the very least my hypothesis—Adorno twice allows himself to get carried away: the first time by the Wagnero-Nietzschean determination of music-drama, conceived as "new tragedy" or as "modern tragedy," the second time by the Hegelian determination of tragedy.

■ Hegel defines tragedy, or more exactly the tragic scenario, as "the struggle of new gods against ancient gods."[14] This is obviously the kind of scenario that Adorno rediscovers in *Moses*: the struggle of monotheism, as he says, against the gods of the tribe. Now as this is also, *mutatis mutandis*, the Wagnerian scenario (that of the *Ring* or of *Parsifal*), it is easy to see how the assimilation of the two is possible. (And this was surely the case, in one way or another, for Schönberg. Even if his true subject lay elsewhere—for as Adorno sees very well, it had to do with the very possibility of art—the rivalry with Wagner, and with Wagnerism, weighed on him with too great a force. Here I must admit that I am allowing myself to be guided by the admirable filmic version of *Moses* by Jean-Marie Straub and Danièle Huillet, for one must recognize that it is their dramaturgical intuition that is, as it happens, decisive. They stage the first two acts, but not that which remains of the third, in a Greek fashion, even if it is, for this production, actually the Roman theater of Alba Fucense in the Abruzzi region. In its original intention, in fact, *Moses* is a tragedy.)

■ But to continue from this point and think that an identity of scenario implies an identity of function, this is a great step. In the direct line of the Nietzsche of *The Birth of Tragedy*, but equally that of the Hegel who analyzes tragedy as a "religious" work of art (which is also to say, a political work of art), Adorno spontaneously thinks of tragedy from the starting point of the chorus, and of the chorus as the bearer of "religion" itself, not so much as fervor or belief, but as being-in-community. The chorus is not the people, or the representative of the people (of the spectators); but it is all the same the index that tragedy is originally a common or communitarian work of art, that it is community in and through the work, that is, a work without an individual or singular subject. That all "great art" is in the last resort the creation of a people, this is a dogma of German aesthetics from Hegel to Heidegger. And despite everything—I mean: despite "critical theory"— Adorno accepts this dogma right up to the moment in which it is revealed that the failure of a music which "extends a hand to the cult" (228) with such force and determination has to do with the fact that such a music, notwithstanding the affirmation of the "obligatory character" of its content, fails in being "substantial" in the Hegelian sense, because it is too "willed." An art can only attain greatness if the subject which carries it is—Adorno of course does not say: the people—society. This is why at bottom Adorno condenses all the questions of *Moses* in this question, itself of a transcendental sort: How is a cultic music simply possible outside of any cult? This is also to say, outside of any religious belonging and of any faith, and above all outside of all (social) effectiveness of the cultic. I attach here, with no commentary, the two following pieces:

The impossibility of the sacred work of art becomes increasingly evident the more the work insists on its claim to be one without invoking the support of any outside authority. With the modesty characteristic of the greatest emotional integrity, Schönberg ventured into this realm. The objection that the individual is no longer capable of the subjective piety which the biblical story calls for misses the mark. Bruckner was presumably a believer in an anachronistic sense and as musically inspired as any composer can be. Yet the Promised Land remained closed to him, and perhaps even to the Beethoven of the *Missa Solemnis*. The impossibility we are speaking of extends right into the objective preconditions of the form. Sacred works of art—and the fact that *Moses und Aron* was written as an opera does not disqualify it from being one—claim that their substance is valid and binding, beyond all yearning and subjective expression. The very choice of canonical biblical events implies such a claim. It is certainly implicit in the pathos of the music of *Moses und Aron*, whose intensity gives reality to a communal 'we' at every moment, a collective consciousness that takes precedence over every individual feeling, something of the order of the togetherness of a congregation. Were it otherwise, the predominance of the choruses would scarcely be imaginable. Without this transindividual element or, in other words, if it were merely a case of what is known as religious lyric poetry, the music would simply accompany the events or illustrate them. The compulsion to introduce into the music a sense of its own intellectual situation, to organize it in such a way that it expresses the underlying foundation of the events described, in short, its high aesthetic seriousness forces it into a collective stance. It must of necessity extend a hand to the cult if it is not entirely to fail its own intention. But cultic music cannot simply be willed. Anyone who goes in search of it compromises the very concept. (227–28; translation slightly modified)

We may legitimately ask what produced the conception of this work in the light of such immense difficulties, which may be compared to those experienced twenty years before in connection with *Die Jakobsleiter*. It is not the product of that misconceived monumentality, that unlegitimated gesture of authority which marks so much of the pictorial arts of the nineteenth century, from Puvis de Chavannes down to Marées. Of course it was Schönberg's own individual make-up that provided the critical impetus. His parents do not seem to have been orthodox in their beliefs, but it may be supposed that the descendant of a family of Bratislava Jews living in the Leopoldstadt, and anything but fully emancipated, was not wholly free of that subterranean mystical tradition to be found in many of his contemporaries of similar origins, men such as Kraus, Kafka and Mahler.

The Enlightenment displaced the theological heritage, shifting it on to the plane of the apocryphal, as we can infer from Schönberg's own autobiographical remarks. In particular, superstition survived tenaciously in his life and he often reflected on it. It is doubtless an instance of secularized mysticism. The experience of pre-fascist Germany, in which he rediscovered his Jewish roots, must have released this repressed dimension of his nature.

Moses und Aron was composed directly before the outbreak of the Third Reich, probably as a defensive reaction to what was about to sweep over him. Later, even after Hitler's fall, he did not return to the score. (232)

■ It is hardly doubtful that a question of the transcendental type is fundamental to *Moses*, and it would probably have been difficult for it to be otherwise if one considers that which in the German tradition regularly associates Kant and the figure of Moses ("Kant is the Moses of our nation," said Hölderlin). But it is perhaps not so certain that this question bears on the possibility of a sacred art in the final analysis.

■ In reality Adorno's demonstration is only possible inasmuch as it attaches itself almost exclusively to the music and remains perfectly indifferent to the rest, which is to say, if you will, to the text. This will not in any way be reduced to the libretto, but implies, beyond the scenario itself (in its strange loyalty to the biblical text, which Adorno greatly underestimates all the same), the dramaturgical structures which this scenario induces (for example, the chorus, which is in effect the people, is not Greek at all and in no way has a relation of the tragic type to the protagonists, despite immediate appearances) and, above all, the poem. Now not only does Adorno pay no attention to the text of Act III, under the pretext that it is not set to music (even so, this is decisive for the meaning that Schönberg expressly wished to confer upon the work, which thus concludes, as it is effectively written, with a pardon), but he systematically minimizes the problem of the relation between thought and language, a relation which is central, by assigning it to an inevitably subjective and profane ("heretical") interpretation of revelation, even though it is perhaps here that the transcendental question is articulated for Moses himself.

■ This exclusive attention accorded the music verifies itself in a privileged manner in the final *Rettung*, which is entirely given over to demonstrating the "success" of the work, which is to say, its adequation, despite the fundamental contradiction between intention and composition which subtends the opera. All of this comes down to displaying an internal adequation of the musical texture itself (identified *in fine* with the final accomplishment, by way of musical genius, of the passage to monotheism),[15] which properly redeems the fault that had consisted in making *musica ficta* serve against the figure. And it is such an adequation which fundamentally re-establishes, beyond the peripeteias of "great art" in the bourgeois era, the enigmatic but unseverable link between music and Jewishness.[16]

■ At the same time, if one pays attention this time to the critical aspect of the analysis, it is still this exclusive attention to the music which explains that besides the main grievance (music would be the image of that which eludes all images), one of the major accusations bears on the "unified pathos" of the work. As Adorno very clearly indicates, the incrimination does not take aim only at the "factitious" character of pathos, which arises because the religious content has lost all "substantiality." As a result of this, the "new language," withdrawing from itself, "speaks as if it were still the old one" (240), according to a compromise of the Wagnerian type between monumentality and musical modernity, which authorizes Adorno to speak of the strangely "traditional" effect of *Moses*. Nor does it take aim only at the insufficient differentiation of the couple formed by Moses and Aaron, the one who speaks and the one who sings, due this time to the "imitative" over-determination of the music. Moses, says Adorno, should not speak, for in the Bible he stutters. He adds that "it highlights the crisis of an art which makes use of this text purely as art and of its own free will" (230). But it essentially aims for obedience to the Wagnerian principle of the unity of language, which "cannot accommodate what the subject matter requires above all: the strict separation of Moses' monotheism from the realm of myth, the regression to the tribal gods. The pathos of the music is identical in both" (241). And it is here, moreover, that Adorno puts his fundamental hermeneutic principle into play, one which is borrowed once again from Benjamin, this time from the Benjamin of the celebrated essay "Goethe's *Elective Affinities*." For he explains that if one wishes to break the "vicious circle" of "entrapment in the coils of myth" which alone justifies the unity of language and technique in Wagner, "the caesura was to be decisive." But, he remarks, "the rupture was to become music" (241). This is evidently not the case:

The undifferentiated unity from which the ruthless process of integration allows nothing to be exempted comes into collision with the idea of the One itself. Moses and the Dance round the Golden Calf actually speak the same language in the opera, although the latter must aim to distinguish between them. This brings us close to the source of traditionalism in Schönberg, an issue which has only started to become visible in recent decades and especially since his death. In his eyes the idea of musical vocabulary as the organ of meaning was still instinctive and unquestioned. This vocabulary imagined itself able to articulate everything at any time. But this assumption was shaken by Schönberg's own innovations. (241–42)

To put it in other words, Schönberg betrays his own modernism. He bases his work on the codified syntax of tonality while his atonality would demand that he break it, in conformity with the subject of the work (which would thus be, one must believe: how is it that only atonal music is adequate to the monotheistic idea?). Because of this, Schönberg would be a victim of his epoch, exactly as Schiller was for Hegel. He would succumb to the bourgeois idea of genius, which is to say—but Adorno, precisely, does not say this and probably could not say this, at least not as crudely—of the sublime. But all the same, it is this which is at stake; the lexicon does not fool us:

This introduces a fictional element into the actual construction which so energetically opposes one. The situation points back to an illusion from which the bourgeois spirit has never been able to free itself: that of the unhistorical immortality of art. It forms a perfect complement to that decorative stance from which the Schönbergian innovations had effected their escape. The belief in genius, that metaphysical transfiguration of bourgeois individualism, does not allow any doubt to arise that great men can achieve great things at any time and that the greatest achievements are always available to them. No doubt can be permitted to impugn the category of greatness, not even for Schönberg. A justified scepticism towards that belief, which is based on a naive view of culture as a whole, is to be found in that specialization which Schönberg rightly opposed on the grounds that it acquiesced in the division of labor and renounced that extreme of the aesthetic, the sole legitimation of art. (242)

A verdict without appeal, but which is all the same astonishing on the part of someone who bases his work on the *past* existence of a "great sacred art" in order to condemn any and all factitious "restorations," as if at the same time, to put it by way of a shortcut, the sublime (grandeur) were a bourgeois invention and "great sacred art" were not a retrospective illusion—a projection—of the educated German bourgeoisie from Hegel to Heidegger, or from Kant to Adorno himself. That "aesthetic extremism" should be "the sole legitimation of art" for us, today, this is not doubtful. Who knows if this was not the case for Sophocles, or for Bach? And who knows if it is not precisely this that Wagner betrayed with his "compromises," but not Schönberg, who, as a victim of the bourgeois mythology of art—as Adorno is right to emphasize—all the same chose to abandon (one can suppose: knowing full well the cause of his decision) *Moses*, to *interrupt* it, rather than present supplementary evidence for the re-mythologization of art and of religion.

■ In any case, the question remains: What exactly does Adorno mean when he declares that the rupture (or the caesura) should have made "itself music"? It is easy to see that what is incriminated here is the too powerful homogeneity of the music, its flawless density which paradoxically (or, rather, dialectically) "redeems" or "saves" it as music to the detriment of the work itself in its project, that is, as a "sacred opera." The opposition of the *Sprechgesang* and the *melos*, to put it otherwise, does not "caesure" the continuity of the musical discourse, nor therefore does it bring out the monotheistic idea. The unity of language is pagan, idolatrous. But is the caesura simply a matter of differentiation internal to language—indeed, of the clear-cut opposition of voices? In what sense, at bottom, does Adorno understand "caesura"? And, an inseparable question: Why does he make so little of the interruption of the work—apparently accidental, "empirical," but does one ever know?—and above all, why does he make so little of the very strange mode in which this interruption comes about? I do not at all wish to suggest that the interruption *is* the caesura, but perhaps rather that the caesura, more inaudible to Adorno's ear than it is invisible to his eyes, masks itself in the interruption—which, from then on, would no longer be thinkable as interruption.

■ Here of course we must credit Adorno, in an analogous manner to that which he uses with the word *Rettung*, for using the word *caesura* in the enlarged but rigorous sense which Benjamin gives it in his essay on Goethe, where it is the technical term forged by Hölderlin for his structural theory of tragedy which is elevated to the level of a general critical (or aesthetic) concept: all works are organized as such from the starting point of the caesura inasmuch as the caesura is the hiatus, the suspension or the "antirhythmic" interruption which is not only necessary, as in metrics, to the articulation and the equilibrium of verse (of the phrase and, by extension, of what one might call the work phrase), but, more essentially, the place whence that which Hölderlin calls "pure speech" surges forth. The caesura, to put it otherwise, is the liberation by default—but a non-negative default—of the meaning itself or of the truth of the work. And from the critical point of view, it is only the caesura that indicates, in the work, the place that one must reach in order to accede to the *Wahrheitsgehalt*.[17]

■ On the basis of this hermeneutic model, Adorno is right to look for the caesura in *Moses*, as in any supposedly great work. Perhaps his only fault is to look for it, by "melocentrism," only in the music. For if one takes stock of what Schönberg effectively *wrote*, one can just as well construct the hypothesis that it is at the very place where the music—but not the work—interrupts itself, that is, precisely where Moses proclaims that the word (speech) fails him: "O Wort, du Wort, das mir fehlt!"

■ Indeed, it is well known that up until the end of the second act Schönberg *simultaneously* composed the libretto and the score. And that at the moment when he was to begin composing the third act—whether it is an accidental cause or not does not matter here—abruptly and without giving any indication exactly why, he only wrote the text of one scene, the scene where Moses, who reaffirms his "idea," pardons Aaron or at least orders that he not be executed. And here again it is necessary to recognize that the dramaturgical choice of Straub and Huillet is particularly illuminating: for not only do they play this merely spoken scene in the unbearable silence which succeeds the unfurling of the music, a silence that Adorno analyzes so well, but they have it played in a place other than that which, since the outset, was properly the stage or the theater. They do this in such a way that it is not only the tragic apparatus as Adorno understands it that collapses in a single stroke, but the entire apparatus which kept *Moses* within the frame of opera or music-drama. And it is here, probably, that religion is interrupted.

■ If such an indication is fair, if, dramaturgically, one must take into account this rupture or this hiatus and the passage to simple speech—for such is the enigma of that which remains of Schönberg's work—then there is indeed a caesura, and it clarifies the truth of the work in another way. In particular, it no longer permits one to refer the difference in enunciation between the two protagonists to Schönberg's submission to the imperatives of *musica ficta* (and of Wagnerian dramaturgy). It is from this principle that the music must despoil itself and remain nothing other than naked speech.

■ Beyond its structural function, in Hölderlin the caesura signifies—and it is because of this that it holds Benjamin's attention—the interruption *necessary* for tragic truth to appear, which is to say, the necessary separation, the necessary cut which must (but in the sense of a *sollen*) produce itself in the process of infinite collusion between the human and the divine which is the tragic flaw itself, hubris. The tragic separation, the uncoupling of God and man (which Hölderlin interprets as *katharsis*), thus signifies the law of finitude, which is to say, the impossibility of the immediate: "For mortals just as for immortals, the immediate is prohibited." An immediate interpretation of the divine (Oedipus) is no more possible than an immediate identification with the divine (Antigone). Mediation is the law [*Gesetz*], a law, moreover, that Hölderlin thinks in a rigorously Kantian fashion (as when he speaks of the "categorical diversion" of the divine which brings about the imperative obligation for man to return toward the earth).[18]

■ From here on, according to this model—and according to the logic of the extension of the concept inaugurated by Benjamin and apparently recognized by Adorno himself—why should we not think that insofar as it strikes and suspends the music in the course of a brief and dry scene, the caesura in *Moses* brutally makes it appear that Moses, the inflexible guardian of the Law and the defender of his own great—of his own sublime—conception of God, is also the one who by virtue of immoderation wants to be the too immediate interpreter of God: the mouth or the organ of the absolute, the very voice of God as its truth. This is why in never ceasing to proclaim the unrepresentability of God, indeed his ineffability, neither will he cease (on the same ground of *musica ficta* where Aaron moves around in all his ease) from striving to sing and not to confine himself strictly to speech, as if, by the effect of a compromise induced by his rivalry with Aaron, he were secretly tempted by the idea of a possible presentation (a sublime presentation, according to the rules of his great eloquence) of the true God, of the unpresentable itself. To the point where, for lack of speech or a word, in the despairing recognition of this lack—and here, precisely at this phrase the caesura is situated—he is swallowed up by his own great audacity and the music interrupts itself. By this one may understand why, in the only scene of the final act, all "sobriety" as Hölderlin would have said, Moses grants his pardon, which is to say that he renounces murder. Thus is verified the profound insight that underlies Freud's *Moses and Monotheism*, according to which the prohibition of representation is nothing other than the prohibition of murder.[19]

■ Such is the reason for which that which interrupts itself along with the music, that which is "caesured," is religion itself, if religion is defined as the belief in a possible (re)presentation of the divine, that is, if religion is unthinkable without an art or as an art (which, happily, does not mean—

"we have passed this step"—that art would be unthinkable without religion or as religion). What is at stake here, in the interruption of that which was without a doubt at the outset the project of a "sacred opera," is the very thing that Adorno considers beyond doubt for Schönberg: the figurativity of music. But in order to recognize this, it would have been necessary for Adorno to have been ready to *read Moses*, and not simply to hear it. Or it would have been necessary perhaps for him to have been able to recognize, in according more credit (or confidence) to Schönberg, the limits of his own musical mysticism.

■ At one moment in his analysis, Adorno notes this:

Schönberg's own need to express is one that rejects mediation and convention and therefore one which names its object directly. Its secret model is that of revealing the Name. Whatever subjective motive lay behind Schönberg's choice of a religious work, it possessed an objective aspect from the very outset—a purely musical one in the first instance. (233)

But is it not the same Adorno who had written some years earlier:

The language of music is quite different from the language of intentionality. It contains a theological dimension. What it has to say is simultaneously revealed and concealed. Its Idea is the divine Name which has been given shape. It is demythologized prayer, rid of efficacious magic. It is the human attempt, doomed as ever, to name the Name, not to communicate meanings.[20]

For Adorno as for Schönberg, music in its very intention would, in short, come under the horizon of that which Benjamin called "pure language,"[21] which is perhaps not without a rapport to that which Hölderlin, on the subject of the caesura, called "pure speech." But the Name, as Adorno well knows, is unpronounceable—and music is a vain prayer, the sublime as such, according to its most tried and true code since Kant: "[Music's] Idea is the divine Name which has been given shape." An art (of the) beyond (of) signification, which is to say, (of the) beyond (of) representation. All the same, under the "O Wort, du Wort, das mir fehlt!" that Moses proclaims in the last burst of music, it is not prohibited to hear resonating an "O Name, du Name, der mir fehlt!" As when Kant takes as his major example of the sublime utterance the very prohibition of representation (the Mosaic law), this is in reality a meta-sublime utterance which tells in a sublime manner—and the passage to the naked word in Act III of *Moses* is absolutely sublime—the truth of the sublime, itself sublime.[22] Ultimate paradox: the naked word—the language of signification itself—comes to tell of the impossible beyond signification, something which Benjamin would not have denied, and to signify the transcendental illusion of expression. This is why *Moses* is not "successful." It is "unsaveable" if for Adorno "to save" never means anything other than to consider artworks according to the scale of adequation, which is to say, of beauty: the religious gesture par excellence. Now what *Moses* says precisely, but despite itself—and one must well imagine Schönberg constrained and forced, which is after all the lot of every modern artist—is that art is religion in the limits of simple inadequation; probably the end, in every sense, of religion. Or to be more just: the caesura of religion.

The Replay's the Thing

Peggy Kamuf

Two sets of subtitles accompanying images on a split television screen. The images are often similar or even the same on one side and the other of the screen's dividing line. The effect is that of a replay. Like the subtitles for a film, the text tries to render in another language the sense of the images passing on the screen. These reproduce for the most part well-known public events of recent memory, whose dates are recalled here:

July 1969	*A man first walks on the Moon (Apollo 11).*
February 1972	*U.S. President Richard M. Nixon, near the end of his first presidential term, goes to China for a summit meeting.*
November 1972	*Nixon reelected to a second term.*
May 1989	*Soviet President Mikhail Gorbachev goes to China for a summit meeting.*
April–June 1989	*The "Beijing Spring."*

As for the other principal event evoked by the subtitles, the opera Nixon in China *(music by John Adams, libretto by Alice Goodman, directed by Peter Sellars) was given its first public performance October 1987 in Houston.*

* * *

"The Replay's the Thing" was written for this volume. Excerpts from Alice Goodman's libretto *Nixon in China* appear by permission of Hendon Music, Inc. Libretto © 1987 by Alice Goodman.

■—"The people are the heroes now . . ." sings the chorus in the opening scene of *Nixon in China*. The people, the chorus stand in regimental order, or move in strict patterns as they recite in unison their lines. They are the people's representatives, probably a delegation of officials, and they have come to the airport in Peking (in 1972 that is still the accepted transliteration) to meet Richard Nixon and his party, the first time a President of the United States has made a State visit to their country. Their mission is to be present at this historic occasion, to let the world see the people's representatives so it will remember who are the heroes of this story. But the people themselves, billions of them, are absent.

—*We watch people amass in the large public square, every day more numerous. The Western camera crews and teams of reporters have gone to Beijing to record the first visit of a Soviet President to the People's Republic since the cooling off of Soviet-Chinese relations. The people in the square have given the cameras an unexpected sight.*

■—Chou En-lai enters and positions himself at the foot of the steps on which the President and Mrs. Nixon (the singer-actors imitate them in dress, in gesture, in expression) will descend from the life-size model of Air Force One. Chou is the Premier, the first among the people's representatives to greet the "leader of the Western world." They clasp hands and are frozen for a long moment in that pose, holding it for the cameras, as if they were already seeing the picture they give of themselves on the front pages of all the world's newspapers the next day. They still have not spoken or sung a word. Then they exchange some rather banal talk about the flight, jet lag, and the Premier pronounces his greeting formula. The chorus lines up behind and to the left of Chou, who turns and begins to introduce them one by one to the President: "The Deputy Minister of Security," "[something

something] of the Army." Chou's presentations are barely audible, although his lips are forming words as he and Nixon move down the line that the chorus has formed.

—Press release: "At mid-morning today, about 30,000 student protesters, supporters, and onlookers were still gathered in Tian An Men Square, where the late afternoon welcoming ceremony had been scheduled. The decision to move the welcoming ceremony to Beijing's old airport terminal marked a return to the old protocol in which visiting dignitaries were greeted immediately on their arrival, rather than later at Tian An Men Square" (Los Angeles Times, *15 May 1989). The image of Deng Xiao-ping and Gorbachev shaking hands will be on to-morrow's front page, of course, but they will look a little dismayed as if they could not re-*

member the lines they'd rehearsed. *They too are watching the people in the square who have forced them to improvise. And the people in the square know as well that the Western cameras have satellite hook-ups which can beam images around the world without delay, "live." Irresistibly, the cameras will be drawn toward the square that is now filled day and night.*

■—Nixon shakes each hand, but he hardly looks at the officials. He is elsewhere, watching the replay of his image and that of the Prime Minister beamed around the world. After each distracted handshake, Nixon turns to face the front of the stage, where the public and the cameras are watching, while he sings:

> News news news news news news news news
>   news news news news
> Has a kind of mystery
> When I shook hands with Chou En-lai,
> On this bare field outside Peking
> Just now, the whole world was listening
> And though we spoke quietly,
> The eyes and ears of history
> Caught every gesture,
> And every word, transforming us
> As we, transfixed,
> Made history

■—Nixon's repetitions translate a nervous excitement, barely able to contain itself, the syntax finally collapsing in the last lines. The first word, "news," is sung over and over to the same note in a syncopated rhythm that gets going so fast it almost trips over itself by the end. As if one were hearing the mechanical clatter of a newsroom, the background soundtrack of television news broadcasts, or the pulsing of a telegraphic signal as it used to be represented in the old newsreels: dit-dit-dit-DIT-dit-dit-dit-dit-DIT. "Dateline Peking, Monday, February 21, 1972: President Richard Nixon was greeted today by Premier Chou En-lai as he arrived in Peking for a five-day State visit. It was history in the making."

■ The rhythms and harmonics of John Adams (did his name destine him to this presidential suite?) are perfectly adjusted to these effects of telegraphic and televisual media, although one ought not invoke here any mimetic or representational model. This is not Vivaldi imitating chirping birds or Beethoven making us hear a thunderstorm (although later, in Act II, the music will in fact imitate a thunderstorm as part of its evocation of *The Red Detachment of Women*). The relation between the musical line and the thematic line is altogether different. They are thoroughly implicated in each other, mediating each other, the one propelling or transmitting the other. Besides, how could the media ever be simply a theme?

■—Turning, then, toward the mystery of the replay, Nixon absents himself from this presentation, which proceeds without him, as it were, *à contretemps*, syncopated, in an off-beat rhythm, just before or behind the beat of the historic moment. He is transported to the other side of the world where he sees his image glowing at the center of a familiar intimacy before it is dispersed into the night:

> *News news news news news news news news*
> *It's prime time in the U.S.A.*
> *Yesterday night. They watch us now;*
> *The three main networks' colors glow*
> *Livid through the drapes onto the lawn.*
> *Dishes are washed and homework done,*
> *The dog and grandma fall asleep,*

> A car roars past playing loud pop,
> Is gone.

Notice the conjunction: the "internal" faculty of imagination, by which Nixon transports himself in his mind, and the "external" technology, which transmits his televised image, are flowing through the same relays. The mental exercise is grafted onto the technical feat; the one relays the other as if, in the "age of telecommunications," that which we call imagination could at last recognize itself in its outside. Turned all inside out, Nixon tries to see himself being seen, to capture his own image in its very dissemination, to listen to the world listening to him: "Just now, the world was listening. / Though we spoke quietly / The eyes and ears of history / Caught every gesture." Like a cat chasing its tail, he is pursuing a "mystery" that withdraws to the precise extent he reaches out to grasp it. The movement is by turns exhilarating (he is at the summit of the world, making history; he says he is "put in mind of our Apollo astronauts / Achieving a great human dream") and threatening, since the pursuer is also pursued. Alice Goodman's libretto succeeds not only in sketching the psychological portrait of this volatile reversibility (in her summary of this scene she writes: "As [the President] sings, the joy of anticipated triumph becomes the terrible expectation of failure") but also in locating its mechanism in a network of relays that are not simply psychological.

—*Richard Nixon's well-known mistrust of the media recalls Walter Benjamin's analysis: The performance of the movie actor before cameras must submit "to a series of optical tests." Since it is the film, and not the actor himself, that presents these performances to an audience:*

this permits the audience to take the position of a critic, without experiencing any personal contact with the actor. The audience's identification with the actor is really an identification with the camera. Consequently the audience takes the position of the camera;

its approach is that of testing. . . . "The film actor," wrote Pirandello, "feels as if in exile—exiled not only from the stage, but also from himself. With a vague sense of discomfort, he feels inexplicable emptiness; his body loses its corporeality, it evaporates, it is deprived of reality, life, voice, and the noises caused by moving about, in order to be changed into a mute image, flickering an instant on the screen, then vanishing into silence." This situation might also be characterized as follows: for the first time—and this is the effect of the film—man has to operate with his whole living person, yet forgoing its aura. For aura is tied to his presence; there can be no replica of it.[1]

Richard Nixon was not a movie actor, but a politician who witnessed the advent of television into politics. Historians of this phenomenon invariably cite 1960 as a watershed year, the year of the first televised debate between American presidential candidates: Richard Nixon and John Kennedy. Nixon, they say, lost the election that year because he lost the "debate," by which they mean that his image—ill-shaven, perspiring, badly made-up (it seems he had the flu)—was a poor match for Kennedy's youthful good looks. Nixon had failed his screen test. The demonstration of television's potential influence on electoral politics was made. For having anticipated it, Kennedy won; Nixon had to learn his lesson the hard way. It is true that eight years later, armed with a new image (the "new Nixon") and no doubt some media consultants, Nixon managed his comeback. However, once it had been flaired, the odor of mistrust never really left Nixon's relation to the media, particularly television with its power to evaporate aura. The "tricky Dick" epithet stuck to him, since one sensed he never fully gave himself up to the image, but held something in reserve. The gap seemed perceptible between his intense awareness of television's now indispensable power and his discomfort at submitting to its manipulation. This gap also measures the difference between Nixon and the successful movie actor president, Reagan. It explains, up to a point, why the former had Watergate and the latter had Teflon. Nixon, it seemed, always had something to hide while Reagan, pure simulacrum, never did and never had. A kind of sullied aura clung to the former's image and denounced it as just an image, that is, a dissimulation or a cover-up.

■—What happened in China that week? The event was recorded and reproduced probably more than any single event in history before then. But is it not precisely by virtue of its reproducibility that this unique and first-

time occurrence, this media event, was already from the first not simply itself, an identifiable unicity? The chorus of witnesses saw Nixon arrive in Peking at the same time as they saw his arrival reproduce itself immediately, without delay, or as we say, "live." They saw the fabulous technical apparatus of the Western press deployed all around them, catching their every gesture and every word. For this "meeting of East and West," the staging was no less elaborate than for the opera whose set designer, Adrianne

Lobel, has remarked: "Every second of Nixon's trip was photographed, and I realized that the China that was presented to him was designed. The trip itself was like a huge, operatic presentation."[2] Indubitably, something happened, and for the first time according to a certain geopolitical symbolics, but what and where and when?

—We know now that these days in May 1989 will be remembered not for the Soviet-Chinese summit but for the popular demonstrations that every day grow more bold in the face of an intransigent State and party leadership. With Gorbachev's departure, these leaders have retreated from the view of the cameras. Intensely public events in Beijing still fill our television screens, but they are now more clearly projected against a background of secret deliberations. The greedy cameras wait for the outcome.

■—A media event, we said. With that term is understood an event staged totally or in part for the media, especially television. As such, it is not identical to or coincident with the event it would appear to be, but at once more and less: more because one of the givens of the event is its "filmability," its occurrence in the presence of cameras, and thus alongside its own duplication; less because, intended for duplication and broadcast, the event does not quite manage to happen there where it takes place, but always at some remove from itself and in its own absence. Televised media events display the fundamental instability within the meaning of an event from the moment it is reproducible, that is, from the moment it is retained, recorded, registered as event. Take an obvious example from the domain of electoral politics where this phenomenon is studied so as to be better exploited. When the candidate for public office schedules a "photo opportunity" in a disadvantaged neighborhood of his or her electoral district, the doubled image of the event makes it immediately prey to incompatible interpretations:

on the one hand, there is the public official extending his or her representative status to a part of the public habitually left out of the representative
process; on the other, there is the same official for whom the former image
is good publicity. By the fact of its reduplication and broadcast, the first image always risks being replaced by the second and thereby emptied of its
intended significance. By "media event" we have come to understand this
sort of empty image in which the camera records its own intervention at
the center of an action that is thereby thrown off-center in an endless di-
vergence from itself. In this sense, media events do not ever happen; they
only recur.

—*Twenty years ago one heard the chant: "The revolution will not be televised." Today in Beijing, the demonstrators applaud the foreign news teams, carry signs in English and French,
and protect the cameramen from police aggression. What exactly are these news teams and
cameras doing by focusing on the crowd and interviewing some of the demonstrators?*

■—By asking, "What happened that week?" we are still trying to sort out
the real event from its mediatized "deviations" or its rhetorical detours. Perhaps that is also Nixon's hope in the opera. Remember that when he steps
off the plane and puts his foot for the first time on Chinese soil, he says he
is "put in mind of our Apollo astronauts"? Interesting association: When
Neil Armstrong became the first human to step onto the surface of the
Moon, the symbolic significance attributed to his act—"one giant leap
for mankind"—remained, despite the aggrandizing rhetoric, indissociable
from a punctual fact, the "small step for a man." It would therefore not occur
to us to question where, when, or whether this event took place because
what took place is almost totally reducible to, precisely, a place, a date, and
an action. The presence of cameras recording the event and transmitting

an image of it as it happened apparently does little to alter these punctual givens. It might, however, lead us to ask whether a man or his reproduced image first made contact with an extraterrestrial body, or even whether we any longer have the means of making that distinction. Nevertheless, that Nixon is "put in mind" of this feat suggests a desire: for geopolitical events to be likewise indissociable from punctual acts that are themselves the result of purely technical calculations. More than that, perhaps, Nixon would like to imagine that his sheer presence on Chinese soil will leave a mark as unambiguous as footprints on the Moon, as if China were utterly free of human traces rather than the most populous country on Earth with one of the oldest written histories. What seems seductive about the astronaut analogy, in other words, is this marking of a "virgin" surface which negates the specter of man's absence. Instead of such a seemingly simple dialectic, however, there is this summit on top of a mountain of metaphor, the one Chou invokes in his banquet toast: "We have begun / To celebrate the different ways / That led us to this mountain pass, / This summit where we stand. Look down / And think what we have undergone. / Future and past lie far below / Half-visible. . . . The virtuous American / And the Chinese make manifest / Their destinies in time." The summit meeting of East and West takes place on this shifting ground of metaphor, which is far more alien and alienating than the surface of the Moon because it is not just a passive support for the marks of a human presence or intentional meaning, but already that which transports the mark of presence outside itself.

■—A mountain or perhaps an abyss that opens up beneath their feet, the abyss precisely of the East/West "opening." This metaphor of passage across borders (geographical, economic, ideological) implies a transfer of the mark, its mediatization or telecommunication, which is anything but a delimitable process intervening in the event and forcing it to deviate from its proper trajectory. For what would be the "proper trajectory" of an event that presents itself in the form, precisely, of an *opening* to the outside, of East to West and vice versa? There is, rather, a dislocation of the very idea of the "proper" which happens. That is what the cameras have come to film. But, by definition, the dislocation does not take place where it takes place, before the cameras, *in* China, since what is opened up is the interiority or immanence of such a spatial, national entity, folded back on itself and recognizing itself in its Maoist or McCarthyite features. The media apparatus on location in China is part of the dislocation that it reports. The historical event and the media event dislocate one another.

—*Political analysts speak of a "boomerang effect," by which they mean the effect of foreign news reports beamed back into the country from which they originated by means of broadcast networks such as the BBC and the VOA. The importance of the effect is such that democratic opposition movements to authoritarian regimes (in Chile, in the Philippines, in South Korea) have even hired media consultants to help them use the foreign press as a pressure on their own media. "In an age of mass communications," remarks one such consultant, "it's difficult to maintain a totalitarian regime."[3] The boomerang effect de-totalizes by bringing the outside back in.*

■—A similar dislocation could account for the fact that Nixon's awareness of the media's operation is accompanied by the anxiety we have already remarked. Here is another example. The President is replying to the Premier's banquet toast:

> No one who heard could but admire
> Your eloquent remarks, Premier,
> And millions more hear what we say
> Through satellite technology
> Than ever heard a public speech
> Before. No one is out of touch.
> No one, no one, no one is out of touch.
> Telecommunication has
> Broadcast your message into space.
> Yet soon our words won't be recalled
> While what we do can change the world.
> We have at times been enemies,
> We still have differences, God knows.
> But let us, in these next five days

Start a long march on new highways,
In different lanes, but parallel
And heading for a single goal.
The world watches and listens. We
Must seize the hour and seize the day.

The dislocation is at work here in an apparent overturning of the order of things. This order prescribes that the media be there because there is an event to be reproduced; here, on the contrary, an event must be produced because the media are there to reproduce it. The production of this first-time event, in other words, is not the condition but the effect of its reproduction. This means that the distinction between the first time and its countless repetitions passes through the event itself which has already, from the moment it occurs, recurred. How, then, to seize this hour or this day if their punctual identities are divided from within and from the first, as it were? Nixon's cliché, "We / Must seize the hour and seize the day," acquires a surprising eloquence in this regard because the very terms with which he appeals for an hour and a day that would initiate a new series, "change the world," fall back into the endless repetition of a cliché. The used-up rhetoric designates nothing so well as the emptying out of the unique position of a first time. When that vacancy is then filled, not by a uniqueness but by a figure of unprecedented repetition ("millions more hear what we say / Through satellite technology / Than ever heard a public speech / Before"), the media event has come full circle. The structure is that of a repetition installed at the beginning or the center of the event, which does not so much unfold as continue to fold back on itself, as if it were on a continuous playback loop: "Millions more than ever heard a public speech before hear me say that millions more than ever heard a public speech before hear me say . . ."

—*Millions of people are in the streets now all over China's cities. Millions more in the world's democracies are captivated by the scenes that are beamed into their proximity. They can read, in English and in French, the slogans of Western revolutions recycled to the other side of the globe. The rhythm of this geopolitical revolution is double; it rotates on two axes. There is the rhythm of the simultaneous or the contemporary that races ahead in the development of telecommunications. Here, the rule is absolute speed that would close any gap marking the time of the other, at a distance. It is the time of both the "global village" and the permanent state*

of virtual war and surveillance analyzed by Paul Virilio.[4] *But by turning faster and faster on
this axis, the technology of the contemporary uncovers disjunctions within the "same time."
Thus, the West can seem to recognize its past resurfacing in the latest news from the East,
as if the world had reversed direction. The positions of the avant-garde and the counterrev-
olutionary cross, forming a configuration in which the political world (in the West as well as*

the East, and from left to right) can no longer orient itself as usual. A politics of the contretemps *is taking shape over against the globalization of time.*

■—*Nixon in China* remarks the conditions of a media event and in so doing reflects the possibility of its own invention in the age of technical reproducibility. How is it possible for opera to reinvent itself as a contemporary of mass telecommunications? What does "contemporary" mean in a context of immediate and limitless reproduction? Can this latter trait still be taken, as it is by Benjamin, for whom technical reproduction spells the destruction of the aura of the work of art, as the mark of the masses and therefore of what is called "popular culture" to be distinguished from "high art" (a thing of the past, said Hegel)? Why these quotation marks? They mark a distinction, but they also alert us to the principle of reproducibility at work within this pair of concepts. In other words, when the certainty of reference is suspended (an effect of the quotation marks) we are reminded of the possibility of all manner of repetition between the two poles of the distinction, including, for example, the quotation of the one by the other.

■ We will come back to this example of quotation in a moment, but for now let's take up the notion of the contemporary. On one level, *Nixon in China* proposes *contemporaneity* as a principle of opera's reinvention. The composer has been quoted in the press to this effect:

John Adams, for his part, believes that opera today has "lost its relevance to our experience"; it is out of touch, and "we hardly need another opera on a Shakespeare play or a Greek myth." Great modern political figures like Nixon and Mao, and Kennedy and Stalin, are "the mythological characters of our time."[5]

The idea of "relevance" invoked here is a deceptively simple one. It supposes a straightforward referential function, a single fold relating "our experience" or "our time" to the work. This too simple account (it is true that, as a composer, Adams has no doubt had little need to think about problems of reference or relevance; what would "relevant" music be?) leaves aside, among other things, the fact that "our experience" and "our time" are themselves already determined by such a fold of relevant reference. That is, the experience of our time, our contemporaneity, is marked by a redundance of relevance: relevance is relevant to our experience.

■ More than any other current technology of reproduction, video technology has become an instrument of this contemporary redundancy. It is deployed, that is, according to the principle of simultaneous, contemporaneous production and reproduction of images, their transmission virtually without delay, "live." Television would be the experience of the contemporary both in the sense of what it gives us to see and hear without delay, in the same time, and as that which marks a distinct historical experience. Thus, an opera, or any other kind of work, that would be *relevant* to this experience (that is, literally, that would arise from it) will have to some extent taken television as the model to be simulated.

■ Is this the event of *Nixon in China* as a contemporary opera?

■—A made-for-TV opera? Consider what happens when a performance of the opera is broadcast on television—prerecorded or "live," it does not matter—as it in fact was in April 1988 (simulcast in FM stereo). The first act concludes with an exuberant round of toasts. There is a gay confusion carried along by the orchestra's racing rhythms and punctuated by popping sounds (champagne corks or flashbulbs). The crescendo builds, Nixon and Chou turn to each other once more, raise their glasses, and as the last chord sounds, the actors hold their pose. As one critic has remarked in commenting on the same scene, it is "as if the hold button had been pressed on a VCR."[6] The analogy to a video effect is anything but fortuitous, however, since the staging is in fact a visual quotation of the moment Nixon and Chou held the same pose for the cameras in 1972. So as to quote the pose more exactly, the stage director would have needed only to consult a video archive. Now, this staging is itself being filmed for the television broadcast of the performance by several cameras placed around the theater and stage. The film editing selects from among the different camera angles, and, as one would fully expect, it cuts to a close-up of the toast and ends with that image, freezing the already frozen pose on the screen. In other words, the filming of the theatrical performance obeys the same rules as the filming of the diplomatic banquet; their frames are superimposed, as if the camera had shot a televised image within the precise dimensions of the screen.

There is a telescoping of all the levels of representation: the actors' pose reproduces the televised image of Nixon and Chou, who have already frozen the frame and given an imitation of themselves. The pose held on the stage becomes the image frozen on the screen which it also already was. It succeeds itself by preceding itself—and vice versa. There is no simple, original referent here that can anchor these leapfrogging effects because the actors' simulation makes reference, undecidably and at the same time, both to an image and to its immediate mediation or reproduction.

■ All these teleoperations carry out or develop (as with a photograph) the reproducibility of the event itself. Traditional theories of representation, which cannot integrate this notion of original reproducibility, are inapt for an analysis of teleoperative effects. A teleoperative effect would be a displacement of the interval that traditionally permits one to distinguish between production and reproduction. The interval is measured as a distance, a difference, a delay, and eventually a deviation, a decadence, a detour. By reducing it to virtual simultaneity, video technology has uncovered the interval of reproducibility *within* the simul-, the same moment and the same event. What falls due in the age of television, of teleopera, and of teleoperations in general is the long-deferred necessity to take into account the irreducible interval or deviation *within* the same event and the event of the same.

■ But such an account-taking requires time, and now it is time that is lacking. Teleoperations make impossible what they make possible, at the same time.

—There were, by one estimate, 1,200 foreign journalists in Beijing at the height of the Soviet-Chinese summit. When the far more compelling events in the square drew the reporters' cam-

eras and microphones into their midst, there was a convergence of the movement for free speech with a free, or liberal, press. Their alliance went without saying, as the saying goes. The terrific force and magnitude of the popular resistance to State censorship was an irresistible mirror held up in front of the Western press. It saw reflected there its own mission: to show and tell things as they are, in short, the mission of Truth. Truth itself, it appeared, had presented itself uncensored, without guise, impelling millions of Chinese workers, students, and bureaucrats to manifest themselves as well. The media's mission never seemed so clear, so determined by the very event they reported; the transmission of images and sounds never seemed more transparent. A constraint had given way: the necessity to calculate the interval between mission and transmission, the presentation of Truth and its representation. It is as if the self-evidence of the thing had managed to break through the deflecting screen of representation and impose itself as such, without external support.

This was not simply an illusion or mirage. A singular force had indeed imposed itself, but its impact did not shatter the screen of an originary reproducibility. Not yet the apocalypse, the end of representation, the event is rather an eclipse into which, for a moment, disappears the potential of its own deflection, deviation, or detour. The Chinese authorities, in the meantime and while taking their time, working by the light of these new satellites, had no difficulty monitoring and taping American television transmissions from Beijing. Edited and rebroadcast on Chinese television, the filmed record of protest against an order of censorship could thus reappear as a powerful instrument of the reimposition of that order. The filmed record of the demonstrations ended up in the police records. (In 1992, the Los Angeles Police Department would make a very similar use of TV camera footage shot during the events that began on April 29.) Between the live broadcast and this sinister replay, this boomerang effect that recalls the original function of the hunter's weapon, the catastrophic interval within the event reasserts itself after the eclipse.

Intractable logic of this sequence: the possibility of the replay is inscribed in the event, but as that whose calculation must be suspended for the event to take place. When, therefore, with a certain delay, the possibility plays itself out, any calculation will be too late.

■—Despite the superimpositions, the quotation of the TV image does not unduly disturb the frame of reference. In Act II, scene ii, however, what begins as a quotation, in the form of a play within a play, soon breaks down into something without identifiable outlines. While we cannot strictly speak here of a *mise en abîme*, because the work quotes another opera rather than trying to frame its own repetition, there is all the same an effect of near implosion as if the work had let itself be drawn into a mirror. When this strange fascination takes over the double scene, one senses that the opera has put in play its own operation, its own invention.

■ We quote from Alice Goodman's summary:

Act II, scene ii: The curtain rises to reveal an audience. Madame Mao in a dark Sun Yatsen suit and black-rimmed men's glasses, sits between the President and Mrs. Nixon. . . . We have only a few seconds to grasp these details before another curtain rises onstage. Three [in the final staging there are in fact four] beautiful young women are chained to posts [finally, only one of them will be chained]. The First Lady sits forward a little, as, indeed, does the President. . . . This is the opening of *The Red Detachment of Women.*

At the opera with the Nixons, we watch the opening of Mme Mao's ballet opera: a vigorous dance, accompanied by singers who denounce the corruption and exploitation of the evil landlords. Enter a man with a cane who approaches the girl chained to the post; as he releases her, he boasts of his latest sexual exploit and mimes lascivious gestures. Despite Groucho-like moustache and eyebrows, we recognize the actor who also plays Henry Kissinger. Pat Nixon is also struck by the resemblance: "Doesn't he look like you-know-who!" she whispers to the President. (The fact that a Kissinger persona can play a role in both operas suggests, of course, the same possibility for any of the other characters.) The unchained girl escapes the clutches of the lusting overseer, played by the Kissinger actor, but not for long. He and his guards capture her and begin to beat her mercilessly. The First Lady is outraged:

Kissinger (as Lao Szu):	*Whip her to death!*
Pat:	*They can't do that!*
Nixon:	*It's just a play*
	She'll get up afterwards, you'll see.
	Easy there, Hon.
Kissinger:	*Whip her to death!*
Pat:	*It's terrible! I hate you both!*
	Make them stop, make them stop!

Pat Nixon then rushes onstage, followed by the President, who tries to restrain her: "Sweetheart, / Leave them alone, you might get hurt." From this point, the presidential couple is drawn into the action of the ballet that proceeds as if their roles were already written for them. Pat comforts the girl and recounts what has happened to her to the Party Representative, who heralds the arrival of the Red Women's Militia. "Thank God you came. Just look at this! / Poor thing! It's simply barbarous! / 'Whip her to death!' he said. I'd like / To give his God-damned whip a crack!" The scene shifts. Nixon, or the actor playing Nixon, reappears at a reception in honor of the lord of the estate. Kissinger (as Lao Szu, the overseer) fawns on the visitor and presents himself, a right-hand man to his boss, in terms that collapse the actor's two roles: the Chinese landlord's overseer and the U.S. President's chief adviser:

> *I have my brief*
> *I flatter myself*
> *I know my man*
> *The sine qua non*
> *The face on the coin*
> *You see what I mean*
> *The empire builder*

. . .

And me, I contrive
To catch a few crumbs—
The ringleaders' names
The gist of their schemes—
Loose change.

At which point, Nixon (as visiting capitalist) tosses some coins in his direction. Nixon and Pat remain onstage to the end of the scene, which is taken over by Chiang Ch'ing, Mme Mao. She intervenes from the audience onstage as the President's wife had done. After issuing a strict reprimand concerning Party discipline, she shoulders Pat aside and replaces the latter's comforting embrace of the peasant girl, now enrolled in the detachment of women, with a stiff hold on her. An enormous portrait of Mao Tse-tung, copied by the set designer from the portrait that hangs in Tian An Men Square, moves into place downstage center. Chiang Ch'ing commands everyone's attention with the emphatic aria that sings her own praises: "I am the wife of Mao Tse-tung / Who raised the weak above the strong / When I appear the people hang upon my words, etc." During the reprise of the solo, the dancers form into groups each around a leader who holds aloft a book and points to it. While a horrified Pat Nixon looks on, some of the dancers chase others down and beat them. By this point it is quite impossible to tell whether the action onstage is still part of *The Red Detachment of Women* or whether the Chinese opera has simply dissolved into an indoctrination session with an audience. The curtain falls.

—*Imagine a more succinct summary of these scenes: the Western spectator, overwhelmed by the image of the Chinese people's struggle against its oppressor, is drawn into this play of forces; but the oppressor has several faces and the earnest Westerner is caught off guard when one of them, who has been watching from the sidelines and has seen everything, comes center stage to take the situation in hand; the spectator is expelled and the scene repeats.*

■—We see Pat Nixon as the naive spectator who forgets that, as the President puts it, "It's just a play," just a repetition, just a representation, not the "real thing." We believe he is right, of course, which is why we don't rush onstage, unlike Pat. The question is, however, why, if he's right, does the play continue as if it had not just been interrupted by the intrusion of a spectator? On the one hand, this seems merely to confirm that melodramatic kitsch must always suppose such a spectator who is thus, in a sense, already inscribed within it. But, on the other hand, it accuses an insufficiency in the formula "It's just a play" (or an opera, movie, television show, and so forth), in other words, a simulation and therefore harmlessly unreal. Can we reliably distinguish the former effect from the latter, a certain naivete from a certain critique? For instance, when Pat can no longer tolerate the spectacle of cruelty, she cries out: "It's terrible! I hate you both!/Make them stop, make them stop!" Her outburst points to a collusion between the two sides of the divided stage: "I hate you both," she says. Between a thing and its representation, the dividing line may always be wholly imaginary and dissolve imperceptibly. As we have been saying, an originary reproducibility precedes any division of the sort that is first staged and then dissolved here when Pat Nixon, naively, rushes to the side of the tormented girl.

■ And with that the scene begins to repeat. *Nixon in China* is no longer simply quoting (or pretending to quote) this other work, *The Red Detachment of Women.* Or, rather, the quoting function is still operating, but it is now unclear both where the quotation marks are exactly and which work is quoting the other. Mme Mao's "popular" ballet is at once partially absorbed and inassimilable, thus not simply part of a whole, a whole which, because it cannot close on itself, is not a whole but also a part. The fascination that draws Pat Nixon into the melodrama can be taken as the figure of a fascination at work on the work itself, drawing the opera toward this point of suspended repetition between its own operation and the operation of popular myth, between the appeal of relevant contemporaneity and the force of demagogic manipulation . . . between, as well, historical opera and the opera(tion) of history.

—The television still turned on, the opera is brought to a close. One last freeze-frame image: "Flanked by military leaders, Deng Xiao-ping delivered a televised speech Friday night. Like the last scene of a Chinese opera in which the emperor reappears surrounded by his generals, it was perceived by many as a message addressed to those who might harbor hopes for change: the regime is still solid, the army is behind it, and the situation is in control."[7]

■—Last scene of the last act: Chou En-lai, who keeps watch in his insomnia, calls to the coming day, the day that is not yet our contemporary and whose work undoes present remedies.

> *How much of what we did was good?*
> *Everything seems to move beyond*
> *Our remedy. Come, heal this wound.*

He sings very softly.

Taking Place: Toward a Theater of Dislocation

Samuel Weber

> Moreover, beautiful objects are to be distinguished from beautiful views of
> objects (which often by virtue of distance can no longer be clearly recognized).
> In the latter case taste appears, not so much in what the imagination
> *apprehends* in this field, as in the occasion it receives to *poeticize* [*dichten*],
> i.e., in the peculiar fantasies with which the mind entertains itself, while
> continually being awakened by the variety that strikes the eye; as, for instance,
> at the sight of the changing figures of a fire in a fireplace, or that of a rippling
> brook, neither of which is in itself beautiful.
>
> Kant, *The Critique of Judgment*

During the initial performances of the Frankfurt Opera's staging of *Aida*
January 1981, two scenes seemed particularly to offend a substantial seg-
ent of the audience. The first was the opening scene of the opera, or,
ther, the scene that preceded the opening of the drama, since it accom-
nied the overture. In this scene, Radames, captain of the Egyptian palace
ard, appears dressed in the civilian clothes of a nineteenth-century Eu-
pean businessman. At a certain moment in what seems to be a dream, he
izes a shovel (implausibly located in what appears to be an office) and
gins to dig in the earth, or, rather, to tear up the floorboards of the stage,
inging to light first sand, then a sword, and finally the sculpted head of
da. (See Photo 1.)
The other, highly provocative scene occurs at the beginning of the second
t, when the rising curtain reveals or, rather, confronts the audience with
mething like its mirror image: the original first-night audience of the op-
a's European premiere at La Scala in 1872. (See Photo 2.) But whereas the

king Place: Toward a Theater of Dislocation" originally appeared in *enclitic* 8, nos. 1–2 (Spring/Fall
84): 124–43. All notes are by the author.

Milan audience was absolutely enchanted by Verdi's opera, recalling the composer thirty-two times, the public in Frankfurt was far less unanimously enthusiastic, interrupting the premiere on several occasions with whistles and catcalls and, on one of the following nights, with a bomb threat.

■ Since such expressions of hostility are relatively rare in opera houses these days, the intense indignation evoked by what was to be the decisive

Photo 1. Radames seizes a shovel and begins to dig. *Aida*, Frankfurt Opera. (Photo by Mara Eggert.)

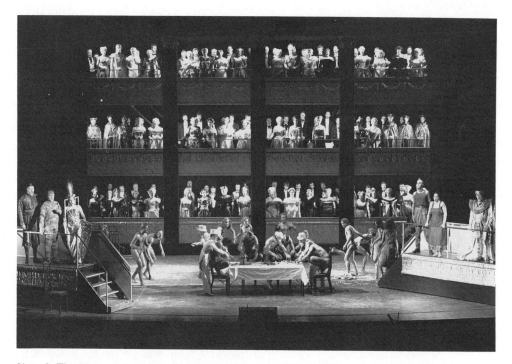

Photo 2. The "triumphal scene" as triumph of the scene. *Aida*, Frankfurt Opera. (Photo by Mara Eggert.)

"breakthrough" of the Frankfurt Opera Company, under the direction of Michael Gielen and Klaus Zehelein, merits attention. If the Frankfurt version of *Aida*, staged by Hans Neuenfels, is generally recognized today, in Germany at least, as one of the high points of contemporary operatic dramaturgy, such recognition has been matched by the indignation and anger of those operagoers for whom the Frankfurt mode of music theater stands as a travesty and betrayal of the tradition to which they feel themselves committed. Such negative voices, although somewhat muted for the time being by the esteem accorded the Frankfurt Opera in the past few years by German music critics, remain clearly audible. All the more reason, therefore, to suspect that the innovative interpretations of this company may perhaps best be understood in terms of the antagonisms they have elicited.

■ If it is safe to assume that those who rejected the Frankfurt *Aida* felt themselves to be acting in defense of an operatic tradition they held to be endangered, such apprehension is, in a certain sense, nothing new to opera. Indeed, it may well turn out to be an integral part of its more recent history which Adorno has described as one of "permanent crisis."[1] Adorno cites three factors as contributing to this crisis. First, the tendency of modern musical composition to develop an ever greater structural *autonomy* has made it difficult for composers to accept the extramusical, literary, and dramatic exigencies of opera.[2] Second, the social function of opera, at least in the eighteenth and nineteenth centuries, was tied to a perspective that tended to exalt the rights of the individual over the conventions of an older, aristocratic order. As the latter came to be replaced by middle-class values, however, the primary locus of dramatic tension was no longer situated in the relation of the individual to society, but rather *within* the private sphere itself, a site less accessible to operatic dramatization. Finally, Adorno relates the crisis of opera to the growing competition of the mass media, which are increasingly able to provide the kind of multimedia spectacle that had been one of the major popular attractions of the opera until the end of the nineteenth century. Adorno, writing in 1960, was thinking in this respect primarily of the cinema, but today it is television, rather than film, that has assumed this function.

■ Perhaps the most remarkable aspect of this crisis, as Adorno describes it, is the dissymmetrical manner in which it has developed. Whereas it seems undeniable that the production of opera has been directly affected by it, the same can hardly be said for its reproduction. In spite of the competition of film and television, opera has succeeded in retaining and even increasing its audiences throughout the Western world. As Adorno writes, opera "presents the paradigm of a form that continues to be an object of uninterrupted consumption, despite the fact, not only that it has lost most of its cultural topicality, but that in all probability it is no longer understood."[3]

■ In short, opera has been able to retain its audience precisely as the result of a certain non-understanding which Adorno analyzes as follows:

> The force that binds people to the opera entails the memory of something long-forgotten, that legendary golden age of the bourgeoisie, whose golden aura itself is only the belated product of the tarnished years that followed. The medium of this unreal memory is the familiarity of individual melodies, or, as in the case of Wagner, of insistent motifs. The consumption of opera becomes to a large extent an exercise in recognition, not unlike that of hit songs, only less precise. . . . Opera lovers watch over the tradition as though it were a valuable possession. Their credo is expressed in statements such as, "It's as beautiful as ever, *Aida.*"[4]

The non-understanding which according to Adorno has been largely responsible for the continued popularity of opera, among a certain audience at least, thus depends upon two factors: nostalgic idealization and identification. The exotic—the distant, heroic, sumptuous Golden Age of the Bourgeoisie—is made familiar by means of that "exercise in recognition" which Adorno sees as common to "high" and "low" culture, to operatic arias as well as to popular songs.

■ This discussion suggests how apt and telling the term "opera *lover*" is: the love of opera, like all love perhaps, is eminently narcissistic. The opera lover is moved by a desire for recognition, which is inevitably also one for self-recognision. This Self, however, is an intrinsically contradictory instance: familiar, and yet distant, exotic, idealized. It is the product of a process of identification, in which the alterity of the object as well as the extraterritoriality of the site in which such identification takes place are simultaneously affirmed and denied: affirmed, in order to permit the all-too-familiar to be idealized, and denied in order that the ideal remain accessible to self.

■ Such a process of identification can therefore hardly avoid a certain ambivalence: its "recognition" of the other inevitably entails the effort to appropriate the latter as an image of the self. This ambivalence aids us in understanding the opera's ability not merely to resist the loss of what Adorno calls its "cultural topicality," but even to profit from it.

■ For it is surely the ability of opera to guard a certain distance from everyday occupations that has allowed it to survive the end of the heroic epoch of bourgeois individualism. In this context, the "gap" described by Adorno as having established itself "between contemporary society, including those that it has mandated to serve as audience, and the opera itself,"[5] assumes its full significance. The figure of the "gap"—in German, *Graben*—denotes literally that which results from digging (*graben*): a trench, ditch, or moat; it thus recalls the gesture of Radames, digging up the floor of the stage.

■ And yet, this very juxtaposition also suggests an important distinction between the two *Graben*. That to which Adorno refers does not merely separate: it also is the condition of the recognition and identification that determine the relation of opera to a large portion of its contemporary audience.

In this sense, the gap also *joins* the audience to the spectacle on stage, confirming that each is in its respective place, while providing the transparent space through which they communicate. Hence, this gap is more akin to an orchestra pit (in German, also a *Graben*) than to a fissure or crack that might call into question the integrity of the scene itself. It is a gap that bridges itself, as it were, thus safeguarding the familiar and well-ordered space of the traditional opera house.

■ If it is possible, therefore, for the audience to gratify the desire of (self-) recognition that traditionally defined the relation of opera to its public, it is because the *object* of that identification has changed. The latter is no longer a represented figure—a hero or heroine, for instance—or a situation, but rather the representation itself, the spectacle as a performance. The audience identifies (with) the spectacle today less for what it represents than for the performances it permits. Today's heroes and heroines of opera are its stars, who have come to replace the works themselves as the primary focus of interest.

■ This shift in interest, from work to performance, is a complex development that has allowed two potentially different, although in fact often related, tendencies to emerge. In addition to the cult of the individual performer, the concern with performance has also permitted the process of staging, the *mise-en-scène*, to acquire new importance. The latter can, of course, merely add a new dimension to the star system: that of the stage director, whose "characteristic style" is then treated as just another distinctive—but above all recognizable—brand of theater. It is possible, however, that the new importance accorded performance can serve to call the individualist attitude toward opera into question, for instance, by performing precisely what the latter generally takes for granted. This is just what the gesture of Radames—and in general the stagings of the Frankfurt Opera—attempt to do.

■ But before proceeding, we should address two potential misunderstandings. It might well be objected that the "star system" in and of itself is nothing new to opera, and that therefore it can hardly be adduced to explain its situation today. If, however, the system itself is not new, what *is*, is the function it has acquired during the past century. In opera, as in society as a whole, the ability to perform is no longer valued primarily as a sign of individual prowess, which, at the formal-aesthetic level, would confirm the traditional *parti pris* of the opera on behalf of the liberated individual. Instead, performers are adulated today precisely for their capacity to function with maximum efficiency in a system of power relations that leaves little place for individual difference and variation. Such virtuosity, indispensable for success in advanced capitalist societies (and in the world they dominate), is dramatized and "individualized" in the star system in general, and in that of the opera in particular.

■ What distinguishes opera stars from their counterparts in sports or film, however, is the cultural context in which they work. That of opera is generally associated with a tradition marked by the continuity of perennial values ("It's as beautiful as ever, *Aida*"). The virtuoso performance of the singer or conductor in an opera is thus regarded as the unmediated realization, by an individual, of universal, eternal aesthetic values. The tradition is thus homogenized and pasteurized, purged of the differentiating ferment of conflict and presented as the neutral space in which timeless situations, moods, and feelings are transmitted by the star to the spectator— that is, from one individual to another. This process, and the semblance of individuation it produces, is powerfully supported by the nondiscursive aspect of musical language, which allows itself to be considered, and indeed consumed, as a purely expressive medium, as the direct exteriorization of disembodied moods or feelings.[6]

■ What is new, in short, in the operatic star system today derives from the growing discrepancy between, on the one hand, a mode of perception, identification, and recognition, the constitutive category of which is the integrity of the individual (whether object or subject is here of secondary importance), and, on the other, the increasingly non-individual structure of the power relations that determine the social context in which opera exists. Opera houses thus remain one of the arenas in which the spectacle of such individualism can still be staged more or less effectively.[7]

■ And this brings me to a second possible misunderstanding. However important the star system may be for the survival of opera as such, it obviously does not work in the same manner everywhere. Frankfurt is not the Metropolitan Opera, and Wiesbaden is not Frankfurt. The vast majority of opera houses cannot afford the luxury of engaging the best-known singers and conductors. This does not mean, however, that the process of individualizing (self-)recognition and identification does not take place in such houses, but merely that its primary object is no longer the internationally acclaimed star. Rather—if the preceding considerations are valid—the object of identification will have shifted, in part at least, from the individual performer to the individual performance: that is, to the performance *as individualized spectacle*. To be individualized, a spectacle must fulfill two conditions: it must be different (i.e., "distinguished"), and it must be the same (i.e., recognizable as the "work itself"). A spectacle is different by distinguishing itself from its predecessors (what we call "originality"). And it is the same by presenting itself as meaningful and self-contained. Only by fulfilling these two conditions can an opera performance meet the demands of those who expect it to be an individualization of the eternal, an actualization of the timeless, and, thus, a proper object of recognition and of identification.

■ Given the relative rarity of internationally known superstars at the Frankfurt Opera, the protests elicited by its *Aida* could only relate to the spectacle itself: beginning with the gesture of Radames, the scene, although more "self-referential" than ever, is no longer self-contained and, hence, no longer a suitable object of identification. Not that recognition is thereby rendered impossible; rather, it is made all too possible. Instead of presenting itself as the idealized, self-enclosed space of an individuation that the functionalism of contemporary society has drastically restricted, the Frankfurt *Aida* begins by calling that space into question—and with it, the possibility of unreflective identification.

■ From this one might be tempted to conclude that we are dealing here with something like a Brechtian strategy of *Verfremdung*, alienation. And yet, the previous discussion should indicate why such an approach could hardly have provoked the sharp reactions that confronted *Aida* in Frankfurt. For if, as suggested, opera involves its audience in a form of identification, the latter can only be of a kind very different from that practiced by the theater against which Brecht reacted. If audiences identify with opera today, it is precisely because of its distance, not in spite of it. Such identification is the result of the exotic artificiality built into operatic form and expected from it. To remind audiences therefore that what they are watching is not reality but a mere show would be utterly superfluous.

■ Moreover, as generally understood, the notion of *alienation* supposes precisely the traditional, Euclidean notion of space that stagings such as the one we are discussing seek to problematize: a space in which distance and proximity are mutually exclusive. Such a space, and the logic of noncontradiction that it implies, is entirely incapable of explaining the force of the two scenes to which I now want to turn.

■ Let us, therefore, return to Radames, dreaming at his desk. What is startling in this scene is not its strangeness, but its familiarity. The latter, however, does not merely consist in the fact that the expected exoticism of ancient Egypt is supplanted by the all too familiar nineteenth century. As a dramaturgical strategy, this kind of historical shift is certainly familiar enough, but it would hardly startle anyone for very long. Rather, it is what goes on in this setting that is unsettling. For, with his shovel and his dream, Radames sets about dismantling nothing less than the traditional, self-contained space of theatrical representation. Or, rather, he does not so much dismantle this theater as disorganize it. In digging up the floorboards of the stage, Radames does not move outside that space—some desire of this sort may have been at work in certain avant-garde groups such as The Living Theatre, but it is not implied by this gesture. Rather, something far more disquieting takes place, something which can no longer be understood in terms of the ultimately reassuring opposition of "outside" and "inside." What is represented onstage is an act that calls the space in which it "takes place" into question. In digging up the stage, Radames undermines the foundations of representation by putting them into (the) play. The material basis of the operatic spectacle thus becomes part of the performance. And that materiality includes not merely the actual floorboards of the stage, but the entire social system upon which the theater depends. This context is no longer checked in the coatroom, in order to be reclaimed after the performance: it has become an integral part of the show itself—or, rather, a dis-integral part. For this part is one that calls the whole into question in a variety of ways.

■ Once the limits of the scene, the foundations of its site, are thus included in the scene itself, the space of representation can no longer simply be taken for granted or unequivocally delimited. Who is to say where it starts, and where it stops? The audience, finding itself on the spot and yet unable to determine where that spot is located, is put out: exasperated by a space in which it is not entirely at home, and yet which it knows all too well. The opera house has ceased to be a home.

■ It is this, above all, that disorganizes the desire of the audience for (self-) recognition: for how can it hope to recognize what it cannot definitively locate? Once the limits of the scene are no longer neutral, the spectacle is no longer securely in place, nor are the spectators. The role of each becomes an open question, and one that can hardly be answered by self-oblivious abandon.

■ The instinctive reaction of the more traditional opera lover to this sort of disquieting solicitation is to invoke the authority of the Work, and through it—since the Work is never directly accessible as such—the intention of the Author, conceived as an absolutely authoritative, determining instance. Thus, in France and Germany these days, after a decade of dramaturgical experimentation and innovation, the cry "Back to the Work (or Text)!" can be heard with increasing frequency. However understandable such a reaction is, given the ineluctable usury of mere ingenuity, whether in theater or elsewhere, the righteous indignation that generally accompanies such demands tends to forget that the so-called return to the text can never be anything but the replacing of one sort of interpretation by another, albeit by one that considers itself to be nothing more or less than an expression of the Work as such.

■ It is this conception of the Work of Art as a meaningful, self-contained entity—which enters time, as it were, only to await realization by inspired but faithful interpreters—that the Frankfurt staging of *Aida* powerfully dislocates. And it does this not by ignoring the text, but by taking that text so seriously that its confines no longer appear to be self-evident. Author, work, staging, and audience no longer constitute discrete parameters in an aesthetic (and ontological) hierarchy. Rather, they emerge as aspects of an interdependent network of relationships in which no one instance can be said to dominate the others, or even to function without them.

■ This disruption can perhaps best be approached by reflecting upon the status of the opening scene of *Aida*, and in particular upon its relation to the opera "itself." The scene takes place during the orchestral prelude: that is, before the start of the actual story as described in the libretto of Ghislanzoni. The audience in Frankfurt would have had no difficulty in confirming this fact: all they needed to do was consult the copious program notes in which the libretto is reprinted. In the same volume of 135 pages, they would also have discovered a number of related documents, not the least interesting of which is the text upon which the libretto was based: the long-lost first edition of Auguste Mariette's version of the story, which called it to Verdi's attention.[8]

■ It is remarkable, then, that those who were responsible for reconstituting the "authentic" history of the text of *Aida* were not averse to imposing a supplementary scene that none of the published texts explicitly prescribe. Such an imposition, however, can only be rejected out of hand if the text—in general and in particular—is considered to be something that can operate independent of its reinscription. If, however, the text is itself already a reinscription and, moreover, one that requires continued revision in order to be implemented, then the clear-cut opposition between original and interpretation can no longer be invoked to condemn such impositions.

■ In the case of *Aida*, as Klaus Zehelein reminds us,[9] the orchestral prelude, which the initial scene in Frankfurt accompanies, is in the most literal sense a revision: it came as a second thought to Verdi. His original overture was far more pompously affirmative, and this, Zehelein suggests, was the reason he replaced it with another version, far more meditative in character. The so-called original then, here as elsewhere, even where the process may be less explicit or evident, is the result of a process of revision, interpretation, and reinterpretation, of writing and rewriting. This is not to say that there is *no* text, of course, but rather that the text, far from being a self-contained structure, articulates itself through a tissue of contradictions and a force field of tensions from which it emerges ineluctably as—to borrow a term from psychoanalysis—a *compromise formation*, the signification of which is inseparable from its reinscription elsewhere.

■ One of the exemplary instances of such compromise formation is, of course, the dream. And it is hardly a coincidence, therefore, that the Frankfurt staging of *Aida* should begin with one. The aptness of this beginning, however, is far more precise than what the "dreamy" quality of Verdi's prelude might suggest. For what is involved here is not a mere mood, but a radically different approach to the aesthetic work—to *opera*—than that to which the traditional aesthetics of the Authorial Work has accustomed us, particularly when we enter an opera house. If such traditional aesthetics can be described as one of representation, the hermeneutics elaborated by Freud, and which also marks many of the Frankfurt stagings, is one of dislocation. In German, the contrast can be expressed more forcefully: the traditional aesthetics of *Darstellung* is replaced by a theater of *Entstellung.*[10]

■ The fact that *Aida* is thus introduced, and then framed—for the final scene returns to the initial setting—by a dream, can be seen to have a double significance. Considered formally and in abstraction from the particular contents of the scene, the dream dislocates the work as a self-contained structure, relocating it in and as the twisted space of conflictual desire. The curious "twist" to this scene is that it is neither simply exterior to the opera (given the belated character of the orchestral prelude) nor simply a part of it. But precisely the same holds for the structure of dreams as analyzed by Freud. Their defining limits can never be definitively determined; the dream proper, for instance, cannot be clearly distinguished from the dissimulating narratives through which it is subsequently articulated. Such indeterminacy (or overdetermination) is reinforced by the content of this particular dream scene. Its setting, that of a nineteenth-century palatial office, is neither part of the fiction of *Aida* nor entirely separate from it, given the conditions of its composition. Like the stage floor, the historical context of its emergence is inscribed in, or rather *as*, the scene that "ushers in" the work; once again the enabling limits of the opera are folded back into the spectacle itself.

■ From this, however, to conclude that the opera's meaning might be reducible to the historical situation in which it was composed would be once again to ignore the fact that texts in general, and theatrical texts in particular, are what they are only when they come to be subsequently inscribed elsewhere as what they are not. It is here that the Freudian hermeneutics of the dream is of particular pertinence. For when Radames takes the shovel—which, with oneiric incongruity, just happens to be ready at hand—

and begins to dig, what comes to light is not merely a number of obviously symbolic objects—sword and sculpted head—but also, and perhaps more important, *the materiality of the scene itself* in all of its equivocal overdetermination. The gesture of Radames forces the spectators to direct their glance at the physical foundation of theatrical representation, the flooring of the stage, the "basis" of the scene. The floorboards that are thus literally dislocated do not in turn become symbols invested with some ultimate meaning; rather, they function allegorically, in the sense given the term by Walter Benjamin, denoting both themselves and an indeterminate number of other objects. The latter can never be exhaustively identified, however, for a very specific reason: they can be determined only by reference to the very theatrical context which they in turn serve to delimit. This is why this dream sequence serves both to introduce and at the same time to dislocate the opera as a work.

■ But if the work is thus dislocated, so are the spectators. The latter have little choice but to simply stop waiting, as it were, for the work to come to rest, in order then to be able to situate themselves with respect to it. Instead of awaiting the work, they are enjoined to begin working themselves— working, that is, not to take those selves simply for granted.

■ To be sure, one can cling to the seemingly secure connotation of sword and sculpture, of glory and art, power and love, in order to orient one's bewilderment. But such orientation is particularly unreliable here, where the image of the Orient is in question. Why does a nineteenth-century, upper-middle-class person dream of digging up an ancient Egyptian sword and the head of an Ethiopian princess—and then write an opera about them? And why do people of the twentieth century, in Frankfurt and elsewhere, put such dreams on the stage, often forgetting, in the process, their dream-like quality?

■ Again, the disturbing force of such questions might be blunted if the initial scene could be taken as an effort simply to historicize *Aida* as a psychological or aesthetic reality. Such an interpretation, however, ignores the way in which this initial representation of a dream also calls into question the site of representation itself: not by virtue of the ontological deficiency of its fictions, but because of the uncertainty of its borders. This uncertainty affects above all the relation of spectator and spectacle. The dreamer, who appears at first to be a mere witness of the dream, is soon revealed to be a participant rather than a viewer, occupying a place that is impossible to situate once and for all. Neither simply author nor purely recipient, the subject of the unconscious confounds activity and passivity in movements that are neither the one nor the other, and that require other categories in order to be adequately described.[11]

■ From this, one might be tempted to conclude that the destabilization of the scene qua self-contained site of representation introduces a new controlling instance, and that instead of the Work it is now the Audience that becomes that determining factor in *Aida*. This very response is anticipated by the second scene I want to discuss, that which opens Act II.

■ In this scene, the curtain rises to reveal a surprising, indeed even breathtaking tableau: the chorus assembled as the elegant audience gathered for the opening night of *Aida* at La Scala in 1872. What quite literally takes one's breath away in this image is not merely the unexpectedness of its content but its location. The chorus, ranged horizontally and vertically in a grid representing the Scala loges and covering most of the visible area, is placed at the very front of the stage, just behind the curtain. The tableau thus deprives the scene of all depth; the appearance of the Milan audience, representing the "original" addressees of *Aida*, is thus staged so as to reduce the scene to a mere surface, very much like that of a mirror. One audience looks at another. And the other stares back. And yet, there is something more complex than a mere specular image at work here. For the stage audience is not quite the same as the "real" one, nor is it utterly different. If the Frankfurt audience applauded the Scala simulacrum, the latter repaid the compliment at the end of its opening chorus, acknowledging the audience with hand waves of its own. And yet, the movement that accompanies those gestures of friendly complicity indicates why the recognition thereby displayed can never be simply reciprocal or mutual.

■ For as the initial chorus, heralding the victory of Radames and the Egyptians over the Ethiopians, concludes, the loges containing the Scala audience gradually withdraw to the rear of the stage, thus liberating the space of what will now unfold as the triumphal scene. Not merely the audience, therefore, but its withdrawal is thereby put forth as the enabling condition of operatic representation. This "triumphal scene" is indeed a triumph of the scene, but of one which takes the place of the audience to which it thereby remains structurally indebted. But if the audience thus emerges as the instance that defines and delimits the space of the scene, the latter in turn also defines and delimits the audience. This noncircular circularity dooms any attempt to reduce the *singular specificity* of theatrical representation to the apparently univocal reality of a "real" audience, determined entirely in socio-historical terms. Such a reduction cannot succeed because the reality of an audience constitutes itself theatrically only through its in-

teraction with the spectacle: that is, with something from which it is inseparable, but with which it is never simply identical.

■ What the opening scene of Act II here demonstrates is that this relation
of inseparable nonidentity is at work even in the process of reflection and
recognition that seems to abolish that difference. To the extent that the audience recognizes itself in the Scala spectators, it is no longer strictly itself.
To "recognize" the audience as an instance that makes way for the spectacle it then witnesses is to problematize the notion of the spectator as a
mere recipient of a preexisting Work. This in turn cannot but alter the process of narcissistic identification. Narcissus, we recall, fell in love with an
image that he did *not* recognize as his own. The suggestion that the triumphal scene of *Aida* might in some way be a mirror image of opera itself—or
rather of the attitude that construes opera to be itself—is already sufficient
to disturb the continued "acting-out" of that attitude.

■ Thus, this scene continues the dislocation initiated by Radames. Whereas
the opening scene draws attention to the foundations of a space that is usually taken for granted, the second scene represents the process of *granting*
as one by which the audience effaces itself, but only to impose its desire all
the more powerfully, albeit unconsciously. To vary celebrated words of
Freud, "Where the audience was, the spectacle shall come to be."[12]

■ If the space of the spectacle is that opened by this "retreat" of the spectators, the *Graben* to which Adorno refers can no longer be regarded as separating opera from its audience, or from a society at large held together, in
part at least, by precisely the self-evidence of a spectator function, which
the Frankfurt staging renders eminently problematic. Instead of the transparent space required by the self-evident spectator, the *Graben* itself is ren-

dered visible. Confronted by its narcissistic double, the Frankfurt audience is impelled to deal with that other of itself, which, like Freud's *uncanny*, should have remained concealed and now begins, not only to emerge, but to circulate.

■ It is this circulation—supplanting the more traditional conceptual oppositions of production and consumption, creation and reception—that is transforming the aesthetic space of the Frankfurt Opera, making it into a theater of dislocation in which *taking place* itself becomes the primal scene.

■ Whereas the previous remarks were directed at an already existing *mise-en-scène*, those that follow were written in the context of a staging yet to come, that of Wagner's *Ring of the Nibelung* at the Frankfurt Opera. The first installment of this new production of the tetralogy, *Das Rheingold*, had its premiere in December 1985; the full *Ring* cycle was performed in March 1987. My discussion of the *Ring*, therefore, will be concerned with its theatrical and dramaturgical aspects, and it will deal almost exclusively with the text of the tetralogy, "bracketing" almost entirely the music. For reasons that will, I trust, become clear as the reading progresses, such an approach is both useful and legitimate. Those who would reject it out of hand, deeming opera to be an exclusively musical form of art, should recall the emphasis and intensity with which Wagner constantly struggled to rehabilitate the *literary* and *dramatic* aspects of opera, the form of which he held to be fatally flawed precisely because of its tendency to subordinate these elements to its musical component.[13]

■ To be sure, any discussion limited to the text of the *Ring* can only be partial and provisional in its conjectures and conclusions. And yet, there is also an advantage in focusing one's attention, initially, on the literary side of the tetralogy. For the text—written before the music was composed—is in and of itself of such extraordinary complexity that a close reading of it, and in particular of its theatrical implications, has almost more to deal with than it can handle, even without including the obviously essential, but additional, complication of the relation of that material to the music. Furthermore, the structural problems of the *Ring* may well be more accessible through a reading that begins with its text rather than with a musical score that often conceals the subtleties of its organization behind a deceptive simplicity. I am thinking here in particular of the manner in which the Wagnerian leitmotif has generally been understood, namely, as a kind of univocal, melodic signal. To assume, however, that the structural significance of these thematic elements is fixed once and for all is to ignore precisely what is most innovative and path-breaking in Wagner's use of melody. As the contemporary French composer and critic André Boucourechliev has observed, Wagner's music, particularly in the *Ring, Tristan,* and *Parsifal,*

abolishes every known formal scheme, every familiar frame of reference, not only of opera—the partitions, the succession of codified "numbers" and the code of their appearances, repetitions, procedures—but of music itself. For it abolishes the function that hitherto had been essential, that of the theme—paradoxically by multiplying themes indefinitely—disengaging it from its traditional dialectical domain, depriving it of the antagonistic role that Beethoven had exacerbated and, according to Wagner himself, "exhausted."[14]

■ Wagner's writing should be approached in a similar spirit. The condescension with which it is often treated—by those who then exalt his music— is generally based upon aesthetic criteria designed to avoid the problems his compositions seek to articulate. To attack or defend the Rhine Maidens' "*Weia! Waga! Woge, du Welle!*" etc. on the basis of whether or not the use of alliterative onomatopoesis serves to further what one takes to be the scene's significance—the rolling sounds of the water, the depiction of a "natural," primeval scene, and the like—is to ignore the possibility that what the scene is about is not "nature," Eden, watery sounds, etc., but rather a certain use of language itself, a children's language game, for instance, and everything it entails.

■ Wagner himself was fully aware of the function of such efforts to disqualify his writing in order to praise his music: that of censuring any attempt to disrupt the established partitions and pigeonholes of the traditional aesthetic grid. And no one understood better than he that the problems with which he grappled required the elaboration of new forms and spaces that would allow the mediums and genres to interact in ways not foreseen or permitted by that tradition, at least in its most scholastic and codified form.

■ This is why an attentive reading of the text of the *Ring*—one which is as free as possible from the certitudes of that all too domesticated tradition—may be the best approach to the problems with which the tetralogy struggles. For it should not be forgotten that *ringen*, in German, means just that: to struggle, physically as well as mentally; to wrestle. Toward the end of *Das Rheingold*, the two giants, Fafner and Fasolt, are described as "wrestling for the ring": "*Sie ringen.*" And, indeed, the *Ring* is not only about such a struggle: it *is* that struggle itself. *Der Ring ringt.* . . . The following remarks try to retrace the arena, the ring in which that *ringen* takes place. This struggle is inevitably one in which place itself is at stake; even more clearly than in *Aida*, it is a struggle to take (the) place. Needless to say, to describe *that* struggle is also to participate in it.

■ The struggle can be said to begin where the Frankfurt *Aida* leaves off:

with the theatrical dislocation of the work. The difference is that whereas in Verdi's opera this dislocation must be imposed by the staging, it is explicitly inscribed in the text of the *Ring*. More than any of his contemporaries, Wagner was concerned with the multimedia aspect of "music theater." From its very inception and conception, the *Ring* was written and then composed with its dramaturgical implications clearly in view. The fact that for many years Wagner was convinced that the project would never reach the stage, and that he often seemed to compose in open defiance of any compromise with existing theater practices, only underscores the significance of theatricality for his work. Theater was far too important to Wagner for him to equate it with the established theater of his time.

■ *Theater* for Wagner retained its Greek connotation of visibility. He once wrote that he "would gladly describe my dramas as visualizations of musical deeds [*ersichtlich gewordene Taten der Musik*]."[15] In the process of writing the text of the *Ring*, however, theatricality becomes something far more complex than the term "visualization" generally suggests.

■ To study this shift at work, we need only turn to the very first scene of *Das Rheingold*, entitled "On the Bottom of the Rhine." The scene is introduced by a remarkable set of stage directions. At first, the picture that emerges seems to have a symmetrical and stable structure: the upper part of the stage is described as filled with water "flowing ceaselessly from right to left" while its lower portion "seems entirely free of water from the ground up," at least far enough for a male figure to take its place (*in Manneshöhe*). When the description reaches rock bottom, however, the setting becomes more confused:

Everywhere, rocky reefs jut jaggedly out of the depths and delimit the space of the stage; the entire bottom is split up into a wild tangle of crags [*in ein wildes Zackengewirr zer-*

spalten] so that it is nowhere completely flat and in the thickest obscurity suggests more profound crevasses, branching out in all directions [*nach allen Seiten hin in dichtester Finsternis tiefere Schluchten annehmen lässt*].

In the middle of the stage, around a reef whose tapered peak juts up into the denser, more luminous [*heller dämmernde*] waves, the daughters of the Rhine swim graceful circles.[16]

■ Read in a cursory fashion, these stage instructions seem to set a scene that is well defined and clearly organized: its upper regions are framed by flowing water, while below there is a kind of clearing, the dimensions of which are cut to the measure of a male figure (*der Raum der Manneshöhe*). In this open space, the events of the scene will take place, presumably with all the required theatrical visibility.

■ And yet, we need only reread those same stage indications with a certain attentiveness in order to discover that this setting is far less settled, and the events it harbors far less visible than Wagner's notion of theater might lead us to expect.[17] The all-important *Grund*, the ground of the Rhine, is described as a kind of arrested volcanic eruption, upon whose precarious solidity the space of the scene itself depends: "rocky reefs *jut jaggedly out* of the depths" and "delimit the space of the stage" (*grenzen den Raum der Bühne ab*). But the German word *abgrenzen*—translated here as "delimitation"—has a connotation that the English word does not. It entails the gesture of demarcation: the space of the stage is not merely defined in itself, contained by and within its borders; it is set apart from something else that, precisely from its position offstage, seems to have frozen the volcanic eruptions into lava-like reefs. It is as though another scene, by virtue of its exclusion, determined the shape of that from which it has been expelled.

■ Traces of this excluded scene can be deciphered in the peculiarities of the river's "bed." First, the ground is described as wildly disordered, rent, uneven. Second, this wild cleavage does not seem to be the result of an event that has taken place once and for all; rather, the syntactic parallelism, in which the "rocky reefs" both "jut" and "delimit" (*ragen . . . und grenzen*) the scene, suggests that the brittle borders of the stage are involved in an ongoing movement that is far from finished. And indeed, as we follow these directions to their conclusion, the scene we have before our eyes is caught up in a dynamics that turns out to be less visible than it first seemed, although not necessarily any less theatrical. Rather, the locus of theatricality shifts offstage, into the audience. For what these stage directions conclude with is a description not so much of a visible scene as of the *effects* that scene is supposed to produce among the spectators, precisely insofar as it is invisible. Thus, the disorder of the riverbed is said to culminate in what cannot be seen but only imagined: "in the thickest obscurity . . . more profound crevasses branching out in all directions."[18]

■ This shift in the stage directions, from a description of the visible scene itself to its invisible but assumed effects, delimits and dislocates the scene it thereby "sets." At the same time that the *Bühnenraum* (the "stage space") is set apart—*abgegrenzt*—from the *Zuschauerraum* (the "spectator space"), the stage is shown to require the latter in order to establish its invisible borders. The onstage scene is thus made a function of *another* scene, provisionally located in the shadowy space of the audience and of its imagination. The latter, however, is in turn not independent of the scene it is supposed to delimit. We are thus confronted with a circularity not unlike that already discussed in regard to *Aida*.

■ Such noncircular circulation, by which the scene itself is set in motion and put into play, constitutes an essential characteristic of a theater of dislocation. What distinguishes this theater from traditional theatrical (re-) presentation (*Darstellung*) is that none of its elements is constituted independent of its interaction and place in a circulation, the trajectory of which can never be fully predicted or exhaustively determined. The scene cannot be entirely determined by what it appears to represent since the latter supposes an imaginative effort of the audience as an integral part of its articulation. The audience thus ceases to function as a pure spectator: it no longer merely registers or reproduces what is shown onstage; rather, by reacting to what is *not* shown, it may in a certain sense be said to complete the scene. In this case, the work, by being more than a simple *Darstellung*, more than a representation in the strict sense, might nevertheless be claimed to control that excess by determining its effects in the audience. Thus understood, the text would be construed as explicitly prescribing just what the spectators are supposed to assume. And to the extent that this prescription is successful, one might assert that we are still operating according to an aesthetics of *Darstellung*, in which the Work, and ultimately the Author, has the first but above all the last word.[19]

■ The question, however, is: Can the audience response to this scene be said to complete its borders? Or does it continue the movement of dislocation? Or perhaps both? And in the latter case, what is the status of a scene that defines itself through such dislocation?

■ Any response to these questions can only come from an analysis of the scene itself. But before we attempt such an analysis it may prove helpful to recall the description of another scene, which in many respects seems closely related to the one we have been discussing. I am thinking of the scene sketched by Freud in *The Interpretation of Dreams*, when he seeks to render visible what he calls the "navel of the dream." The play of light and dark he describes, as well as the centrifugal movement that results from it, will by now have a familiar ring:

Even in the best interpreted dreams, there is often a place that must be left in the dark, because in the process of interpreting one notices a tangle of dream-thoughts arising which resists unravelling but has also made no further contributions to the dream-content. This then is the navel of the dream, the place where it straddles the unknown. The dream-thoughts to which interpretation leads one are necessarily interminable *and branch out in all directions into the netlike entanglement* of our world of thought. Out of one of the denser places in this network, the dream-wish rises like a mushroom out of its mycelium.[20]

Freud's formulation describing the movement of the dream is identical to that found in Wagner's stage directions: like the invisible gorges, his dream thoughts "branch out in all directions"—*nach allen Seiten hin*—losing themselves in the web of our waking thoughts. This centrifugal movement tends to dislocate the scene of the dream in a manner very much like what we have discerned at work in the beginning of *Das Rheingold*. Were such a process allowed to develop unimpeded, the very status of the dream itself as an objectifiable entity would be threatened. For how could one ever hope to control its overdetermination sufficiently to distinguish it—to demarcate it—from the "world of thought" (*Gedankenwelt*) that characterizes conscious life in general?

■ It is therefore all the more remarkable how in both cases—in Freud's description of the dream-navel no less than in Wagner's setting of the Rhine—the threatened dislocation or dissipation of the scene is held in check by the emergence of a new phenomenon rising above the proliferation of shadows to provide the badly needed bright new center of attention. This phallic figure—reef or "mushroom"—is designated by Freud as the *dream-wish*.

■ And since, as we all know, Freud designates the dream as a wish-fulfillment, it would seem that its integrity as a phenomenon and an object is thereby reestablished. The dream could thus be held to take place, and to take its (proper) place, as a form of presentation, as a *Darstellung*.

■ The only problem with this version—as Freud himself had to acknowledge while writing the dream-book—is that it ignores the specificity of the dream as a singular form of articulation. For the dream is not merely the fulfillment of a wish, but rather the distorted, dislocated—*entstellte*—fulfillment of a conflictual desire. The dream, as Freud remarks in a long footnote at the end of his chapter entitled "Dream Work," is not to be construed as the expression of a "latent content," not as the figuration of a dream-wish or of its fulfillment, but as the disfigurement of a fulfillment that in turn is inseparable from the irreconcilably conflictual nature of the wish itself.

■ The dream-wish, then, which arises out of the dream-navel, endows the interminable proliferation of dream-thoughts with a certain structure. But at the same time this structure recenters the dream around "the unknown," around the overdetermined conflictuality of which the dream is a self-dissimulating dissimulation. The emergence of the phallic dream-wish therefore does not abolish what I have elsewhere described as the *thallic* dynamics of the dream—it merely gives its dislocation a focus.[21]

■ Something very similar occurs at the very beginning of *Das Rheingold*. If the stage directions tend to delimit the scene they set, the Rhine daughters, swimming about the reef that lodges the gold, serve to recenter the scene. But this recentering turns out to repeat the scenic dislocation, although now in a dramatized form—that is, in a form that is tied to identifiable figures. Instead of the stage being determined by its other scene, that is, by a *Zuschauerraum* that it can never entirely integrate or dominate, an effort is made to assimilate this spectator space to the scene by bringing spectating itself onstage, and thereby making it into a visible spectacle.

■ For whatever else Alberich may be, he makes his initial appearance first and foremost as a spectator. And indeed, it would hardly be an exaggeration to see the entire *Ring* as resulting from his inability to remain one.

■ Emerging from the obscure depths, Alberich is immediately confronted— and captivated—by the sight of the swimming maidens. Fascinated, he watches them playing, and his gaze transforms their game into a *Schauspiel*, a theatrical spectacle: "*Er schaut dem Spiele zu.*" What he sees, however, does not permit him to retain the role of a mere observer. He is carried away, like a child seeking to play with children he hardly knows. The desire that carries him away—away from the position of spectator—can be described with some precision. It is a desire not merely to possess what it sees, but to imitate it. Alberich attempts to do what he sees the Rhine daughters doing: catch, seize, lay hold of the others. In this imitative gesture, the desire that will fashion the ring—and keep it in motion, until the end—demonstrates its narcissistic character. It is a narcissism that will be characteristic not merely of Alberich but of all the figures in the *Ring*, with a single, equivocal exception to which I shall have occasion to return. It is more than an archaism of language, therefore, if throughout the text of the tetralogy, "desire" and "envy" are confounded in a single word: *Neid*.

■ The fate of Alberich then is the fate of the spectator whose narcissism does not permit him either to remain outside the spectacle he views or to find his place within it. The irregular shapes and slippery surfaces of the uneven riverbed make it impossible for Alberich to get a firm footing, catch hold of the nymphs, or master his movements. He slips and slides about, unable to hold on to anything, least of all the fata morgana of his lubricious desire. Expelled from his place in the dark below, humiliated and furious above, Alberich cuts a sorry figure indeed. It is as though his name catches up with him: ein *albernes Ich*, a ludicrous Ego caught in a nightmare (*Alptraum*).[22]

■ It is precisely at the moment when Alberich is quite literally beside himself with rage and desire—having lost his security as spectator and gained nothing but humiliation in return—that another spectacle intervenes, allowing him to reassume briefly his initial role before the cycle of dislocation resumes. This spectacle is nothing less than the primal scene of the *Ring*. Once again, Alberich's gaze is drawn to a *Schauspiel* that consists in a highly symbolic play of light: "From above, an ever brighter glow penetrates the waves, and, at a point toward the top of the central reef, gradually ignites into a blindingly bright, golden light." That the penetrating rays should be said to gradually ignite (*allmählich entzündet*) testifies to the tension of the desire at work in this description. The ensuing dialogue of the Rhine daughters indicates just what is at stake in this spectacle of desire.

Woglinde:	*Look sisters! she who wakes*
	[die Weckerin] *laughs to the depths.*
Wellgunde:	*Through the green wave she greets the happy sleeper* [den wonnigen Schläfer].
Flosshilde:	*Now she's kissing his eye, so that he opens it.*
Wellgunde:	*Look, it's smiling in the bright light.*
Woglinde:	*Through the flood its radiant star flows out.*

■ Once we restore the play of genders to translations that generally ignore such differentiations, the particular quality of this scene, which the Rhine Maidens describe, comment on, and explain to Alberich (and to all the other spectators), emerges as an effect of the confusion of conventional sexual roles. The ray that penetrates and "awakens" the dormant gold with its embrace, the intense light that "gradually ignites" in a kind of spontaneous combustion—but one that also involves a certain reflection—is designated in German as feminine, whereas the somnolent gold is masculine (*den wonnigen Schläfer*). Such an inversion or perversion of sexual roles repeats the situation of Alberich, who has already been reduced to passivity by the play of the Rhine Maidens.

■ With this second spectacle, Alberich puts an end to his passivity, temporarily at least. And yet, what he "curses" and renounces is not so much *Minne*, love—for how can one renounce what one does not have and cannot acquire?—but rather the spectator role itself. What he could not achieve with the undines he now attempts with their gold: laying hands upon it, touching it, "he tears the gold out of the reef, with dreadful force [*mit furchtbarer Gewalt*]": castration and defense against castration at once.

■ As Alberich grasps the gold, the stage is plunged into darkness. The primal scene is concluded, the scenario can begin. The basic machinery, however, is in place. Reduced to the role of an impotent spectator, powerless to remain an observer, and incapable of gratifying his desire, Alberich seizes the spectacle itself: the specular, spectacular phenomenon that is the gold, and that promises its possessor "measureless might." The dream of unlimited power, *machtlose Macht*, implies the wish to do away entirely with the Other, with all others. It is also the dream of the spectator, who seeks to appropriate the spectacle—and, indeed, the conditions of all sight.

■ It is no accident, therefore, that the first thing Alberich does to consolidate his power is to have Mime weld him the *Tarnhelm*, the magical casque that enables Alberich to change shape. But this casque is also Alberich's undoing: for although it allows him to assume different forms, it does not permit him to disappear entirely; only such a power, however, could make him truly invulnerable. That he should confuse the two—the power to disappear and the power to change shape—indicates the conflictual force at work in his desire—and in the *Ring*. For the narcissistic denial of alterity plays itself out first and foremost not in the relation to other persons, but on the stage of the body as such.

■ It is not surprising, therefore, that the fate of the gold should be bound up with that of the body. The role of the latter, however, is to appear less as an image of wholeness than as a site of dislocation and of dismemberment, from the sadistic cruelty of Alberich and Siegfried (toward Mime) to the exuberant violence of the Walkyries. The deformations of the Nibelungs, Alberich, and Mime (their "ugliness"), the wounds of Siegmund (but also of Wotan, who has lost an eye to desire), the "dis-arming" of Brünnhilde, the fatal vulnerability of Siegfried, the ferocious but fragile strength of the Walkyries: these are all elements of the corporeality of the *Ring*, no less at work in the ubiquitous crevices into which the male figures are incessantly disappearing, than in the bodies represented as such.

■ In this context, the *Ring* emerges as the narcissistic nightmare of the dismembered body and as the effort to contain its dismemberment. This container is the ring. When Alberich seizes the gold, whose initial appearance is that of a passive, reflecting mirror of light, an object is fashioned whose circular shape is meant to contain the movement of a dislocating desire. In this sense, Alberich's act is an allegory of the *Ring* itself: he seeks to create what he then can appropriate, the self-enclosed space of a self-contained work. And yet, far from confirming the integrity of its Author and Owner, the spectacle of the ring only unleashes what it sought to defend against: the disfiguring, dislocating, dismembering circulation of a desire that can never be appropriated or put in its proper place. This is the narcissistic desire of the other, known in the *Ring* as *Neid*.[23]

■ Thus, as the lights go out on the bottom of the Rhine, they go on up above. The rays that lit up the gold down below now rise to illuminate Walhalla. By putting an end to this primal scene, Alberich's theft inaugurates the spectacle proper. But as the musical transition in its uninterrupted flow suggests, the show goes on. Whatever the distance that separates the Nibelungs from the gods, Alberich from Wotan, the two are part of the same world, as distant and different from one another as a mirror image from the body it reflects. In *Siegfried*, Wotan will acknowledge as much when he refers to himself as "Light Alberich."

■ This remark, startling in its abruptness, is all the more significant for its utter lack of justification, whether in terms of its motivation or of its consequences. It exemplifies what is perhaps the determining structural feature of the *Ring*: its oneiric quality. The *Ring* resembles a dream not simply in the symbolic aspects of what it represents, but in its manner of representing: not only in gorges and crevasses that outstrip the eye, but in the fissures and gaps that rend its own narrative, whether the latter is setting the scene, as at the beginning of *Das Rheingold*, or referring to a situation, as in this remark of Wotan's.[24]

■ The most striking instance of such oneiric dislocation probably occurs at the very beginning of the second scene of *Das Rheingold*. In its content this scene repeats the primal scene it both supplants and continues: Wotan is awakened by Fricka, but what he discovers glinting in the rays of the morning sun is the dream itself, Walhalla. Or, rather, the dream-wish itself, rising high like a mushroom out of its mycelium (or like a reef out of the abyss).

■ But this "awakening" from the dream is more like a dream of awakening.

For the dream does not vanish when Wotan opens his eyes. Rather, in becoming reality it discloses the conflicts that it dissimulates and articulates. The fulfillment of Wotan's dream-wish is the beginning of the nightmare. He wakes to find "the eternal work" that he has "*borne* in my dreams" (*wie im Traum ich ihn trug*). The verb *tragen* has in German the same connotations as "bear" does in English: Wotan thereby describes himself as the Creator and Author of the Work, its father and mother at once.

■ And yet, Wotan appears onstage less as a creator, or even as a producer, an artisan like Alberich or Mime, than as a passive spectator of his desire, utterly dependent upon others for its fulfillment. And this desire, in turn, is quickly revealed to be a function not only of such dependency but of the incapacity to assume it.

■ For the denial of sexual difference is only one of the forms that Wotan's narcissistic repudiation of alterity assumes. Its most explicit form is his disavowal of the debt he has contracted with the Giants in exchange for their labor in constructing Walhalla. Nowhere is the self-destructive force of the *Ring*'s narcissistic desire more in evidence than here, at the risk of compromising all semblance of plausibility. For what Wotan has done is nothing less than to seal the fate of the gods, even before the curtain rises. In promising the Giants Freia, he has mortgaged the figure upon whom the gods depend for their very survival. Freia, who nourishes the gods with her "golden apples," is the *Ur-* mother long before Erda appears. Without her they are doomed, literally, to fade away, the negative fulfillment of that invisibility to which Alberich in vain aspires.

■ Wotan's fate is thus sealed long before the curtain rises, or rather—since in *Das Rheingold* the curtain only rises once, to reveal "the bottom of the

Rhine"—long before he is awakened from his dream. And indeed, the sense of fatality that pervades the tetralogy indicates that its effective, effectuating force resides not in any particular event or act, but rather in the structure of desire that reveals itself to be a defense against anxiety. The narcissistic desire staged by the *Ring* emerges, in *Das Rheingold* and throughout, as a flight from the anxiety of losing oneself in alterity. This refusal of alterity entails not simply its repression: Wotan "knows," as Fasolt reminds him, that "what you are, you are through contracts," that is, through the negotiated relationship to others. He *knows* this, he carries it around with him everywhere he goes, as much (or as little) a part of him as the text that is etched into his spear. But he cannot accept its consequences. And in his efforts to escape them, he renders them reality.[25]

■ If Wotan can thus be said to continue the game that began with Alberich, he also radicalizes it. Taking the suggestion of Loge, who tells him what he wants to hear, Wotan sees no problem in taking the ring away from Alberich, unable to discern any difference in their respective relations to it. And yet the difference is clear. Alberich steals the ring, but he also gives up something for it. And even if what he gives up is also what he could not have, even if cursing something may not be the same as renouncing it, Alberich's gesture does imply a recognition of alterity of which Wotan by contrast is utterly incapable. For Alberich is still in a position to acknowledge the other, albeit only as a subject to be subjugated or dethroned. Wotan, on the other hand, is unable to give up anything or acknowledge anyone. As a monarch who would be absolute, he resembles nothing so much as a spoiled child.[26]

■ In his long "self-dialogue" with Brünnhilde, in *Die Walküre*, Wotan describes his dilemma with the utmost lucidity:

> *How can I create a free agent,*
> *whom I never protected,*
> *whose own defiance*
> *would be most dear to me?*
> *How could I make another,*
> *who, no longer myself,*
> *would do on his own,*
> *what I alone desire?*

And his response is no less categorical:

> *O divine despair!*
> *terrible shame!*
> *With disgust I find*
> *only myself, eternally,*
> *in everything I do!*
> *The other for which I yearn,*
> *that other I will never see,*
> *For the free man must make himself;*
> *My hands mold only slaves!*

■ Lucid as to his dilemma, Wotan still clings to the ideal of "the free man" who is *self-made*. Precisely this Enlightenment ideal of the autonomous subject is what the *Ring* plays out in all of its self-destructive circularity, which no semblance of "redemption" can fully obscure.

■ It is of course a commonplace to point to Brünnhilde's love and self-sacrifice as the sign of just such a possibility of redemption. Although the question is too complex to be dealt with adequately here, it should be obvious that the significance of Brünnhilde's final gesture, leaping into the flames, cannot be separated from that of the fire itself. And in regard to the role of fire throughout the tetralogy, a powerful case can be made for the argument that it entails precisely the convergence of disfigurement and desire that marks the emergence of the theater of dislocation. In conclusion, then, I want to discuss briefly three notable occurrences of fire, limiting myself again to *Das Rheingold.*

■ The first instance is to be found in the opening scene. Alberich describes himself as set on fire by the spectacle of the nymphs, not merely by the lust that the sight of them elicits, but also by the fury that their ridicule provokes:

> How in my limbs
> the ardent passion
> burns me and glows!
> Fury and love,
> wild and potent,
> excite my spirits!

The fire that consumes Alberich produces a very precise result: the *body* of the Nibelung, already deformed, is even more *disfigured* by his passion. To be dislocated as spectator, therefore, involves much more than a mere change of venue: the displaced subject risks losing its bodily integrity together with its proper place vis-à-vis the spectacle.

■ All the more reason to remark that the reemergence of the *Schauspiel*, this time as the primal scene of the awakened gold, also entails a shift of the fire from the spectator back to the spectacle. The awakening of the gold is, as already mentioned, described in the oxymoronic style of the unconscious: the descending light "gradually ignites into a blindingly bright, golden light" (*sich . . . allmählich zu einem blendend hell strahlenden Goldglanze entzündet*). The fire here works to reestablish the coherence of the spectacle, previously threatened by that same fire. Fire will also be the means and medium by which the gold is then forged into a ring. And it will also provide the medium through which Siegfried reassembles the fragments of his father's sword, Notung.

■ In short, fire both protects and endangers representation and figuration. Fire protects the sleeping Brünnhilde, just as it consumes her. Fire frames the picture of the gods in Walhalla, as it destroys and effaces them. As visibility, theater requires the proximity of fire.

■ Yet nowhere, perhaps, are the ambivalent dramaturgical implications of fire as extensively staged as in the enigmatic figure of Loge, demigod of fire, Germanic cousin to Hephaistos. Loge, who appears as the servant of Wotan, reveals the fatal dependency of the gods upon him at the same time that he demarcates himself from them. "House and hearth tempt me not," he informs the master of Walhalla. For unlike the other gods, Loge has no desire to have a place of his own; he alone seems untouched by the desire of appropriation and of autonomy: he has nothing and wants nothing. Loge's strategy—and he is the only strategist among the gods—is one of total submission. He gives the others what they (think they) want, and this gift only accelerates their self-destruction.[27]

■ It is therefore entirely consistent that Loge, having played his part in *Das Rheingold*, should henceforth vanish from the scene, at least as a distinct, identifiable figure. For his interest is merely to reflect and illuminate the conflicts that the more prominent figures seek to conceal. And yet, in the peculiar ephemerality of this figure, the passage from a drama of figuration to a theater of disfiguration traces its course. For Loge designates not merely the impersonal personification of "fire" but also the homonym for *loge*: a form of "spectator space" that allowed the audience to intrude into the space of the stage, and that would have no place in Wagner's Walhalla, otherwise known as Bayreuth. In Bayreuth, the stage was to be clearly and definitively separated from the audience, for only so could the *theatron* desired by Wagner be fully realized. What was required was "a space calculated for nothing other than the view, to be looked into, namely, in the direction in which one's place points."[28] The place of the spectators has to be fixed in order for their gaze to be directed properly. To accomplish this, it was absolutely indispensable that the spectators be kept at a proper distance from the stage. This is why there could be no loges at Bayreuth—and also why Wagner was horrified at every tendency to reduce the separation of spectator and spectacle. He violently condemned the dramaturgical practices of his time, for instance, which tended to bring the scene so close to the audience "as to place it within the grasp of the spectator."[29]

■ And yet, if Wagner was so profoundly revolted by such tendencies to undermine the clear-cut separation of *Bühnenraum* and *Zuschauerraum*,[30] it was doubtless also because his own writing tends precisely in this direction. The figure of Loge is evidence of this tendency: neither interested actor nor disinterested spectator, at home neither with the gods nor with humans, Loge is nonetheless indispensable for the entire *Ring*. No hero, he elicits the decisive acts; no author, he guides the others to their doom. Loge's role can best be compared to that of a stage director or a dramaturg, an interpreter who transmits faithfully the discourse and desire of the principal figures, and who thereby dislocates them irremediably. As the disfiguring power of repetition, Loge does dramatically what the orchestral prelude to *Das Rheingold* accomplishes musically: the dismemberment of identity through its repetition. Just as the reiteration of the E-flat Major chord tends to decompose its tonal unity through the pulsations of its harmonic overtones, the repetitive gestures of Loge displace what they replicate.

■ In so doing, Loge gestures toward that other theater that resonates in the interstices of the text of the *Ring* and in the recurrences of its score: a theater of dislocation. The drama of this theater can no longer be described as the visualization of events on a stage; the space of the spectacle can no longer be taken for granted, for its structuring partitions partake in the scene they permit to take place. It is, in short, the drama of *taking place*.

■ The concluding scene of the entire tetralogy exemplifies this drama at work in the *Ring*. The conflagration into which Brünnhilde springs threatens to engulf the entire stage (and, by implication, the theater as well). The endangered limit between spectacle and spectators is represented, onstage, by the men and women gathered to witness the final scene: "Beside themselves [*entsetzt*] they crowd toward the extreme foreground" of the stage, their bodies serving as the ultimate barrier between the flaming spectacle and the audience. The menace is temporarily averted by the rising waters of the Rhine, coming full circle to reclaim the ring. But the fire is far from extinguished: as the water recedes, it flares up once again, this time to illuminate the final image of the gods, gathered silently in Walhalla: "Bright flames seem to burst into the hall of the gods. As they are entirely covered by the flames, the curtain falls."

■ The curtain falls. But does it put out the fire? Or only cover the still life of a theater that cannot stand still?

Monteverdi's *L'Orfeo*:
The Technology of Reconstruction

Klaus Theweleit

Blanching Stars

■ Europe's head honchos celebrated the exit of the darkened Middle Ages with a festival of light, noise, and colors. The festival lasted three centuries . . . no single person lasted that long . . . Clans, races, towns kept it going, as long as they weren't busy keeping themselves in the saddle, mixing poison and alliances, stealing gold, sustenance, and women, plunging Europe back into darkness, depopulating entire regions: exhausting the repertoire of gang warfare.

■ Otherwise they were celebrating, says Richard Alewyn. In halls, churches, grottoes, and public squares, on streets, rivers, and seas, under canopies as well as in the open air, publicly or in private, with the constant deployment of all available arts, with music, poems, theater, water ballet, and innumerable extras amid huge, painted sets. The crowd teems with gods—it's their first big sell-out show. All the myths are playing in Florence,

"Monteverdi's *L'Orfeo*: The Technology of Reconstruction" appears here for the first time in English translation. It is taken from of Theweleit's *Buch der Könige*, vol. I, *Orpheus und Eurydike* (Frankfurt am Main: Stroemfeld/Roter Stern, 1988). The translation is by David J. Levin. Text and notes have been slightly abridged.

Venice or in Paris, London, Antwerp, Madrid. Artificial springs shoot forth from the ground, opera houses are burned down, and fireworks are set off:

The night transforms itself into an artificial day, lights everywhere, houses, paths, canals are lined, the wave of light surges toward the heavens, cones of fire shoot into the night and the stars blanch.[1]

Just as the reader blanches in the twinkle of such a sentence.

■ The Renaissance princes did not restrict themselves to the occasional bottle rocket launched into the Roman, Florentine, Milanese, or Mantuan airspace—to a mere theater of light. They intervened more forcefully among the stars, undertook corrections, shifted hierarchies of light, disempowered constellations, installed new ones.

■ One of those constellations able to make entire galaxies blanch was catapulted into the sky at the court of the Gonzaga Princes of Mantua on February 22, 1607, and was christened *Euridice.*

■ At the same time a new star is born to the earth—"the star"—and christened *Orfeo.*

■ New stars tend to come from new media—is there one here? There is: this *Favola in Musica* (= Courtly Festival-Play with Music)—a designation employed by the Mantuan court conductor Claudio Monteverdi for his composition *L'Orfeo*—later gains the status of being Europe's "first real opera,"[2] which is to say, the first real opera, period.

■ (Why and to what end does the new medium Opera emerge around 1600 in Italy? Why is it ignited by the constellation Orpheus/Eurydice?)

. . . A Lover Disappears

■ The first scene of the opera shows an artist and a woman who declare their love for each other and marry. They marry under the sympathetic (and surveilling) eyes of "friends"—the shepherds and nymphs—who have broken into dance and applause on account of this marriage, as if it had transported one and all into love.

■ The bride loves her groom precisely *because* of his art. For weeks his lyre playing had gone unrewarded (according to the commentaries of the shepherds), but finally it moved and softened her, until she finally surrendered herself. It is *this* event that they celebrate: the heartening, heartwarming, heartfelt power of "music."

■ "Music" brings about love, says the first act.

■ Monteverdi/Striggio knew that they were working on a reconstruction of the Orpheus figure.

Act I: Eurydice has yielded to Orpheus' wooing. They are wed among the shepherds and nymphs (=amid the court society). All's well in the world. Dances.

Act II: Orpheus reflects on how empty and how sad life was without Eurydice. Smack dab in the middle of his reflections the "messenger" arrives with news that Eurydice has died from a serpent bite. Orpheus is petrified, becomes mute—then the lament.

Act III: Orpheus before the gates of the underworld. Charon is plied with music to let Orpheus in. That seems to fail. Eventually, Charon falls asleep. Orpheus steps into Hades.

Act IV: The gods of the underworld are moved to give Eurydice back to the singing lover. Orpheus violates the condition that he not turn around. Eurydice is lost again.

Act V: Orpheus' mourning. Orpheus' wish to die. Orpheus' call for Eurydice's irreplaceable ear. Orpheus' rescue by Apollo.

■ As a singer, Eurydice appears only in Acts I and IV. Without a doubt, Orpheus is the figure through whom the opera wants to work something out. He appears in every scene.

■ From the start, the pair is imbalanced: even in the mutual declaration of love at the outset, Orpheus sings about three times as long as Eurydice.

■ What he sings is later called an "aria." What Eurydice sings cannot be so named. Her singing has the character of song. She sings a nice, three-minute, modest little song.

■ On the steps, after Orpheus will have turned around, she has another such three-minute song of lament. That's all she has to sing in the whole opera. (Orpheus sings for over an hour.)

■ Nonetheless, one can say that the opera is centered on the "love" of the two; thematically no other strain of the Orpheus figure is of any importance.

■ Orpheus begins his declaration of love with a question addressed to the sun: whether it has ever seen a happier lover.

■ Then, to Eurydice:

> *Blessed was the day,*
> *my beloved, on which I first saw you,*
> *and happier still the hour*
> *when I sighed for you,*

> *since you returned my sighs;*
> *happy the moment*
> *when you gave me your white hand*
> *as a pledge of pure faithfulness. (8)*[3]

■ Centered around the concept of "faithfulness," this text is a typical example of the propagation of monogamous marriage by European courtly societies around 1600.[4]

> *Had I as many hearts*
> *as eternal heaven [has] eyes and these*
>   *pleasant hills*
> *leaves in green May,*
> *all would be full and overflowing*
> *with the joy that has made me happy*
>   *today. (8)*

Heaven's "many eyes" seem a bit odd. Perhaps the rest of the text will provide an explanation.

■ Eurydice answers Orpheus' revelation of his love—which is capable of making millions of hearts overflow—with the admission that she herself has no heart left at all:

> *I will not say how great*
> *my bliss is, Orpheus, at your bliss,*
> *I do not bear my heart within me,*
> *it remains with you together with my love;*
> *ask it if you would hear*
> *how it rejoices and how much it loves you. (8)*

■ She has given it to *him*, it's already *beating* in his breast. At this point no one can imagine how seriously the opera will follow through with this heart transplant. But at this point that's the "whole truth" and Eurydice's whole text as well.

■ The two are not alone onstage for a single second. "Nymphs/shepherds" are always around them; their wedding is a courtly, a societal event.

■ Act II shows Orpheus, content, among the shepherds—the guys—while Eurydice amuses herself upon other meadows with her "companions."

■ There is no explanation given for their separation, but Eurydice has to be offstage so that news of the serpent bite and her death can be delivered.

■ In his Zurich production of the opera,[5] the stage director Jean-Pierre Ponelle had Eurydice's "friend" who brings the news appear dressed in a serpent costume herself (suggesting that the other women are not interested in Eurydice's function as "the singer's one and only," or even that they are jealous of her):

> . . . when a treacherous serpent,
> hidden in the grass,
> bit her in the foot with its poisonous fangs. (10)

■ (In Vergil, as in Poliziano's *Orfeo* [1471] and later in Jacques Offenbach, there is another man—Aristaios/Aristaeus—who is mixed up in the bite. Eurydice flees through the fields in the hot midday sun as he chases after her, trying to seduce her. In the course of this flight, she is bitten "by the serpent"—a turn of events which smacks of rape. That is missing here—there is no "other man," there are no threats, no temptations.)[6]

> And behold, suddenly
> her beautiful face turned pale, and her eyes
> lost that brilliance for which the sun envied them.
> And now we, all horrified and woeful,
> ran to her and tried

> *to reawaken the spirit that had fled*
> *with fresh water and powerful spells;*
> *but all in vain—ah, wretched am I—*
> *for she briefly opened again her dying eyes*
> *and calling you, Orpheus,*
> *after a deep sigh*
> *expired in these arms; and I remained*
> *with my heart full of anguish and fear. (10)*

The Messenger/Serpent's song bearing *the news* is longer than everything that Eurydice herself sings in the opera.

■ Orpheus is rendered speechless—before he speaks up, the "shepherds" do. "Ah, bitter occurrence!" "So overcome by grief, he cannot lament," . . .

> *You are dead, my life, and I am breathing?*

■ Orpheus begins with the trademark claim of one who occupies the "Survivor" position (or the "S" position):[7]

> *No, if my verses have any power at all,*
> *I will surely go down to the deepest abysses*
> *and, having softened the heart of the King*
> > *of the Shadows,*
> *lead you back with me to see the stars. (10)*

Whoever pays close attention may be surprised that Orpheus wants to give the evening sky back to her, and not sunlight or the light of day.

■ Should this fail, he wishes for his own death.

■ The act closes with the complaint of the "nymphs and shepherds" to the gods that they have interfered with the loving couple—"ah, unjust stars, ah, miserly Heaven"—out of jealousy and ill will.

■ Then Orpheus stands at the gate to Hades. Speranza, the muse of hope, has guided him thus far.

Orpheus: *You, my companion and guide in such*
            unfamiliar and unexplored paths, have
            strengthened my feeble and trembling steps,
            wherefore I hope again today
            to see again those blessed eyes
            which alone bring day to my sight. (11)

It is the *sparkle* in Eurydice's eye, he says, that animates him.

■ "So may a great heart and a beautiful song aid you," sings La Speranza: "un bel canto." "Bel canto" was at that time not yet the professional term for dazzling opera coloraturas. It could be that the word appears here in this way for the first time, designating the mode of singing/song with which Orpheus should convince/lull/outfox Charon into opening the gates of Hell for him.

■ La Speranza herself may not go farther, "since a stern law forbids it" (11),

            a law inscribed with iron in the hard stone
            of the gateway to the deepest kingdom of terror,
            expressing its fierce meaning in these words:
            Abandon all hope, ye who enter here. (11)

■ "Iron" and "stone"? Words had strange destinies back then. It may be that Pluto, Ruler of the Underworld, also had a welcome-verse mounted upon the gates of Hades—but the one quoted here was written, with a feather upon paper, by Dante, 300 years before the Mantuan event. Over the years, the feather had (through book printing) metamorphosed into "iron" and the paper had become "stone." Striggio immediately demonstrated further reverence for Dante's printed power by having Orpheus, who now enters Hades, continue his song in Dante's meter.

■ (*L'Orfeo* in Mantua [1607] is separated from Dante by 300 years, and from us by about 385; it falls right around the middle.)

■ Hades is described by La Speranza as a city, *città dolente*, Pain City. This too is Dante's coinage (*Inferno* 3,1) and underscores that *The Divine Comedy* is one of the bibles of Renaissance mythologies.

■ The words "un bel canto," a beautiful song, were not merely a chance directive to Orpheus, but a directive concerning a mode of singing, a programming directive: *Ms. Hope* sang these words, *the only* words of her farewell, in *coloratura*, thus demonstrating what she considers to be "a beautiful song."

■ Orpheus, having received an order, does his darndest to carry it out. He floods Charon with coloraturas to make your ears ring. As many as fifty tones occur on a single textual syllable. Thus art's regal road to the cold heart of Hell's doorman is to be festooned, not with a spoken plea, but with musical flourishes.

■ Around 1600, those instances where singers were given the opportunity to demonstrate their vocal talents were marked in the scores merely by *outline tones*; the singer did the embellishing himself. Not so here. Contrary to all tradition, at the point where Orpheus seeks to convince Charon, Monteverdi wrote out the music for his coloratura note for note. This was not going to be just any old coloratura, but one which in its dramatic course makes clear *what* the singer is doing here: employing musical virtuosity in order to get someone to do something against his will.

■ The orchestra assists with sound tricks and echo games: it's the compositional high point of the opera in terms of the display of *musical means*. The echo of a violin, a flute, a trumpet, each very quietly repeats from "behind" what the same instrument "up front" played loudly, thus bringing the *beyond*, which Orpheus seeks to enter, as a presence into the ear of the listener—as if he were already over there, since the *tones* already are.

■ All of this is unleashed in the service of persuasion. For his part, Orpheus resorts to every trick in the book, including the most extreme flattery. Charon is addressed as:

Mighty spirit and powerful divinity (12)

even though he isn't even *close* to being a god; he's only the highest-ranking slave (he himself has to spend a year in Hades as punishment for having failed to block Heraclitus' entrance).

■ Coloratura and the magic of musico-instrumental artistry are thus deployed as a means of deception—and neither works.

■ Charon remains ice cold. The application for transit privileges is denied.

■ Orpheus, in whom the pain of losing his loved one is mixed with the pain caused by the failure of his song, is seized by wrath, desperation, and mourning (this time "for real")—he runs out of "bel canto," tricks, effects, and all.

■ Monteverdi switches to a very direct, emotionally laden song, an emotional *outburst* on Orpheus' part. The text, which had been buttering up Charon ("For it is only the sweet strings of a golden lyre / I use as a weapon / against the stern souls to whom it is vain to implore" [12]), also switches to direct emotion:

Does impious fate thus will it
that I, in this horror of death,
far from you, my beloved,

call your name in vain
and waste away in imploring and weeping?
Give me back my love, gods of Hell! (12)

■ The switch to direct emotion doesn't work either, insofar as Charon still doesn't grant him transit; but he expresses his lack of jurisdiction in the face of this outburst—by falling asleep.

■ Orpheus, opening his eyes which he had closed in pain, sees before him a slumbering Charon: his song has traversed the Styx, has reached *godly ears* and they in turn have shut off Charon, the doorman-function. Orpheus steps inside:

Let daring prevail where entreaties were vain. (12)

■ In *La Musica*'s Prologue it was said that music moves feelings. Does Monteverdi want to demonstrate that—in this game—only music corresponding to a player's feelings has this effect upon the affects? It seems that he does: Orpheus's wished-for success comes about only when he forgets his listeners and his musical *ends*.

■ In fact, whenever someone seeks to express emotions directly in this opera, coloratura is missing. When someone speaks openly, coloratura doesn't appear. There isn't a single "embellishment" in Eurydice's song.

■ Only when someone is not sure of himself, where there are exaggerations, mistakes, calculations, stratagems, there too one finds vocal coloratura.

■ This must be based upon a theory that straightforward feelings can be expressed in music.

■ Just such a reliable sense of self speaks out of the regular bass tempi that give the song of Pluto, the Prince of Hades, something definitively authoritative. Orpheus' tenor and Pluto's bass relate to one another—as far as Orpheus' coloraturas go—according to the model "the son makes the faces (interesting), but father makes the rules."[8]

■ In the coloraturas, Monteverdi takes Orpheus to the verge of parody or beyond it. In the line:

To her I have turned my path through the dark air (12)

half a hundred notes are devoted to the embellishment of the word "her" (*lei*). "She," ostensible goal of his song, therewith recedes to an ever-greater distance (just as, during the course of this sort of song, the singer seems to move farther away from himself, seems to lose himself in his own voice).

■ It's only when he laments and makes demands that a *moving* song results.

■ In Hades itself the work of musical persuasion is transferred to Proserpina, the ruler of Hades. With good reason too, since Monteverdi/Striggio would have been in a pinch had they been forced to make Orpheus now repeat for Pluto's ears his whole song from the Styx.

■ Proserpina pleads Orpheus' case; she has heard his song, i.e., she must have been eavesdropping in the background as Orpheus was trying to persuade Charon.

■ Ponelle made use of this in order to clarify the function of the "high women" in the opera: Orpheus, eyes closed, *missed the moment* during which Charon fell asleep, and he *wasn't* the one who put him to sleep. While Orpheus sings, Ponelle has La Musica/Proserpina perform a few hypnotic hand gestures in Charon's direction; his boss prescribes the requisite sleep for him. (Orpheus takes the credit himself.)

■ Pluto, god of the Underworld, allows himself to be persuaded by Proserpina to give Eurydice back to Orpheus. And again Orpheus will take the credit himself, crediting his lyre, which, strictly speaking, only softened Proserpina's ear.

■ Proserpina for her part catches Pluto's ear with a declaration of love:

> *Oh, if you have drawn*
> *the sweetness of love from my eyes,*
> *if my gentle brow has pleased you*
> *which you call your Heaven, wherefore you have sworn*
> *not to envy the fate of Jupiter,*
> *I implore you by that sweet fire*
> *with which Cupid kindled your great soul,*
> *let Eurydice again*
> *enjoy those days*
> *which she spent in rejoicing and song,*
> *and console the laments of wretched Orpheus. (13)*

■ Here is the true love scene between the true pair of lovers in the opera (the scene between Orpheus and Eurydice in Act I was so strangely short and imbalanced).

■ Pluto answers:

> *Although stern and immutable fate*
> *opposes your wishes, beloved wife,*
> *nothing indeed shall now refuse*
> *such beauty combined with such entreaties.*
> *His beloved Eurydice*
> *Orpheus shall find again, contrary to*
> *   the decrees of fate. (13)*

It is as a favor to *his* wife that Pluto agrees to cancel the power of death this one time. The First Spirit remarks this fact with the following words:

> *O mighty king of the eternal realm of shadows,*
> *your sign be our law. (13)*

■ Ponelle is right to have this spirit appear in a skeleton costume: made visible as "death," the spirit now exits, leaves the scene.

■ Now Pluto announces the condition of "no turning around." But it is not the only condition of the episode. The second one is addressed to Proserpina. Proserpina had greeted Pluto's concession with a joyful cry:

> *Blessed be the day on which I first pleased you,*
> *blessed be the abduction and the sweet deceit*
> *through which, to my good luck,*
> *I won you while losing the sun. (13)*

■ This refers to Proserpina's history: Pluto, in search of a wife who would join him in the netherworld,[9] *abducted* her from Earth and forcibly made her his wife. Jupiter, the more powerful god, punished him for this by granting to Proserpina the right to spend half of the year above ground, among humans, in the sunlight. This right is annulled by Pluto at this moment:

> *Your sweet words revive anew*
> *the old pangs of love in my heart.*
> *So may your soul nevermore*
> *long for heavenly delights*
> *so that you abandon your marriage bed. (13)*

■ In this moment, Pluto and Proserpina, the rulers of the underworld, become the whole-year couple that they had never been before. This happens with explicit reference to "Amor," who had incited Pluto's "great soul" to the abduction; i.e., to the abduction of a woman whom he had not previously *known.* We will soon see what role this plays when we hear Orpheus singing of Amor.

■ The Chorus of Spirits concludes this section with the words:

> *Pity and love have today triumphed in Hell. (13)*

■ Then Eurydice is brought in and placed behind Orpheus' back.

■ There he stands—lyre in hand, woman behind him, at the foot of the stairs—and he looks up into the light at the end of the tunnel.

First Spirit *(= disempowered death):*
> *Here is the gentle singer,*
> *leading his wife to the skies above. (14)*

A sky that remains at an unattainable distance for all who are "led" by a back (death—who else?—seems to know this).

■ There is no dialogue between Orpheus and Eurydice. No question: "Are you there? Can we go?" She also cannot take him by the hand; the hand is occupied. What thus follows is a demonstration of the fact that Orpheus (in every sense) has been occupied for a long time. He speaks to his instrument:

> *What honor is worthy of you,*
> *my omnipotent lyre,*[10]
> *that you have, in the infernal realm,*
> *been able to overcome every hardened spirit? (14)*

The zither begins to tremble beneath the adjective of godliness: *onnipotente.*

> *You will find a place among the most beautiful*
> *images of Heaven,*

> *and to your sound the stars will*
> *dance in circles, now slowly, now quickly. (14)*

"Dancing stars"; the sound[11] (*tuo suon*) moves the universe. Every listener knows the constellation of Lyra, knows that Orpheus speaks "true."

> *I, made perfectly happy through you,*

—only here, after it has been made clear that he and the lyre are the couple that is leaving Hades, does Eurydice enter the picture—

> *will see the beloved brow.*
> *On the white breast*
> *of my lady I shall rest*
>   *today. (14)*

The words "see," "white," "rest" do not bode well. A strange thought takes shape in his mind:

> *But while I am singing, alas, who*
>   *will assure me*
> *that she is following? Who keeps*
> *the beloved eyes hidden from me? (14)*

(Always the eyes.)

■ Of course he cannot hear her, since she is still a ghost and thus makes no sound. But he wouldn't be able to hear her even if she were already corporeal: his ear is occupied by his song.

> *Perhaps pierced by envy*
> *the gods of Avernus*
> *forbid me, so that my happiness will not be complete*
> *through looking at you,*

> *blessed happy lights*
> *that can make others blessed with one glance alone. (14)*

■ (The impression grows that he is seeking the glitter in her eyes as a form of applause for his song. An applause that he "hears.")

> *(with surging voice:)*
> *What do you fear, my heart?*
> *What Pluto forbids, Cupid [Amor] commands.*
> *A more powerful divinity*
> *who conquers men and gods*
> *I must obey.*
> *But what do I hear, alas?*
> *Do the Furies, madly in love,*
> *attack me with such rage[12]*
> *to rob me of my beloved? And I allow it? (14)*

■ Thus with the effect of his actions on his tongue, he turns around.

■ He passes off his action as a command from the god Amor. "This Orpheus is pretty weird, he's a hopeless case," everyone in the audience will probably have thought upon hearing these lines.

■ Amor is a blind god, and this hybrid constantly coughs up sentences about how much he wants to see his lover's eyes.

■ More: not only is Amor blind, but Orpheus, the philosophical Orpheus of Neoplatonism, is his prophet. "Orphic love," as Edgar Wind explains in a long chapter in *Pagan Mysteries in the Renaissance*, does not require eyes.[13]

That the supreme form of Neoplatonic love is blind was plainly asserted not only, as we have seen, by Marsilio Ficino, by Pico della Mirandola, by Lorenzo de' Medici, but the idea was expanded to inordinate lengths in the *Eroici furori* by Giordano Bruno,

(whose burned body leaves a powerful stench in the Zurich production) who distinguished no less than nine kinds of amorous blindness. The ninth and highest of these is the sacred blindness produced by the immediate presence of the deity: "wherefore the most profound and divine theologians say that God is better honored and loved by silence than by words, and better seen by closing the eyes to images than by opening them: and therefore the negative theology of Pythagoras and Dionysius is so celebrated and placed above the demonstrative theology of Aristotle and the Scholastics."

. . . Among Renaissance theologians it was almost a commonplace to say that the highest mysteries transcend the understanding and must be apprehended through a state of darkness in which the distinctions of logic vanish. (57)

. . . In defining the blindness of supreme love as Orphic, Pico relied on a Platonic text: he remembered an allusion to Orpheus in Proclus's *Commentary on the Timaeus* (33C). In explaining the creation of the world, Plato had written that an all-embracing body would not require eyes to see, nor ears to hear, since all things would be within it, and none outside. Proclus inferred from this statement that the highest mysteries must be seen without eyes and heard without ears, and he claimed that Orpheus meant to refer to that secret when he "said Love to be eyeless." (60)

Edgar Wind wrote his book as part of a movement that was intended to go beyond Panofsky's account in *Studies in Iconology* of "blind Amor" and his outrageous deeds.[14]

■ Amor is a complicated figure. There is the Amor of "heavenly" as well as the Amor of "worldly," of "profane" love; he appears as blind and seeing; sometimes he strikes the right people, sometimes he strikes with deadly consequences. At that point in time there were innumerable pictures and texts in circulation on the subject.[15] It is by no means clear which sensory organ best serves to open the bodily gates for the arrow's piercing entrance. Usually, a mixture of blindness and seeing, of hallucination and perception transports one into a state for which the likes of Amor is responsible.

■ It would be overstated to claim that the courtiers of Mantua (familiar with more than one version of Amor) saw with Wind's eyes how Orpheus transgresses here the highest laws of "Orphic love" (which of course are also a display of the gods). But they will not have failed to notice that this singing Orpheus is ruled by a *fury of wanting to see*, that his justification for turning around is very one-sided.[16]

■ When Orpheus cries out upon seeing the face of his love, or when he invokes Amor, people must have thought something along the lines of: "The man is daring . . . a bit beside himself . . . to put so much faith in a visual Amor."

> *O sweetest lights, I can indeed see you,*
> *I can, but what eclipse, alas, obscures you? (14)*

(Amor immediately takes revenge and makes Eurydice invisible.)

> *You have broken the law and are unworthy of mercy.*

So announces the Spirit to the jarring bass tones of the regal.[17] A musical thunderclap.

■ One can see that Striggio/Monteverdi are not proceeding blindly insofar as Proserpina invokes Amor in Pluto's presence, but Orpheus and Eurydice don't mention him in Act I when they declare their love for one another.

■ Pluto's soul was inflamed by Amor: blind Amor shot the arrow and he fell in love.

■ With Orpheus it was different:

> *Blessed was the day,*
> *my beloved, on which I first saw you. (8)*

A contrast to the methods of blind Amor in every respect. It was Orpheus himself who awakened this love within himself; he did it with the help of his eyes (the organs that a traditional Amor precisely does not use and does not need). Orpheus and Eurydice did not invoke him; this couple seems to be a test case for a newer, more direct form of love, one which involves selecting a loved one, making decisions rather than relying upon Amor's unpredictable arrow. The point here seems to be to bring this form of love into play, if only then to discredit it.

■ Pluto's injunction not to turn around, not to touch through glances, seems like a test of the real heat of the singer's love, a test in the principles of Old Amor.[18] If Orpheus loves Eurydice in and through the eyeless god, then he will not turn around, then he will not have to *see* his loved one,

> *for even only a single glance*
> *will condemn him to eternal loss. (13)*

■ (That Pluto's words here are not to be taken simply as the proclamation of "the Hades Law" along the lines of Vergil, Ovid, or Poliziano could be seen in the Florentine *Euridice* of 1600: Rinuccini kept Orpheus from turning around, since a tragic ending did not fit in with the courtly festivities; at that time, one took such liberties.)[19]

. . . A Media Technologist Appears

■ Eurydice takes her leave with the words:

> *Ah, sight too sweet and too bitter;*
> *so by too much love you thus lose me?*
> *And I, poor one, lose*
> *the happiness of returning to light and life, and lose at the same time*
> *you, dearest of all possessions, my husband. (14)*

The screenplay requires that she accept her own murder—perpetrated with skewed rationalizations—as love.

■ A couple, comprising two naive people, that is split apart?

■ In the following lines, it becomes clear that Orpheus doesn't "do" all of this himself, as a "person." Something happens to him ... he "wants to die," but is *not allowed* to:

> What secret power of these horrors
> drags me from these beloved horrors
> against my will, and leads me
> to the hateful light? (14)

A secret power (less secret to us than to him) catapults him into the "S" position.[20]

■ The newborn European artist stands before us as a rationalizing "S" man, filled with half-foreign affects, a dizzy man who plays the lyre well.

■ The second member of the couple, the one with whom Orpheus joins in order to conceive artificial realities is, instead of a woman, the instrument in his arm.

■ The philosopher / the prophet / the lover have been taken out of him, surgically removed.

> Orpheus overcame Hell and was
> overcome by his passions.[21] (14)

Thus comments the Chorus of Spirits.

■ The singer succumbs to false affects—and yet for Monteverdi music is the medium in which true affects should attain expression and victory. This noteworthy contradiction should be kept in mind.

■ The beginning of the last act shows Orpheus training himself in mourning, i.e., in good music. Songs of lament sweep through the hall, heartrending ones.

■ And who answers? A new woman? Yes. Not a corporeal one, but the one whom Narcissus spurned, who is in this instance a natural phenomenon (and a compositional achievement): the nymph Echo repeats Orpheus' last word, "lament." And Orpheus, happy to hear a voice, answers:

> *Kind, loving Echo,*
> *who are disconsolate*
> *and wish to console me in my grief,*
> *although these eyes of mine*
> *through so much weeping are made two fountains,*
> *in my serious misfortune*
> *I have not yet wept enough, not yet enough. (15)*

And Echo protests:

> *Enough! (15)*

■ Orpheus is training himself to be alone with his medium; alone as a *couple*. (The two fountains that his eyes become are a straight quote out of Dante's *La Vita Nuova*.)

■ Narcissus' error, according to McLuhan, was that he became the servo-mechanism of his own image in the water; that he became the servant of his self-extension in the mirror.[22]

■ Something similar threatens Orpheus here. He serves Echo with cues (with the lyre, his self-extension) and waits to hear how she will return them. In this self-involvement Orpheus would become precisely the "closed system" which McLuhan perceived in Narcissus.

■ But Monteverdi/Striggio did not envision such an end for their newly designed artist. After Echo has repeated a further word, "sorrow," Orpheus goes off the deep end:

> *If you have pity for me in my suffering, I thank you*
> *for your kindness.*

> Yet while I lament
> why do you answer me
> only with the last syllables?
> Give me back my entire laments. *(15)*

■ You may laugh, but here in 1607, as he seeks to install music upon the throne of enlivening media, Orpheus is asking for Edison. He is calling (into the woods and into the chasms and down the stairs) for something that will record his song and return it to him *wholly*.

■ He is serious, he isn't joking with Ms. Echo, and he is not simply mourning for his various loves: he himself *creates* this recording medium and he creates it out of his dead lover, Eurydice:

> But you, my soul, if ever your cold shadow
> visits these amiable banks,
> receive from me this last song of praise,
> for I dedicate to you my lyre and my song,

(he's not talking about *his* soul)

> as I already, on the altar of love,
> brought you my burning soul as a sacrifice.
> You were beautiful and wise,
> Heaven granted you
> generously all its gifts,
> while to every other it gave too little.
> The praise of every tongue is becoming to you,
> who housed in a beautiful body a more beautiful
> soul, the less haughty, the more worthy of honor.
> All other women . . . *(15)*

■ If it is not yet clear, it becomes clear here: Orpheus is speaking of Eurydice's soul. He is leaving the sound of his lyre and his song *to her* on this riverbank. The ear/the soul of the dead woman on the banks of the Styx become the tape into which Orpheus' sounds engrave themselves; the meadows of the Styx are in Monteverdi's staff paper. And Charon will sleep forever where the tones and the soul of dead Eurydice cross the river in order to meet for recording/resuscitation.

■ What follows is an outburst of hatred on Orpheus' part toward all other women, an outburst that first struck me as very arbitrary and unmediated. What did they do to him? Nothing. But the media hookup that he has just established with the body of his dead "one and only" requires an exclusion: that is, it requires that love for a real woman be excluded from the *Recording Device of Feelings.*

> All other women are proud and perfidious
> toward their adorers, heartless and inconstant,
> devoid of sense or noble thoughts,

(=do not return his tones, do not store them)

> wherefore their deeds are rightly not praised;
> it will never happen that through a common woman
> Love [Amor] will pierce my heart with a golden arrow. (15)

■ *Now* the mention of Amor makes sense: the love launched by his arrow can no longer reach the body of the new artist. (Monteverdi did not remarry after his second wife, the young girl–singer, died). All he did now was *make music.* Exactly what McLuhan terms: *"in love with his gadgets"* (41ff.).

■ As for "misogyny," I don't see it in him.

■ I prefer to say: Orpheus attaches himself to the pole of anesthesia, as far as "all other women" are concerned.

■ It may seem strange that Eurydice's ear/the soul of a dead lover become a recording component; it's an unfamiliar idea, and one might feel inclined to ask, "How's that supposed to work?"

■ One is (read: I am) not engineer (and not artist) enough to be able to answer this without hesitation. The "history" of technical invention does, however, provide an answer, indeed an answer in the spirit of Monteverdi/ Striggio. It turns out that human and/or animal body parts were used for the invention of the gramophone and the telephone, the first technical devices for sonic recording and sonic transmission before Edison successfully made the leap into a purely technical device. In 1829 Willis uses elastic tongues, modeled on human tongues, for a speech machine that transforms input oscillation frequencies into audible tones.

■ For the first visualization of spoken tones as a trace, Edouard Léon Scott in 1857 makes use of a swine bristle as a precursor to the gramophone needle which, attached to a membrane, writes the trace of the tones on a lamp-black glass plate.

■ And Bell and Clarke build the first prototype of our telephone receiver with the eardrum of a human corpse as membrane (1874).[23]

■ In the search for an *echo* that will *wholly* reproduce Orpheus' laments, Monteverdi/Striggio come upon exactly the same idea.

■ In the space reserved for the most adequate hearing and the preservation of their music, they place—this is a fact—the ear of this dead person, to whom *Heaven generously granted all its gifts*. In other words, the place of the best possible reception of their music and of a hoped-for *transmission* is *encoded* with a woman's soul. To describe the relationship to this (vanished) "soul" as "love" is a translation of the physiological functions of the eardrum. They thus *translate* the quality of Eurydice's wonderful ear into a quality of her "soul."

■ Just as Renaissance painters encode the gaze upon countrysides that are intended to be seen as "beautiful" or "harmonic" with a calculated female body, the musicians here encode the site of appropriate hearing/precise reproduction of their music with the ear/the soul of the "most beautiful" woman.

■ They do this—apparently—because they do not have the apparatus that *would in fact do* what they have in mind.

■ They build an *approximation* of such an apparatus out of a disassembled woman's body.

■ They manufacture (in the work of art) the dead woman that they need for this, simultaneously lamenting her irreplaceable loss (a social tribute) and resorting to inherited "mythological" recording and representational apparatuses.

■ In the course of its performance, the expiring artwork draws its notoriety for a certain sacredness not least (indeed, perhaps first) of all from its ritual sacrifice of the most beautiful woman before the eyes (and in the ears) of all. But amid the sacrifice it is primarily the *reconstruction* of recording devices and perceptual occurrences that is staged with the help of the dead body.

■ Accordingly, "beauty," "wisdom," "all of Heaven's gifts," "beautiful soul," all designate a real, unexploited excess in the body of women deployed in this manner, as they designate physiological-technical inventions that have yet to be created.

■ That is to say: a horse or a dog won't do. In any case, they aren't used here.[24]

■ In 1880, the echo that plays a similar role in the construction of Orpheus' wish for recording and reproduction appears accordingly in one of the first theoretical texts on Edison's invention, "Memory and Phonograph" by the French philosopher Marie Jean Guyau:

If the phonograph were to hear itself, it would learn the difference between the two voices: first, the one that comes from outside of itself and is violently imposed upon it, and second, the voice that it itself produces and that is a simple echo of the first, upon an already beaten trail.[25]

Orpheus' music plays with the echo in this function: "upon an already beaten trail" (namely, that of written music), the same instrument *quietly* (=farther back in the room) plays *back* what its visible likeness farther forward in the room initially played *loudly*. In 1607, in Mantua, *L'Orfeo* simulates scenically and musically a gramophone effect.

■ They take a "woman in Hades" "as membrane," as "needle" they take an echo in the instruments according to the notation. *Echo-Eurydice* vanquishes the Styx.[26]

■ The circuit intended to create auto-recording is connected thus—it is no mere circuit *game*.

■ I cannot tell, however, whether this circuit *requires* dead bodies lying around—not only in but also outside the works; whether the artist needs them, or whether he couldn't *make do* without them. Or perhaps there is a punishment involved, imposed upon him by a plague or power, so that he too gets his fair share of suffering. All I see is that they're lying there.

Eurydice Torn Up, Numerous Couples, a Leftover Star

■ What the circuit still needs in order to function is the connection to courtly power. At precisely the moment when Orpheus is ready, Apollo/ Prince Gonzaga[27] steps forward as if he had been standing in the wings watching until Orpheus had made himself into a couple (by linking himself to his lyre) and into a recording device (by linking himself to pieces of the dead woman), and had "sworn off" all living women:

> *Why do you give yourself over to rage and grief*
> *as prey like this, O son? (15)*

Plain and simple, a physician, this Dr. Prince. He wants to heal Orpheus' sorrows. His first medicine: one must not serve one's feelings (*servir al proprio affetto*):[28]

Apollo: *Now listen to me, and you will have fame and life.*

Orpheus: *. . . Heavenly father: command and I will obey.*

Apollo orders Orpheus to join him "in heaven."

Orpheus: *So shall I never again see*
             the sweet eyes of my beloved Eurydice?

Apollo: *In the sun and the stars*
             you shall recognize her beautiful likeness. (15–16)

■ This is the second partitioning of Eurydice's body after her death. It's not Orpheus who is "torn apart," she is. While her ear/soul remain in Hades / at the Styx, the glitter of her (audience's) eyes moves on to heaven.[29] At the same time Orpheus is ordered to the court, seated to the right of Apollo, who puts him on display before his court audience, before the shining eyes of the courtly women who are hooked up to the new European affects by way of the music.

■ (The Prince wants to be loved like that as well, just as perhaps a Eurydice from one of those weird bourgeois families might love her Orpheus: with "feelings.")

■ He will do everything in order to block and to ruin the possibilities of such a love. The conclusion of this opera documents this programmatically.

Apollo and Orpheus (rise singing to Heaven):
> *Let us rise, singing, to Heaven,*
> *where true virtue*
> *has its own reward: joy and peace. (16)*

This shabby fraternalization must have been too much for Monteverdi (personally)—he wasn't maneuvered into this position by the Gonzagas; he only approaches it in Venice. He shook a sack full of coloraturas into the score and Orpheus and Apollo vanish from the stage amid musical contortions and a display of vocal-garbage flourishes.

■ The two couples that triumph as producing couples in the end—one consisting of man and his instrument; the other consisting of artist and a power—overshadow the pair of lovers O & E.[30]

■ What do they "produce"? Since they aren't a "factory." Or are they?

■ They produce prototypes, societal model couples of the couple artist/ prince, of the couple artist/medium, of the two-man couple that works on mediums, of the couple artist/wife—and they test each of the prototypes for its potential suitability for serial production (this holds for those couples we have seen to this point, but that isn't all of them).

■ They produce structures of reality and amorous relationships (with and without a return ticket across the Styx).

■ The Florentines were very impressed.

■ Jean-Pierre Ponelle is very impressive too. The last image of his television recording is given over to death, laughing.

■ The reconstruction that Monteverdi attempts with the dead body of Eurydice must not have been noticed by the Gonzagas. Their interest is in elevating music, in gaining an "artistic victory" for their court (and blocking any loving couples who are not on the royal level).

"The Wound Is Healed Only by the Spear That Smote You": The Operatic Subject and Its Vicissitudes

Slavoj Žižek

The Answer of the Real

■ At the origins of opera there is a precisely defined intersubjective constellation: the relationship of the subject (in both senses of the term: autonomous agent as well as the subject of legal power) to his Master (King
or Divinity). The hero's recitative (the counterpoint to the collectivity em-
bodied in the chorus) is basically a supplication, an entreaty, addressed to
the Master, a call to him to show mercy and to make an exception (to forgive
the hero his trespass).[1] The first, rudimentary form of subjectivity is this
voice of the subject beseeching the Master to suspend, for a brief moment,
his own Law. The dramatic tension of subjectivity consists in the ambiguity
between power and impotence that pertains to the gesture of grace by
means of which the Master answers the subject's entreaty. As to the official
ideology, grace expresses the Master's supreme power, the power to rise
above one's own law: a Master must be really powerful to be able to afford

" 'The Wound Is Healed Only by the Spear That Smote You': The Operatic Subject and Its Vicissitudes"
was written for this volume. All notes are by the author.

mercy. What we have here is a kind of symbolic exchange between the human subject and his divine Master: when the subject, the human mortal, by way of his offer of self-sacrifice, surmounts his finitude and attains the divine heights, the Master responds with the sublime gesture of grace, the ultimate proof of *his* humanity.[2] Yet this act of grace is at the same time branded by the irreducible mark of a forced empty gesture—the Master ultimately makes a virtue out of necessity, he promotes as a free act what he is in any case compelled to do: if he refuses clemency, he takes the risk that the subject's entreaty will turn into open rebellion. . . . It is here that we already encounter the intricacies of the dialectic of Master and Servant elaborated later by Hegel: is not the Master, insofar as he depends on the other's recognition, effectively his own servant's servant?

■ For that reason, the temporal proximity of the emergence of opera to Descartes' formulation of the *cogito* is more than a fortuitous coincidence: one is even tempted to say that the move from Monteverdi's to Gluck's Orpheus corresponds to the move from Descartes to Kant. At the formal level, this entails a shift from recitative to aria; at the level of dramatic content, what Gluck contributed was a new form of subjectivization. In Monteverdi we have sublimation in its purest form: after Orpheus turns to cast a glance at Eurydice and thus loses her, the Divinity consoles him. True, he has lost her as a flesh-and-blood person, but from now on, he will be able to discern her beautiful features everywhere, in the stars in the sky, in the glistening of the morning dew. Orpheus is quick to accept the narcissistic profit of this reversal: he becomes enraptured with the poetic glorification of Eurydice that lies ahead of him. (This, of course, throws another light on the eternal question of why he looked back and thus screwed things up. What we encounter here is simply the link between the death drive and creative sub-limation: Orpheus' backward gaze is a perverse act *stricto sensu*. He loses her intentionally in order to regain her as the object of sublime poetic in-spiration.)[3] With Gluck, the denouement is completely different: after look-ing back and thus losing her, Orpheus sings his famous aria "Che farò senza Euridice," announcing his intention to kill himself. At this precise point of total self-abandonment, Love intervenes and gives him back his Eurydice.[4] This specific form of subjectivization—the intervention of grace, not as a simple answer to the subject's entreaty, but as an answer in the very mo-ment when the subject decides to put his life at stake—is the twist added by Gluck.[5]

■ Opera's development thus reaches its first full circle: all the elements for Mozart are here. That is to say, Mozart's "fundamental matrix" consists in precisely such a gesture of subjectivization whereby the affirmation of the subject's autonomy (our readiness to sacrifice ourselves, to go through with it, to die, to lose all) gives rise to a gesture of mercy in the Other. This matrix is at work in its purest form in his first two masterpieces, the *opera seria, Idomeneo,* and the *Singspiel, Abduction from the Seraglio*: when, in *Seraglio,* the two lovers, prisoners of Pasha Selim, express their fearless readiness to die, Pasha Selim shows mercy and lets them go. All Mozart's subsequent operas can be read as so many variations or permutations of this matrix. In *Le Nozze di Figaro,* for example, the relationship is reversed: the Master—Count Almaviva—is not prepared to grant mercy to his wife and Figaro when he thinks that he has caught them in adultery. Yet when he walks into the trap and his own deceit is exposed, he is himself forced to beg for mercy and the community of subjects forgives him—a unique utopian moment of reconciliation thus occurs, where the Master is integrated into the community of equals. *Don Giovanni* brings this logic of mercy to its inherent negation: in it, we find neither entreaty nor mercy. Don Giovanni proudly refuses the Stone Guest's call to repent (i.e., to ask for mercy), and what then befalls him instead of clemency is the most cruel punishment: he is swallowed by the flames of Hell; the ideal balance of autonomy and mercy is here perturbed by the emergence of an autonomy so radical that it leaves no space open for mercy, an autonomy in which it is not difficult to discern the contours of what Kant called "radical Evil."[6] After this moment of utter despair, when the whole economy of mercy is suspended, the register miraculously changes and, with *The Magic Flute*, we enter the domain of fairytale bliss. Here we also twice encounter the gesture of subjectivization through a readiness to die (both Pamina and Papageno are about to commit suicide), yet the agency which intervenes and prevents the accomplishment of the act is not an imposing Master or Divinity but the three *Wunderknaben.*

■ The temptation to be avoided here is to conceive this Mozartian co-dependence of autonomy and mercy as a compromise formation, as an illusory point of equilibrium between the not-yet-subject who still relies on the Master's grace (the subject of enlightened absolutism in his relationship to the Monarch) and the fully autonomous subject, master of his own fate. If we succumb to this temptation, we lose the fundamental paradox of how *autonomy itself, in its very self-affirmation, relies on "mercy," on a sign of the Other, on an "answer of the real"*:

The empirical mind sees the response of mercy as an alien caprice, or just coincidence. Bondage to fate can, absurdly enough, be broken only by the favor of fate; the individual can round his existence into a whole only, as Goethe put it, "if quite unexpected things from outside come to his aid." Piously believing it and bitterly accepting it, Goethe entrusted self-realization in his life to the "daemon," in his major work to the devil.[7]

In Mozart, of course, the bourgeois subject, with his utilitarian, instrumental, cunning dexterity, is at work from the very beginning (the element of *opera buffa*). The motto "The Lord helps those who help themselves" attains its full value here: the subject is never a mere applicant; by way of his subterfuge, he prepares the ground in advance, arranges the plot, so that all that is left to God-Master is to nod his assent after the fact, like the Hegelian monarch. But the more it becomes clear that, at the level of content, the subject's subterfuge has already taken care of the final outcome, the more the true enigma of form becomes palpable: why does the subject still need mercy, why does he not also assume the formal act of decision, why does he still rely on the Other?

■ The further feature which apparently contradicts the first is that the Other intervenes at the very moment when, in a suicidal act of abandonment, the subject expresses his readiness to risk everything in a gesture of defiant renunciation and thus disavows all the cheap tricks of instrumental reason. As long as I endeavor to bargain, as long as I propose my self-sacrifice so to speak with my fingers crossed, counting on the last-minute intervention of grace, the Other will not respond. Grace is a case of what Jon Elster called "states which are essentially a by-product":[8] it occurs at the very moment when we abandon all hope and cease to count on it. The situation is here ultimately the same as that of Abraham's acceptance of God's command to sacrifice his son: because he accepted it, he did not have to carry it out—*but he could not know that in advance.* And does not the same paradox define so-called mature love: our partner will really appreciate our love only if we somehow let him know that we are not childishly dependent on him, that we are able to survive without him? Therein consists the ordeal of true love: I pretend that I'll leave you, and only if and when you demonstrate your ability to endure my loss, do you become worthy of my love. As was pointed out by Claude Lefort,[9] a similar confidence in the answer of the real is at work in democracy, which entails the symbolic dissolution of social links (in the act of elections, the future fate of society is made dependent on a play of numeric contingency); the underlying hypothesis that—in the long term, at least—the result will be in the best interest of society can never be directly proven, it always relies on a minimum of miraculous coincidence, i.e., to refer to the Kantian terms, the status of this hypothesis is strictly regulative, not constitutive, like that of teleology in Kant. (It is precisely this gap which opens up the space for the totalitarian temptation to impose on society the solution which is "in its best interest.")

■ One of the "postmodern" myths concerns the phantom of the so-called Cartesian paradigm of subjectivity: the era of modernity now reaching its end was allegedly marked by the all-devouring monster of the absolute, self-transparent Subject, reducing every Otherness to an object to be "mediated," "internalized," dominated by technological manipulation, etc., the ultimate result of which is the present ecological crisis. Here, reference to the history of opera allows us to denounce this myth by way of demonstrating how, far from postulating an "absolute subject," philosophy from Kant to Hegel, this apogee of "modern-age subjectivity," struggled desperately to articulate the paradoxical conjunction of autonomy and grace, i.e., the dependence of the very assertion of the subject's autonomy on the sympathetic response of an Otherness.[10]

Subjectivity and Grace

■ This answer of the real on which we rely, this support in the big Other whose gesture of response "subjectivizes" the abyss of the pure subject, is what Hegel has in mind when he speaks of the "cunning of reason." The subject's readiness to "sacrifice everything" is conceived by Hegel as "the return of consciousness into the depths of the night of the I = I, which distinguishes and knows nothing besides itself. This feeling is therefore in fact the loss of substance and its standing over and against consciousness."[11] The commonplace reproach to Hegel is that, in the "closed economy" of his idealism, this loss reverts automatically to the new positivity of the self-identical Subject-Substance—but we must be particularly careful not to miss the paradox of this inversion. On the one hand, the sacrifice is in no way feigned, i.e., part of a game in which one can rely on the Absolute guaranteeing a happy outcome. Hegel is here quite clear and unambiguous: what dies in this experience of the return into the night of the I = I is ultimately Substance itself, i.e., God qua transcendent agency which pulls the strings behind the scenes. What dies is thus precisely God qua Reason, which, by way of its "cunning," guarantees the happy outcome of the historical process—in short, absolute Subject-Reason, the notion of which is usually imputed to Hegel. Hegel's interpretation of Christianity is here far more subversive than it may appear; that is to say, how does Hegel conceive the Christian notion of the becoming-man of God, at what level does he place the sign of equality between God and man? At the radical opposite of the usual view which conceives the "divine" in man as that which in him is eternal, noble, etc.—when God becomes man, he identifies with man qua suffering, sinful mortal. In this sense, the "death of God" mean that the subject verily finds himself alone, without any guarantee in the substantial Reason, in the big Other.

■ On the other hand, however—and therein consists the paradox—we are here as far as we can possibly be from any kind of existential despair, from the "openness" of the radical risk ("when everything is put at stake, grace can either intervene or not"): the reversal into mercy follows automatically, it takes place as soon as we *truly* put everything at stake. Why? More precisely: why is the standard Derridean question ("What if the reversal does *not* arrive, what if no 'answer of the real' follows the radical loss?") here totally out of place? There is only one possible explanation: the reversal of loss into salvation by way of grace is an act of purely formal conversion, i.e., *the intervention of grace is not something distinct from the preceding loss, but is this very loss, the same act of self-renunciation, conceived from a different perspective.* With regard to Christianity, this means that the death of Christ is simultaneously a day of grief and a day of joy: God-Christ had to die in order to be able to come to life again in the shape of the community of believers (the "Holy Spirit"). Instead of the "substance" qua God-Master, the inscrutable Fate which reigns in its Beyond, we obtain the "substance" qua community of believers. In this precise sense, "the wound is healed only by the spear that smote you": the death of God *is* his resurrection, the weapon which killed Christ *is* the tool which created the Christian community of the Holy Spirit.

■ Subjectivity thus involves a kind of loop, a vicious circle, an economic paradox which can be rendered in a multitude of ways, Hegel's, Wagner's, Lacan's. Lacan: castration means that the Thing-Jouissance must be lost in order to be regained on the ladder of desire, i.e., the symbolic order recovers its own constitutive debt; Wagner in *Parsifal*: the wound is healed only by the spear that smote you; Hegel: the immediate identity of the substance must be lost in order to be regained through the work of subjective mediation. What we call "subject" is ultimately a name for this economic paradox or, more accurately, short circuit whereby *the conditions of possibility coincide with the conditions of impossibility.* This double bind which constitutes the subject was for the first time explicitly articulated by Kant: the I of transcendental apperception can be said to be "self-conscious," can experience itself as a free, spontaneous agent, to the very extent to which it is inaccessible to itself as the "Thing which thinks"; the subject of practical reason can act morally (out of duty) to the very extent to which any direct access to Supreme Good is barred to him; etc. The point of these paradoxes is that what we call "subjectivization" (recognizing oneself in interpellation, assuming an imposed symbolic mandate) is a kind of defense mechanism against an abyss, a gap, which "is" the subject. The Althusserian theory conceives the subject as the effect of ideological (mis)recognition: the subject emerges in an act which renders invisible its own causality. Reference to opera enables us to discern the contours of a certain vicious circle which defines the dimension of subjectivity, yet is not the Althusserian circle of interpellation: the Althusserian moment of the closure of the circle, of the (mis)recognition in interpellation, is not the direct effect of a "process without subject," but an attempt to heal the very wound of subjectivity.

■ Kant's merit consists thus in the very feature that is the usual target of his critics: by means of one and the same gesture, his philosophy opens up the space (the possibility, the need) for a thing and makes this thing inaccessible and/or impossible to accomplish—as if the opening is possible only at the price of the instantaneous crossing-out.[12] Salomon Maimon, Kant's contemporary, was the first to point out that Kant's dualism between reason and sense both creates the need for the transcendental turn (to escape Hume's skepticism) and makes it impossible; along the same lines, Kant is usually reproached for conceiving Things-in-themselves as a necessary presupposition of our knowledge (providing the "material" to be formed by the transcendental grid), but at the same time making them inaccessible to our knowledge; on another level, the pure ethical act is unconditionally imposed by the moral imperative and something that, for all practical purposes, remains impossible to accomplish, since one can never be quite certain of the total absence of "pathological" considerations in any of our acts. This entity, necessary and impossible in one and the same movement, is the Lacanian Real.[13]

■ And does not this same absolute simultaneity of positioning and prohibiting define the Lacanian *objet petit a*, the object-cause of desire? In this precise sense, Lacan can be said to accomplish the Kantian critical project by supplementing it with a fourth critique, the "critique of pure desire," the foundation of the first three critiques.[14] Desire becomes "pure" the moment it ceases to be conceived as the desire for a "pathological" (positively given) object, the moment it is posited as the desire for an object whose emergence coincides with its withdrawal, i.e., which is nothing but the trace of its own retreat. What must be borne in mind here is the difference between this Kantian position and the traditional "spiritualist" position of striving after infinity, freed from every attachment to sensible particularity (the Platonic model of love which elevates itself from love for an individual person toward love for the Idea of Beauty as such): far from amounting to another version of such spiritualized-ethereal desire, the Kantian "pure desire" is confined to the paradox of the subject's finitude. If the subject were able to trespass the limitations of his finitude and to accomplish the step into the noumenal domain, the very sublime object which constitutes his desire as "pure" would be lost (we encounter the same paradox in Kant's practical philosophy: it is the very inaccessibility of the Thing which makes us capable of moral acts).

From Mozart to Wagner

■ Yet the story is far from over at this point. The line of Mozart's operas from their fundamental matrix through its variations to the final reversal into the bliss of *The Magic Flute* is repeated, on a different level, in Richard Wagner. The missing link between Mozart and Wagner is provided by Beethoven's *Fidelio*. On the one hand, we find in it the intervention of Mercy which follows the gesture of self-sacrificing subjectivization in its purest form: when Pizarro, the evil governor of the prison, wants to dispose of the noble Florestan, Leonora, Florestan's faithful wife, masked as a man and employed as the jailer's assistant under the false name of "Fidelio," interposes herself between the two, protecting Florestan with her own body, and reveals her true identity. At the very moment when Pizarro threatens to kill her, a trumpet sounds, announcing the arrival of the Prime Minister, the messenger of the good King who is here to free Florestan. On the other hand, we already encounter here the key moment of Wagner's fundamental matrix: man's redemption through woman's willing self-sacrifice.[15] One is even tempted to say that *Fidelio*, this apogee of the exaltation of the bourgeois couple, is entirely directed toward the sublime moment of the woman's redemptive sacrifice, the consequences of which are double. Because of this exalted ethical enthusiasm, *Fidelio* has always been surrounded by a kind of magical aura (as late as 1955, when its performance marked the opening of the renovated Vienna opera house, wild rumors began to circulate in Vienna about cripples regaining their ability to walk and blind men their sight). Yet this very obsession with the ethical gesture entails a kind of "ethical suspension of the esthetic" which seems to sap the opera's stage potential. At the crucial moment, the curtain falls and the opera proper is supplanted by a symphonic interlude, alone capable of rendering the intensity of the sublime exaltation (the overture Leonora III, usually performed between the denouement—the Minister's arrival—and the jubilant finale)—as if this exaltation fails to meet the "considerations of representability," as if something in it resists the *mise-en-scène*.[16]

■ For the shift to Wagner's universe to take place, we only have to brand both man and woman with a certain stain of "pathology": the man to be delivered is no longer an innocent hero, but a suffering sinner, a kind of Wandering Jew who is not allowed to die, since he is condemned for some unspeakable past transgression to unending roving in the domain between the two deaths. (In contrast to Florestan who, in his famous aria which opens the second act of *Fidelio*, prior to the spectral appearance of Leonora, repeats almost obsessively how he "has done his duty" [*ich habe meine Pflicht getan*], the Wagnerian hero *failed* to act in accordance with his "duty," his ethical mandate.) At the same time, the woman, his redeemer, acquires the unmistakable features of hysteria, so that we obtain a kind of redoubled, mirrored fantasy. On the one hand, *The Flying Dutchman* "could be reduced to the moment when the Dutchman steps beneath—one could almost say, steps out from—his picture, as Senta, who has conjured him up as Elsa had conjured up the knight [in *Lohengrin*], stands gazing into his eyes. The entire opera is nothing more than the attempt to unfold this moment in time."[17] (And is the great last act of *Tristan und Isolde* not an inversion of this spectral fantasy? Is not Isolde's appearance conjured up by the dying Tristan? For that reason, the two recent stagings of Wagner which displaced part of the action into the imagination of one of the persons onstage are deeply justified: Harry Kupfer's interpretation of the Dutchman as Senta's hysterical vision; Jean-Pierre Ponelle's interpretation of Isolde's arrival and ecstatic death as the vision of the dying Tristan.)[18] On the other hand, this figure of the woman ready to sacrifice herself is clearly an ostentatious male fantasy, in this case, Wagner's own. Suffice it to quote the following passage from his letter to Liszt apropos of his love affair with Mathilde Wesendonk:

The love of a tender woman has made me happy; she dared to throw herself into a sea of suffering and agony so that she should be able to say to me "I love you!" No one who does not know all her tenderness can judge how much she had to suffer. We were spared nothing—but as a consequence I am redeemed and she is blessedly happy because she is aware of it.[19]

Thus, one is quite justified in considering *The Flying Dutchman* as the first "true" Wagner opera: the suffering man, condemned to wander in the domain "between the two deaths," delivered by the woman's self-sacrifice. It is here that we encounter the fundamental matrix in its purest form, and all Wagner's subsequent operas can be generated from it via a set of variations.[20] Here, also, the elementary form of the song is the entreaty—man's complaint whose first paradigmatic case is the Flying Dutchman's monologue in which we learn about his sad fate, eternally sailing on a ghost ship. The most powerful moments in *Parsifal*, Wagner's last opera, are also the two supplications of the Fisher King Amfortas; here, as in the case of the Dutchman, the content of the entreaty is almost the exact opposite of the entreaty which opens the history of opera: in Wagner, the hero bemoans his very inability to find peace in death, i.e., his fate of eternal suffering.[21] The gesture of grace, the "answer of the real," which closes *Parsifal* is an act of Parsifal himself, who intervenes at the last minute, preventing the knights from slaughtering Amfortas and using the spear to deliver him from his torments. Here is the outline of the story:

The holy Grail, the vessel with Christ's blood, is kept in the castle Monsalvat; yet its ruler Amfortas, the Fisher King, is maimed: he betrayed the sanctity of the Grail by letting himself be seduced by Kundry, a slave to the evil magician Klingsor, who castrated himself in order to be able to resist the sexual urge. While Amfortas was in the embrace of Kundry, Klingsor snatched away from him the sacred spear (the one with which Longinus smote Christ on the cross) and wounded him in the thigh. We have already encountered the special character of this wound: it condemns Amfortas to a life of eternal suffering. The young Parsifal enters the domain of Monsalvat and kills a swan, unknowingly committing a crime; the wise old Gurnemanz recognizes in him the pure fool who—so the prophecy goes—will deliver Amfortas; he takes him into the temple of the Grail, where Parsifal witnesses the ritual of the Grail's disclosure painfully performed by Amfortas. Parsifal is unable to make anything of it, and Gurnemanz chases him away. In Act II, Parsifal enters Klingsor's magic castle, where Kundry endeavors to seduce him; in the very moment of her kiss, Parsifal experiences compassion for the suffering Amfortas and pushes her away; when Klingsor throws the sacred spear at him, Parsifal is able to stop it by raising his hand—since he resisted Kundry's seduction, Klingsor has no power over him. By making the sign of the cross with the spear, Parsifal dispels the magic and Klingsor's castle disintegrates into dust. In Act III, Parsifal, after many years of wandering, returns on Good Friday to Monsalvat and reveals to Gurnemanz that he has recovered the stolen spear; Gurnemanz anoints him as the new king; Parsifal baptizes the repentant Kundry, experiences the inner peace and elevation of Good Friday, then again enters the temple of the Grail where he finds Amfortas surrounded like a wounded, entrapped animal by enraged knights. The knights want to force him to perform the Grail ritual; unable to do it, he implores them to kill him and thus relieve his suffering; but at the last moment, Parsifal enters, heals his wound by a touch of the spear ("The wound is healed only by the spear that smote you"), proclaims himself the new king, and orders the Grail to remain revealed forever, while Kundry silently drops dead. How can one avoid here, as a first spontaneous reaction, amazement at the strange set of central characters, an amazement expressed by, among others, Thomas Mann:

One advanced and offensive degenerate after another: a self-castrated magician; a desperate double personality, composed of a Circe and a repentant Magdalene, with cataleptic transition stages; a lovesick high-priest, awaiting the redemption that is to come to him in the person of a chaste youth; the youth himself, "pure" fool and redeemer.[22]

The way to introduce some order in this apparent mess is by simple reference to the four elements of the Lacanian discourse matrix: the maimed king Amfortas as S_1, the Master; the magician Klingsor as the semblance of knowledge, S_2 (the semblance pertaining to Klingsor's status is attested to by the spectral character of his magic castle: as soon as Parsifal makes the sign of the cross, it falls to ruins);[23] Kundry as $, the split hysterical woman (what she demands from the other is precisely to refuse her demand, i.e., to resist her conquest); Parsifal, the "pure fool," as *objet petit a*, the object-cause of Kundry's desire, yet totally insensitive to feminine charms. The next mystery is the lack of any proper action in the opera. What actually takes place is a succession of negative or empty, purely symbolic gestures: Parsifal *fails to understand* the ritual; he *refuses* Kundry's advances; he *makes the sign* of the cross with the spear; he *proclaims* himself king. Therein consists the most sublime dimension of *Parsifal*: it dispenses wholly with the usual "action" (with positively "doing something") and limits itself to the most elementary opposition between the act of renunciation/refusal and the empty symbolic gesture.[24] Two of the above-mentioned gestures are decisive: in Act II he rejects Kundry's advances, and in Act III, at what is perhaps the crucial point in the opera, he proclaims himself king, accompanied by the fourfold beat of the drum ("that he may greet me today as king"). In the first case, we have the act qua repetition by means of which Parsifal identifies with Amfortas' suffering, takes it upon himself; in the second case, we have the act qua performative by means of which Parsifal assumes the symbolic mandate of the King, the keeper of the Grail.[25] So, what can this set of eccentrics and their (non-)deeds tell us?

"I Am Going to Talk to You About the Lamella"

■ Let us begin by taking a closer look at the mysterious wound which prevents Amfortas from finding peace in death. This wound, of course, is another name for its opposite, for a certain surplus of *jouissance*. According to Lacan, the symbolic order "stands for death" in the precise sense of "mortifying" the real of the body, of subordinating it to a foreign automatism, of perturbing its "natural" instinctual rhythm, *thereby producing a certain surplus*: the very symbolic machine which "mortifies" the living body produces by the same token its opposite, the immortal desire, the Real of "pure life" which eludes symbolization. Let us recall the role of the magic love potion in Wagner's *Tristan und Isolde*. In what, precisely, does its effect on the (future) lovers consist?

Wagner never intends to imply that the love of Tristan and Isolde is the *physical conse-quence* of the philter, but only that the pair, having drunk what they imagine to be the draught of Death and believing that they have looked upon earth and sea and sky for the last time, feel themselves free to confess, when the potion begins its work within them, the love they have so long felt but have concealed from each other and almost from them-selves.[26]

The point is therefore that after drinking the philter, Tristan and Isolde find themselves in the domain "between the two deaths," alive, yet delivered of all symbolic ties—*as such*, they are able to confess their love. In other words, the "magical effect" of the philter is simply to suspend the "big Other," the symbolic reality of social obligations (honors, vows). Is this domain "be-tween the two deaths" not thus the space where imaginary identification, as well as the symbolic identities attached to it, are all invalidated, so that the excluded Real (pure life-drive) can emerge in all its force, although in the form of its opposite, the death drive? According to Wagner himself, the passion of Tristan and Isolde expresses the longing for the "eternal peace" of death. The trap to be avoided here, however, is to conceive this pure life-drive as an entity subsisting prior to its being captured in the symbolic net-work: it is, on the contrary, the very mediation of the symbolic order which transforms the organic "instinct" into an unquenchable longing which can find solace only in death. In other words, this "pure life" beyond death, this longing which reaches beyond the circuit of generation and dissolution, is it not the *product* of symbolization, so that symbolization itself engenders the surplus which escapes it? The Symbolic itself opens up the wound it professes to heal. What one should do here, in the space of a more detailed theoretical elaboration, is to approach in a new way the Lacan-Heidegger relationship: in the 1950's, Lacan endeavored to read "death drive" against the background of Heidegger's "being-toward-death" [*Sein-zum-Tode*], conceiving death as the inherent and ultimate limit of symbolization, which provides for its irreducible temporal character; with the shift of accent toward the Real from the 1960's onwards, however, it is rather the indestructible life sprouting in the domain "between the two deaths" which emerges as the ultimate object of horror. Lacan delineates its contours toward the end of Chapter 15 of his *Four Fundamental Concepts of Psycho-Analysis*, where he proposes his own myth, constructed upon the model of Aristophanes' fable from Plato's *Symposium*, the myth of *l'hommelette* (little female-man—omelette):

Whenever the membranes of the egg in which the foetus emerges on its way to becoming a new-born are broken, imagine for a moment that something flies off, and that one can do it with an egg as easily as with a man, namely the *hommelette*, or the lamella.

The lamella is something extra-flat, which moves like the amoeba. It is just a little more complicated. But it goes everywhere. And as it is something . . . that is related to what the sexed being loses in sexuality, it is, like the amoeba in relation to sexed beings, immortal—because it survives any division, any scissiparous intervention. And it can run around.

Well! This is not very reassuring. But suppose it comes and envelops your face while you are quietly asleep . . .[27]

I can't see how we would not join battle with a being capable of these properties. But it would not be a very convenient battle. This lamella, this organ, whose characteristic is not to exist, but which is nevertheless an organ . . . is the libido.

It is the libido, *qua* pure life instinct, that is to say, immortal life, or irrepressible life, life that has need of no organ, simplified, indestructible life. It is precisely what is subtracted from the living being by virtue of the fact that it is subject to the cycle of sexed reproduction. And it is of this that all the forms of the *objet a* that can be enumerated are the representatives, the equivalents. The *objets a* are merely its representatives, its figures. The breast—as equivocal, as an element characteristic of the mammiferous organization, the placenta for example—certainly represents that part of himself that the individual loses at birth, and which may serve to symbolize the most profound lost object.[28]

What we have here is an Otherness prior to intersubjectivity: the subject's "impossible" relationship to this amoebalike creature is what Lacan is ultimately aiming at by way of his formula $\$ \lozenge a$. The best way to clarify this point is perhaps to allow ourselves the string of popular-culture associations that Lacan's description must evoke. Is not the *alien* from Ridley Scott's film of the same title "lamella" in its purest form? Are not all the key elements of Lacan's myth contained in the first truly horrifying scene of the film when, in the womblike cave of the unknown planet, the "alien" leaps from the egglike globe after its lid splits off and sticks to John Hurt's face? This amoebalike, flattened creature which envelops the subject's face stands for the irrepressible life beyond all the finite forms which are merely its representatives, its figures (later in the film, the "alien" is able to assume a multitude of different shapes), immortal and indestructible (it suffices to recall the unpleasant thrill of the moment when a scientist cuts with a scalpel into a leg of the creature which envelops Hurt's face: the liquid that drips from it falls onto the metal floor and corrodes it immediately, nothing can resist it).[29]

■ The second association which brings us back to Wagner is a detail from Syberberg's film version of *Parsifal*, the way Syberberg depicts Amfortas' wound: externalized, carried by the servants on a pillow in front of him, in the form of a vaginalike partial object out of which blood is dripping in a continuous flow (as, *vulgari eloquentia*, a vagina in an unending period). This palpitating opening—an organ which is at the same time the entire organism (let us just recall a homologous motif in a series of science-fiction stories, like the gigantic eye living a life of its own)—this opening epitomizes life in its indestructibility: Amfortas' pain consists in the very fact that he is unable to die, that he is condemned to an eternal life of suffering; when, at the end, Parsifal heals his wound with "the spear that smote it," Amfortas is finally able to rest and die. This wound of Amfortas, which persists outside himself as an *undead* thing, is the "object of psychoanalysis."

The Wagnerian Performative

■ If, then, *The Flying Dutchman* renders the fundamental matrix of Wagner's universe—man's redemption through woman's self-sacrifice—*Parsifal*, his last opera, is to be conceived as the concluding point of a series of variations, the same blissful point of exception as Mozart's *Magic Flute*.[30] The parallel between *The Magic Flute* and *Parsifal* is a commonplace. Suffice it to recall a nice detail from Bergman's film version of *The Flute*: during the break between Acts I and II, the actor who sings Sarastro studies the score of *Parsifal*. In both cases, a youthful, initially ignorant hero, after successfully enduring the test, takes the place of the old ruler of the temple (Sarastro is replaced by Tamino and Amfortas by Parsifal); Jacques Chailley even composed a unique narrative in which all we have to do in order to obtain either the story of *The Magic Flute* or of *Parsifal* is to insert the proper variables: "(Parsifal/Tamino), a prince from the East, has left his (mother/father) in search of the unknown (knights/kingdom)," etc.[31] What is even more important than these parallels in the narrative content is the *initiatory* character of both operas: the events which, at first glance, are nothing but meaningless peripeteias (Parsifal's bringing down of the swan, Tamino's fight with the serpent; the momentary loss of consciousness which follows this confrontation; etc.) become intelligible the moment we conceive them as elements of an initiatory ritual. In both *The Magic Flute* and *Parsifal*, the price to be paid for the reversal into bliss is thus the "transubstantiation" of the action: external events change into mysterious signs to be deciphered. Most interpreters fall into this trap and try to provide a secret code for the reading of *Parsifal* (Chailley sees in it the staging of the Freemasonic initiatory ritual; Robert Donington offers a Jungian reading: *Parsifal* as an allegory of the transmutations of the hero's psyche, of his inner journey from the initial breaking out of the incestuous closure to the final reconciliation with the "eternally feminine.") Our aim, however, is to *resist* this temptation. How, then, are we to proceed?

■ The way out of this impasse is offered by the Lévi-Straussian differential approach: our attention should be centered on those features which differentiate *Parsifal* from Wagner's previous operas, as well as from the traditional version of the Grail myth. The difference from the *Dutchman* is that here the suffering hero—the Fisher King Amfortas—is delivered by a "pure fool," Parsifal, not by the woman. Whence the difference, the misogynist reversal? The main enigma of—and at the same time the key to—Wagner's *Parsifal* is that Wagner leaves unexploited the crucial component of the original legend of Parsifal, the so-called Question Test. When Parsifal first witnesses the Grail ceremony, he is perplexed by what he sees—the maimed King; the display of a strange, magic vessel—but out of respect and consideration he abstains from inquiring about the meaning of it all. Later, he learns that he thereby committed a fateful mistake: by simply asking Amfortas what is wrong with him and for whom the Grail is intended, he would deliver him from his torment. After a series of ordeals, Parsifal again visits the Fisher King, asks the proper question, and thus delivers him. Furthermore, Wagner simplifies the Grail ceremony by reducing it to the display of the Grail vessel. He leaves out the uncanny dreamlike scene which accompanied the display in the traditional version of the legend: a young squire frantically and repeatedly runs across the hall of the Fisher King's castle during the dinner, displaying the spear with blood dripping from its tip and thus provoking ritualistic cries of horror and grief from the knights present. What we have here is the compulsive ritual in its purest sense, similar to that of a thirty-year-old married woman, described by Freud: "She ran from her room into another neighboring one, took up a particular position there beside a table that stood in the middle, rang the bell for her housemaid, sent her on some indifferent errand or let her go without one, and then ran back into her own room."[32]

■ The solution: during her wedding night, her husband had been impotent; he had come running repeatedly from his room into hers to try once more. Next morning, out of shame that the housemaid would not find the traces of blood (the sign of his success in deflowering the bride), he poured some red ink over the sheet. The key to the present ritualistic symptom is that on the table beside which the woman took up the particular position was a big stain. By assuming this strange position, the woman wanted to prove to the Other's gaze (epitomized by the housemaid) that "the stain is there," i.e., her aim was literally to attract the Other's gaze to a certain stain, a little fragment of the real which proves the father's (man's) sexual potency. (At the time that the symptom occurred, the woman was in the process of obtaining a divorce from her husband: the aim of the symptom was to protect him from malicious gossip about the true cause of the divorce, i.e., to prevent the Other from registering his impotence.) And, perhaps, the compulsive displaying of the bleeding spear in the traditional version of the Parsifal myth is to be read along the same lines, as proof of the King's potency (if we accept the interpretation of the bleeding spear as the condensation of the two opposing features: not only the weapon which deals the wound, but at the same time the phallus which, as is proven by the blood on its tip, successfully performed the deflowering).

■ By virtue of the Question Test, *Parsifal* functions as a complementary opposite to Wagner's *Lohengrin*, the opera centered on the theme of the forbidden question, i.e., on the paradox of self-destructive female curiosity. In *Lohengrin*, a nameless hero saves Elsa von Brabant and marries her, but enjoins her not to ask him who he is or his name—as soon as she does so, he will be obliged to leave her (the famous air "Nie sollst du mich befragen" from Act I); Elsa cannot stand it and asks him the fateful question; so, in an even more famous air ("In fernem Land," Act III), Lohengrin tells her that he is a knight of the Grail, the son of Parsifal from the castle of Monsalvat, and then departs on a swan while the unfortunate Elsa collapses dead.[33] How not to recall here Superman or Batman, where we find the same logic: in both cases, the woman has a presentiment that her partner (the confused journalist in *Superman*, the eccentric millionaire in *Batman*) is really the mysterious public hero, but the partner puts off as long as possible the moment of revelation. What we have here is a kind of forced choice attesting to the dimension of castration: man is split, divided into the weak everyday fellow with whom sexual relations are possible and the bearer of the symbolic mandate, the public hero (knight of the Grail, Superman, Batman); we are thus obliged to choose: as soon as we force the sexual partner to reveal his symbolic identity, we are bound to lose him.[34] Here, it would be possible to articulate a general theory of the "Wagnerian performative" reaching from *The Flying Dutchman* (when, at the end, the offended unknown captain publicly announces that he is the Flying Dutchman wandering the oceans for centuries in search of a faithful wife, Senta throws herself from a cliff to her death) to *Parsifal* (when Parsifal takes over the function of the King and reveals the Grail, Kundry drops dead). In all these cases, the performative gesture by means of which the hero openly assumes his symbolic mandate, reveals his symbolic identity, proves incompatible with the very being of woman. The paradox of *Parsifal*, however, is the exact contrary to *Lohengrin*: the fateful consequences of a *failure* to ask the required question.[35] How are we to interpret it?

Beyond Phallus

■ What we encounter in the Question Test is a pure case of the logic of symptom in its relationship to the big Other qua the symbolic order: the bodily wound—symptom—can be healed by being put into words, i.e., the symbolic order can produce an effect upon the real. Parsifal thus stands for the big Other in its ignorant neutrality: the enunciation of a simple "What's wrong with you?"—somewhat like Bugs Bunny's famous "What's up, Doc?"—would trigger the avalanche of symbolization, the King's wound would be healed by being integrated into the symbolic universe, i.e., by way of its symbolic realization.[36] A symptom—therein consists perhaps its most elementary definition—is not a question without an answer but rather an answer without its question, i.e., bereft of its proper symbolic context. This question cannot be asked by the knights themselves, it had to come from outside, from somebody who epitomizes the big Other in its blessed ignorance. One is tempted to evoke an everyday experience: a stuffy atmosphere in a closed community where the tension is suddenly resolved once a stranger asks the naive question of what is actually going on.[37]

■ Yet Wagner left this line unexploited: why? The first, superficial, yet quite accurate answer is: the second act. That is to say, it would be easy to transpose the traditional myth into an opera in two acts; what takes place between Mozart and Wagner is simply *the second act*: between Mozart's traditional two acts (the formula also followed by Beethoven in *Fidelio*) another act creeps in, and it is here, in the second act (of *Lohengrin, Die Walküre, Götterdämmerung, Parsifal*), that the crucial shift occurs, namely, the step into "hystericization" which confers on the action the "modern" touch.[38] One is thus even tempted to arrange the inherent logic of the three acts of *Parsifal* by reference to Lacanian logical time:[39] the first act involves the "instant of looking"—Parsifal looks, witnesses the ritual, but does not understand anything; the second act marks the "time for understanding"—through meeting Kundry, Parsifal gets the meaning of Amfortas' suffering; the third act brings about the "moment for concluding," the performative decision—Parsifal delivers Amfortas from his suffering and takes his place.

■ The cause of this interpolation of a supplementary act is a certain change in the status of the big Other:[40] in Wagner, the "pure fool" Parsifal is no longer a stand-in for the big Other, but—what? Here, a comparison between *Parsifal* and *The Magic Flute* can be of some help. In *The Magic Flute* the old king Sarastro retires in full splendor and dignity, whereas in *Parsifal*, Amfortas is maimed and therefore unable to officiate, to perform his—let us say—bureaucratic duty; *The Magic Flute* is a hymn to the bourgeois couple in which, notwithstanding the numerous male-chauvinist "wisdoms," it is ultimately the woman—Pamina—who leads her man through the fire-and-water ordeal, whereas in *Parsifal* woman is rejected—the hero's capacity to resist her is precisely what is at stake in the ordeal. (Also in *The Magic Flute*, Tamino's crucial test concerns his ability to remain silent when faced with Pamina's desperate pleas and thus to endure her symbolic loss; yet this loss functions as a step toward the constitution of the couple.)[41] In *Parsifal*, woman is literally reduced to a symptom of man—she is caught in cataleptic torpor, roused only by her master's voice or injunction. "Woman is a symptom of man" seems to be one of the most notoriously "antifeminist" theses of Lacan. There is, however, a fundamental ambiguity as to how we are to read it: this ambiguity reflects the shift in the notion of the symptom within the Lacanian theory. If we conceive the symptom as a *ciphered message*, then, of course, woman-symptom appears as the sign, the embodiment of man's Fall, attesting to the fact that man "gave way as to his desire." For Freud, the symptom is a compromise formation: in the symptom, the subject gets back, in the form of a ciphered, unrecognized message, the truth about his desire, the truth that he was not able to confront, that he betrayed. So, if we read the thesis "Woman is a symptom of man" against this background, we inevitably approach the position that was most forcefully articulated by Otto Weininger, Freud's contemporary, a notorious Viennese antifeminist and anti-Semite from the turn of the century, who wrote the extremely influential best-seller *Sex and Character*[42] and then committed suicide at the age of twenty-four. Weininger's position is that, according to her very ontological status, woman is nothing but a materialization of man's Sin: in herself, she does not exist, which is why the proper way to get rid of her is not to fight her actively or to destroy her. It is enough for man to purify his desire, to rise to pure spirituality, and, automatically, woman loses the ground under her feet, disintegrates. No wonder, then, that Wagner's *Parsifal* was Weininger's basic reference and that Wagner was for him the greatest man since Christ: when Parsifal purifies his desire and rejects Kundry, she loses her speech, changes into a mute shadow, and finally drops dead. She existed only insofar as she attracted the male gaze.

■ This tradition, which may appear extravagant and outdated, reemerged more recently in film noir, where the femme fatale also changes into a formless, mucous slime without proper ontological consistency the moment the hard-boiled hero rejects her, i.e., breaks her spell upon him—witness the final confrontation of Sam Spade and Brigid O'Shaughnessy in Hammett's *Maltese Falcon*. We have thus the male world of pure spirituality and undistorted communication, communication without constraint (if we may be permitted to use this Habermasian syntagm), the universe of ideal intersubjectivity, and woman is *not* an external, active cause which lures man into the Fall—she is just a *consequence*, a result, a materialization of man's Fall. So, when man purifies his desire of the pathological remainders, woman disintegrates in precisely the same way as a symptom dissolves after successful interpretation, after we have symbolized its repressed meaning. Does not Lacan's other notorious thesis—the claim "Woman doesn't exist"—point in the same direction? Woman exists not in herself, as a positive entity with full ontological consistency, but only as a symptom of man. Weininger was also quite outspoken about the desire compromised, betrayed when man falls prey to a woman: the death drive. After all the talk about man's superior spirituality, inaccessible to women, etc., he proposes, in the last pages of *Sex and Character*, collective suicide as humanity's only path to salvation.

■ If, however, we conceive the symptom as it was articulated in Lacan's last writings and seminars—as, for example, when he speaks about "Joyce-the-symptom"—namely, as a particular signifying formation which confers on the subject its very ontological consistency, enabling it to structure its basic, constitutive relationship toward *jouissance*, then the entire relationship is reversed. If the symptom is dissolved, the subject himself loses the ground under his feet, disintegrates. In this sense, "Woman is a symptom of man" means that *man himself exists only through woman qua his symptom*: all his ontological consistency hangs on, is suspended from, is "externalized" in, his symptom. In other words, man literally *ex-sists*: his entire being lies "out there," in woman. Woman, on the other hand, does *not* exist, she *insists*, which is why she does not come to be through man only. There is something in her that escapes the relation to man, the reference to the phallic enjoyment; and, as is well known, Lacan endeavored to capture this excess by the notion of a *"non-all" feminine jouissance*.[43] This, however, opens up the possibility of a different reading of *Parsifal*: Syberberg was again right when, after the crucial moment of conversion (i.e., after Parsifal refuses Kundry's kiss), he replaced the male actor playing Parsifal with a woman. Woman is the symptom of man, caught in the hysterical game of demanding that he refuse her demand, precisely to the extent to which she is submitted to the phallic enjoyment. Wagner's fundamental matrix appears thereby in a different perspective: *woman redeems man by renouncing phallic enjoyment*.[44] (What we have here is the exact opposite of Weininger where man redeems/destroys woman by overcoming his phallicity.) This is what Wagner was not able to confront, and the price to be paid for this avoidance fully to assume the "feminization" of Parsifal after he enters the domain "beyond the phallus" was the fall into perversion.[45]

■ More precisely, what Wagner was not able to confront is the "feminine" nature of Parsifal's identification with Amfortas at the moment of Kundry's kiss: far from being reducible to a case of successful (symbolic) communication, this "compassion" is founded on the identification with the *real* of Amfortas' suffering, it involves the *repetition* of Amfortas' pain in the Kierkegaardian sense. On that account, Syberberg's decision to alternate two actors, a male and a female, in the role of Parsifal should in no way entrap us in the Jungian ideology of hermaphroditism, according to which the figure of mature Parsifal stands for the reconciliation, the unification, of male and female "principles." This alternation, rather, functions as a critical sting aimed at Wagner, a reminder that *Parsifal is not feasible as a unique, psychologically "coherent" personality*:[46] he is split into himself and "what is in him more than himself," his sublime shadowy double (Parsifal-woman first appears in the background as the ethereal double of Parsifal-man and then gradually takes his place).[47] In the course of this transmutation *the voice remains the same* (Parsifal continues to be sung by a tenor); we thus obtain a kind of negative of Norman–Mrs. Bates from Hitchcock's *Psycho*: the monstrous apparition of an apathetically cold woman using a man's voice (the true opposite of the caricature-image of a transvestite, of a man dressing up as a woman and imitating the heightened feminine voice). Parsifal-woman is a man who has cast off the phallic semblance, like a snake getting rid of its skin. What is subverted thereby is the ideology of "femininity as masquerade" according to which man is "man as such," the embodiment of the human genus, whereas woman is a man from whom something is missing (who is "castrated") and who resorts to masquerade in order to conceal this lack: it is on the contrary the phallus, the phallic predicate, whose status is that of a semblance, so that when we throw off its mask, a woman appears. Here, again, the key is provided by comparison with the history of opera: in Gluck, Orpheus is sung by a woman, and this sexual ambiguity continues up to Mozart, in whose *Le Nozze di Figaro* the role of Cherubino, the principal rival and "obstructionist" of the Count, this agent of pure sexuality, is sung by a soprano.[48] Perhaps we could conceive the couple Amfortas-Parsifal as the last permutation of the couple Count-Cherubino: in *Le Nozze* the counterpoint to the Count (to this helpless, yet in no way crippled, but on the contrary quite prepotent Master) is a man with a feminine voice, whereas in *Parsifal* the counterpoint to the maimed king Amfortas is a woman with a masculine voice. This change allows us to measure the historical shift that separates the end of the eighteenth century from the end of the nineteenth century: the objectal surplus of the intersubjective network is no longer the elusive semblance of pure phallic sexuality but rather the embodiment of the saintly, ascetic *jouissance* beyond phallus.

Safekeeping God's 'Jouissance'

■ The parallel between the gestures of grace preventing the hero's suicide in *The Magic Flute* and in *Parsifal* should therefore not blind us to the crucial difference: in *Parsifal* the subjectivization is strictly perverse, it equals its opposite, namely, self-objectivization, conceiving oneself as an instrument of *jouissance* of the big Other. It is here, in this notion of the Other's *jouissance*, that we should seek the roots of Wagner's anti-Semitism: what he resisted was the idea of a formal, empty Law, i.e., the Jewish prohibition against filling God's Name with a positive content. As Lacan put it, pre-Jewish, pagan Gods belong to the Real: we gain access to them through sacred *jouissance* (ritualistic orgies), their domain is that of the Unnameable. What the Jewish religion accomplishes is the radical evacuation of *jouissance* from the divine domain, the crucial consequence of which is a kind of reflective reversal of the prohibition: the prohibition on naming the sacred Real is inverted into the prohibition against filling God's Name with a positive bearer, with His image. In short, what is now prohibited is not to name the unnameable Real but to attach any positive reality to the Name: *the Name must remain empty*. This reversal concerns, among other things, the very notion of democracy: as was shown by Claude Lefort, democracy implies the distinction between the empty symbolic locus of power and the reality of those who, temporarily, exert it; for democracy to function, the locus of power must remain empty, nobody is allowed to present himself as possessing the immediate, natural right to exert it.[49] And the idea of the Grail as the vessel containing the blood of Christ has to be read against this background: this blood which continues to shine and give life, what is it ultimately if not *the "little piece of the real" which immediately legitimizes power*, i.e., which "naturally" belongs to and defines the locus of power? This part of Christ which remained alive, which did *not* expire on the cross, designates the remainder of the divine *jouissance*, the part of it which was *not* evacuated from the domain of the big Other. In short, to spell out the theological consequences: Wagner's radically perverse idea was to "get Christ down from the Cross, or rather stop him getting on it": "I have no doubt that Robert Raphael is right when he says that Parsifal, 'having now redeemed himself by insight and empathy, symbolizes a Christ who *does not have to die*, but lives.' The point about not having to die is that Wagner . . . is repelled by the idea of the Second Person of the Holy Trinity dying in order that the First Person should allow man into Heaven."[50]

■ This is what Wagner ultimately has in mind by the "redemption of the redeemer": Christ does not have to die in order to redeem us. As such, *Parsifal* bears witness to a deep perturbation in the "normal" relationship of life and death: the denial of the will to life, yet simultaneously the fantasy of a life beyond death, beyond the circuit of generation and dissolution. The death toward which the Wagnerian hero tends is the "second death," the denial not of the "natural" life circuit but of the "lamella," of the indestructible libido. The gulf separating Wagner from Christianity is here effectively insurmountable: in Christianity, the eternal life is the life beyond death, the life in the Holy Spirit and as such an object of adoration, whereas in Wagner, this indestructible life entails a vision of endless suffering. Now we can see why, enraptured by the magic of Good Friday, Parsifal is able to perceive the innocence of nature: this nature, caught in the simple circuit of generation and dissolution, is delivered from the pressure of the indestructible drive which persists beyond death.[51] The political consequences of these seemingly abstract ruminations affect us all: the replacement of Amfortas by Parsifal is the replacement of the traditional patriarchal authority by the totalitarian object-instrument of the Other's *jouissance*, the safekeeper of God's Enjoyment (epitomized by the Grail).[52]

■ This political background emerges in precisely those features of *Parsifal* which pose such a problem to traditional interpreters, since they stick out as a kind of uncanny surplus, disturbing the apparent symmetry between the two kingdoms, the bright kingdom of the Grail and Klingsor's kingdom of the dark, attesting to an obscene, dark obverse of the kingdom of the Grail itself. According to Lucy Beckett, for example, *Parsifal* twice reverts to an incomprehensible, out-of-place morbidity: the cruel, inexorable pressure exerted by the Grail knights on Amfortas in the finale of Act III (like a wounded animal, he is encircled by them), which runs counter to the peaceful, blessed nature of the Grail community; the morbid dialogue between Amfortas and his father Titurel in the finale of Act I (Titurel demands that Amfortas perform the required ritual and uncover the Grail in order that he be able to survive—Titurel qua living dead no longer needs earthly food but lives solely off the enjoyment procured by sight of the Grail; Amfortas desperately proposes that Titurel himself perform the ritual and that he be allowed to die). In Titurel, we have the purest personification of the superego: he is literally a living dead, lying in a coffin, kept alive by the sight of the Redeemer's blood, i.e., by the substance of pure enjoyment; never seen onstage, he is present as *la voix acousmatique*, a free-floating voice without bearer[53] which persecutes his son with the unconditional injunction "Accomplish your duty! Perform the ritual!"—the injunction Titurel pronounces *in order to secure his own enjoyment*. The obscenity of Klingsor's "black magic" has therefore its strict correlative in the superego obscenity of Titurel's "white magic": Titurel is undoubtedly the most obscene figure in *Parsifal*, a kind of undead father parasitic on his own son. This morbid, cruel side of the Grail's temple is what Christian interpreters are quite justified in being apprehensive of, since it renders manifest the true nature of *Parsifal*: a work whose ultimate accomplishment is to confer upon a Christian content the form of pagan ritual.[54]

■ With the new notion of the hero—an innocent, ignorant, pure fool, who eludes the splitting constitutive of subjectivity—the circle is in a way closed, we find ourselves again in the domain of unconditional authority: Parsifal's becoming King is not a result of his heroic deeds, he is not qualified for it by any positive feature; quite the contrary, he was able to withstand Kundry's advances because, from the very beginning, he was the Chosen One.

However, this new authority differs from the traditional one in its relationship to the big Other of the Law: the traditional authority addressed by the hero's entreaty from Monteverdi to Mozart was so to speak capable of stepping on its own shoulders and suspending its own Law in the act of mercy—here, the agency of the Law coincides with the agency of its momentary suspension, i.e., the Other is at the same time the Other of the Other. Already in Wagner's *Ring*, however, the God (Wotan), interpellated by the two giants in *Das Rheingold* as the guarantor of the social contract, gets so entangled in his own inconsistencies that the only solution he can envisage is an act of redemption accomplished by a totally ignorant hero who will have nothing to do with the domain of the Gods. Therein consists Wagner's crucial shift: "the wound can be healed" only by a free act which, in a radical sense, *comes from the outside*, i.e., is not engendered by the symbolic system itself. Apropos of Mozart's *Don Giovanni*, Nagel refers to Kierkegaard's famous reading of it in order to be able to jump immediately to modern totalitarianism, via Kierkegaard's reaffirmation of blind, unconditional authority:

After Kierkegaard, the disabled self survives the annihilation of the autonomous subject, which it announces, by excepting itself (as a political theologian or mythologist) from the common fate: to be the self-appointed spokesman of mute domination. It prophesies, propagates a new world of sacrifice, whose murderous law is impenetrability—and whose murderous impenetrability will be called law. Soon, Franz Kafka's tales and Carl Schmitt's jurisprudence will mock the enlightened demand for clear and accessible laws as liberal hairsplitting; indeed such querulous claims of the individual will constitute, for the court of mythical willfulness, proof of his guilt, the very reason for his condemnation.[55]

Wagner's *Parsifal* thus provides the answer to the question, What happens when the subject takes upon himself the symbolic gesture, the "prerogative of mercy," which, in Mozart and Beethoven, still belonged to the big Other?

This gain is paid for by the loss of "actual" power: all that is left to the subject is the empty, formal act of assent, the tautological performative by means of which he appoints himself the "spokesman of mute domination." What is thus missing in Nagel's account is precisely Wagner as the link that fills in the gap between the apotheosis of the bourgeois couple in *The Magic Flute* and *Fidelio* and totalitarianism proper, rendered from different perspectives in the works of Kafka and Schmitt.

The Perverse Self-Instrumentalization

■ At the level of libidinal economy, totalitarianism is defined by a perverse self-objectivization (self-instrumentalization) of the subject. But where then is the difference between perversion and the most elementary ideological act of self-legitimization in which we also encounter a kind of "redemption of the redeemer"? Lincoln's Gettysburg Address is deservedly so famous because it accomplishes in an exemplary way this act of self-legitimization. It first defines its task: we are here to commemorate the dead, to dedicate the sacred place of their death. Then it proceeds to invoke the inherent impossibility of performing this task: "in a larger sense" we cannot do it, since those who died here have already done it with their glorious deeds in a way far superior to what we can do with mere words. Their sacrifice has already consecrated this battlefield; it would be arrogant for us even to pretend that we are in a position to consecrate them. What then follows is the crucial reflective inversion of subject and object: "It is for us the living, rather, to be dedicated here," that is to say, to dedicate ourselves to the task of continuing their work, so that they "shall not have died in vain." (For that reason, it is not sufficient here to distinguish the two levels by saying that "in a narrower sense" we dedicate the battlefield, whereas "in a larger sense" we dedicate ourselves: this "larger sense" is simply the sense *tout court*, i.e., it is this very reflexive reversal which brings about the sense effect.) The result of this inversion is a circle of dedication whereby the two poles support each other: by dedicating ourselves to the task of successfully bringing to an end the work of those who sacrificed their lives, we will make sure that their sacrifice was not in vain, that they will continue to live in our memory; in this way, we will effectively commemorate them. If we do not accomplish this task of ours, they will be forgotten, they will have died in vain. So, by consecrating their memory, what we actually do is dedicate, legitimize, ourselves as the continuators of their work—we legitimize our own role. This gesture of self-legitimation through the other is ideology in its purest form: the dead are our redeemers, and by dedicating ourselves to continuing their work, we redeem the redeemers. In a sense, Lincoln makes himself visible to the dead, his message to them is "here we are, ready to go on." Therein consists the ultimate sense of the Gettysburg address.

■ Yet is Lincoln for all that a pervert? Does he conceive of himself as an object-instrument of the *jouissance* of the dead heroes? No: the crucial point here is to maintain the difference between this traditional ideological vicious circle and the loop of the perverse sacrifice. Let us recall our first example: Orpheus who looked back and thus intentionally sacrificed Eurydice in order to regain her as the sublime object of poetic inspiration. This is, then, the logic of perversion: it is quite normal to say to the beloved woman, "I would love you even if you were wrinkled and mutilated!" A perverse person is the one who intentionally mutilates the woman, distorts her beautiful face, so that he can then continue to love her, thereby proving the sublime nature of his love. An exemplary case of this short circuit is Patricia Highsmith's early masterpiece, the short story "Heroine," about a young governess extremely eager to prove her devotion to the family whose child she is taking care of; since her everyday acts pass unnoticed, she ends up setting the house on fire, so that she has the opportunity to save the child from the flames. This closed loop is what defines perversion. And is not the same closed loop at work in the Stalinist sacrificial production of enemies: since the Party fortifies itself by fighting rightist and leftist deviations, one is forced to produce them in order to fortify Party unity. Kant himself gets caught in this circle of perversion in his *Critique of Practical Reason*: at the end of Part One, he asks himself why God created the world in such a way that things-in-themselves are unknowable to man, that the Supreme Good is unattainable to him because of the propensity to radical Evil that pertains to human nature. Kant's answer is that this impenetrability is the positive condition of our moral activity: if man were to know things-in-themselves, moral activity would become impossible and superfluous at the same time, since we would follow moral commands not out of duty but out of simple insight into the nature of things. So, since the ultimate goal of the creation of the universe is morality, God had to act precisely like the heroine from the Highsmith story and create man as a truncated, split being, deprived of insight into the true nature of things, exposed to the temptation of Evil.[56] Perversion is simply the fulfillment of this sacrificial act which establishes the conditions of Goodness. Therein consists also the secret shared by initiatory circles like the Grail community at Monsalvat: the perverse reverse of Christianity, the intentional killing of Christ, enabling him to play the role of the Redeemer.[57]

■ Consequently, Parsifal's "the wound is healed only by the spear that smote you" amounts to something quite different from what this same phrase may have meant within the horizon of Kant and Hegel. Insofar as, in Kant, the "wound" can only be the inaccessibility of the Thing and its "healing" the teleological *Schein*, the point here is that what appears as "wound" is actually a positive condition of "healing": the inaccessibility of the Thing is a positive condition of our freedom and moral dignity. Yet for that very reason, Kant is as far as possible from allowing any finite subject to assume the role of the instrument which "smote you" in order to enable realization of the Good. *This, however, is precisely what takes place in Wagner* where we witness the emergence of the perverse subject who willingly assumes the "dealing of the wound," the accomplishment of the crime which paves the way for the Good.

World-Breath: On Wagner's Media Technology

Friedrich Kittler

■ Even in the arts, Germany's nineteenth century produced giant enterprises. But only one of them survives without subventions or interventions of state power: Wagner's Bayreuth.

■ Unlike all the programs of aesthetic education, unlike all redemptions through the eternally feminine, music-drama remains contemporary. Wagner, with his nose for public relations, knew only too well that it would have been possible and successful in America too. Otherwise he would not have envisaged emigrating from Bayreuth to a Hollywood *avant la lettre*. But this can only mean that music-drama is the first mass-medium in the modern sense of the word. Its contemporaneity with our senses results from its technology.

■ Arts—to adopt an old word for an old institution—entertain only symbolic relations to the sensory fields they presuppose. Media, by contrast, correlate in the real itself to the materiality they deal with. Photo plates inscribe chemical traces of light, phonograph records inscribe mechanical traces of

For Erika.

"World-Breath: On Wagner's Media Technology" is a revised and expanded version of an essay which previously appeared in English translation in *Wagner in Retrospect: A Centennial Reappraisal*, edited and with an introduction by Leroy R. Shaw, Nancy R. Cirillo, and Marion S. Miller (Amsterdam: Editions Rodopi, 1987). The translation is by the author in collaboration with David J. Levin.

215

sound.[1] This distinction between arts and media was clear to Wagner. In "The Artwork of the Future," an unambiguous title, he made the ironic remark that poetry merely offered its readership the catalog of an art gallery but not the paintings themselves.[2] In order to fill this technological gap, Wagner invented the first artistic machine capable of reproducing sensuous data as such.

■ At one fell swoop, reflection and imagination, education and literacy—all of those celebrated psychic faculties necessarily presupposed by classical poetry in order to reach people by means of its pages—became obsolete.[3] For in the revolutionary darkness of the *Festspielhaus*[4]—to which all the darknesses of our cinemas date back—the medium of music-drama began to play with and upon the public's nerves.

■ *The Ring of the Nibelung* stands for power, not for money.[5] And the only power that is not ruined when twilight befalls the Gods at the end of the tetralogy, is a technical one. The great engineer Alberich, inventor of a magic cap that makes him as invisible as the conductor in Bayreuth's orchestra pit, survives as an invisible yet unvanquished power. Thus Alberich—and not his divine antagonist Wotan, who of course merely improvises Wagner's corporate politics of establishing a family—is the allegory of the *Festspielhaus*. Neither Wotan nor Wagner could ever prevent rebellions by traitors among the offspring, like Siegfried or Wieland—even if they were programmed to be unconsciously loyal. But the invisible power that Alberich exercises with his whip,[6] or that conductors wield with their baton over Nibelungs, musicians, and audience, remains as a physiological inscription in bodies and nerves.

■ The innovations of Alberich, alias Wagner, are easily shown. A comparison of music-drama as a medium with traditional drama and traditional opera already suffices. But there is no reason to differentiate these three genres of art according to form, content, and meaning, that is, with the standard means of philosophical reflection. They are to be seen simply as media, and that means they are to be seen with a stupidity that distinguishes Wagnerian heros, above all Siegfried.

■ In light of this stupidity, classical drama was little more than an exchange of verbal information between people who, it goes without saying, could talk and listen. They knew each other by name or, if they had not yet met, at least by sight. When for dramatic reasons the perfect transparency of this verbal and optical data-stream was muddied, two and only two forms of interference came into play: on the one hand, misleading words, especially names; on the other, masks. But even then, the meaning of words spoken and heard still did not disappear amid the roar of the real. And even the power of masks to de-face did not go so far as to change their bearers into the invisible voice that Wagner's Alberich becomes beneath his magic cap. The acoustic field as such, with its senseless noises and disembodied voices, had no place in drama.

■ No doubt, opera acted as an acoustic data-stream. But not all its parameters were so well defined. A more or less rudimentary interaction, mapped out in the recitativo passages, followed the dramatic model: speech and/or sight informed the characters of their respective positions in the play. However, when they sang arias and thus entered the acoustic field, they did so in order to express so-called affects, which for their part had but little repercussion upon the dramatic interaction. It was only in exceptional instances that sounds (like signals or cries) transported information on the interpersonal level as well. Thus, opera was based upon a separation between verbal and acoustic data, recitatives and arias, which in the final analysis may have simply duplicated the division of labor between libretto and score, between text supplier and composer.

■ Wagner's technical program can only be reconstructed in contrast to the tradition of drama and opera. Two art genres with different sensory fields could not simply be glued together. In order to reach the materially adequate structure of modern mass media, music-drama had to intervene in the materiality of data-streams themselves. In contrast with drama, the figures' interactions needed to be motivated by acoustic events. In contrast with opera, the acoustic events, whether vocal or instrumental, needed to be motivated by dramatic interaction. These are two reasons why Wagner's texts are not simply opera libretti and why his scores include so many stage directions.[7]

■ None of the traditional data-streams, not meaningful words, eye contact, or psychological affects, could guarantee this reciprocal motivation of different sensory fields. One and only one phenomenon is capable of popping up simultaneously in text and score, in drama and music. All of us (except the Wagner experts) know what it is—breathing.

■ *Siegfried*, Act III. The hero has walked through the circle of flames and there in the middle of the circle he discovers a body in full armor lying on the ground. Siegfried does not know whether this body is dead or only asleep. Nor does he know whether it is a man or a woman. Life/death, man/woman: these two oppositions, fundamental to every culture, must first be reestablished. The dramatic scene—one of the most beautiful Wagner ever wrote—begins as a primal scene in every sense of the term.

■ Through this field of total indeterminacy comes one single hint, one single bit of information. Siegfried's ears hear that the body is breathing. Which is why the hero, approaching more closely, celebrates in song the "rising breath" as a sign of life. "He draws his sword, and with gentle caution cuts the chainmail on both sides of the armour," thus freeing the breathing from its "constricting breastplate."[8] But only in order to discover beneath the breastplate the signs of womanliness as well. That is why Brünnhilde's breathing, sign of life and erotics, eventually becomes itself an erotically desired object: "the blissful warm fragrance of this breath," as Siegfried calls it (92). And for good reason. For whatever the hero said and did before, he could not awaken the sleeper. Brünnhilde will only return to the "perception of earth and heaven" when Siegfried "absorbs life into himself from the sweetest of lips"—even "should" he "expire in death" (92, 93).

■ To awaken in Wagner always means to sing. The materiality of musico-dramatic data-streams is based upon the intensity of life in the diaphragm, lung, throat, and mouth. That is why singing is the last and most important metamorphosis of breathing. With the same breath that Siegfried's kiss gave her or perhaps also took from her, the reawakened Brünnhilde begins her salutation of sun, light, and earth, the three mediums of physiological life. Without a doubt, this radiant song becomes increasingly verbal, meaningful, and psychological. Awakened by Siegfried's desire or breath, Brünnhilde begins to explain to her lover how she is, on the one hand, his dead mother and thus subject to the taboo on incest, and how, on the other hand, she is a living woman with whom he can sleep. But as the aria originated in breathing itself, it remains on that physiological level whose theory was first formulated by Wagner's contemporaries. (Acoustics and the physiology of voice began with Ellis in England, Helmholtz in Germany, Brücke in Vienna.)⁹ So for the first time in literary history, a meaningful, articulated speech meets with a pronounced refusal. Here is how Siegfried responds to Brünnhilde's declaration of a love that is equally eternal and chaste:

> It sounds like wonder,
> what blissfully you sing,—
> but its meaning seems obscure to me.
> The sparkle of your eyes
> I see lucidly;
> The waft of your breath
> I feel warmly,
> Your voice singing
> I hear sweetly:—
> but what you, singing, tell me,
> amazed, I do not understand it.
> What is remote I cannot
> grasp its sense,
> when all my senses
> see and feel only you—
>   (Siegfried, 95, trans. modified)

■ The burning presence of a desire instead of eternal or platonic love; "sound"¹⁰ (in the exact sense of Jimi Hendrix) instead of verbal meaning; physiologically aroused senses instead of a psychological mother-imago: Siegfried's response defines music-drama itself. For it speaks only of those media that Bayreuth presents: optics, acoustics, lighting, and rustling breath. In traditional art, such a response would have created a scandal. Dramatic plots could not have developed at all without that strange form of understanding which essentially locates meaning in words (and does not hear their breathing). The *belcanto* of Italian opera, even when it verges on incomprehensibility, was not meant to reveal the physiological sources of song in respiration. Rather it concealed them behind melodic figurations and vocal virtuosity. That is also why no opera could allow itself a finale like that of *Siegfried*, which essentially brought the love-act in its physiology onto the stage.

■ Put in Lacanian terms, the "respiratory eroticism"[11] at play between Brünnhilde and Siegfried is by no means exceptional in Wagner's music-dramas. The same primal scene appears repeatedly: one dramatic figure listening to another's breathing. That's what happens at the outset of *Die Walküre* between Sieglinde and the fainting Siegmund, and, at the end of this love, between Siegmund and the unconscious Sieglinde.[12] That's what happens with the dying Tristan, first when the servant Kurwenal "bends over him in grief" and "carefully listens to his breathing," and finally when Isolde laments before Tristan's corpse that she no longer hears "a single fleeting flutter of his breath."[13] Repeatedly, the other's breathing becomes the diagnostic sign of life or death, of being able to sing or of becoming mute. Conversely, one's own breathing becomes the necessary condition for acts that are always both musical and dramatic. In the first act of *Siegfried*, the hero's unarticulated cries and his refrain "blow, bellows, blow the fire!" (40) accompany the bellows during the kindling of a fire in what amounts to an industrial smelting furnace. In Act II, the same breath activates Siegfried's horn and reed-pipe (59–61). In Act III, finally, the breath swells into an articulated love song. Thus, in Wagner's music dramas, music itself, whether vocal like the love song or instrumental like the horn and reed-pipe, is motivated and generated by the plot.

■ And yet, most critics ignore or scorn Wagner's so-called libretti. Perhaps they have eyes only for the letters, but no ears for all that breathing, rustling, and storming that Wagner's poetry discovered. Perhaps they are also blinded by the framework of a loud-mouthed philosophy such as Wagner constructed around his very simple texts. In any case, the facts of physiology and media technology remain too dumb or too unconscious for critics.

■ But in mass media, whatever is unconscious becomes the focal point itself. Consciousness can hook up and disconnect the information channels of traditional arts. Those who gave a speech or understood it could also choose not to. Those who sent or received glances could also shut their eyes. "Sound,"[14] on the contrary, pierces the armor called Ego, for among all of the sensory organs, the ears are the hardest to close. That is why Alberich succeeds, in *Götterdämmerung*, in getting his sleeping son Hagen to "listen" and even in issuing orders to his "sleep."[15] The all-pervasive power of sound sustains Wagner's artistic imperialism. And the plots of the music-dramas also betray that Wagner was every bit as aware of this power as was his media technician, Alberich.

■ Critics have repeatedly remarked that on the whole *The Flying Dutchman* is based upon an optical hallucination: Senta's "dreamily" fascinated gaze at the Dutchman's wall-portrait results in his materialization.[16] Yet no one seems to have realized that with *Lohengrin*, that is, with the onset of Wagner's maturity, acoustic hallucinations take the place of optical ones. Their content is no more and no less than the all-pervasive power of acoustics itself. Elsa, Lohengrin's future bride, says (and sings) so:

> *Alone in troubled days*
> *I appealed to God*
> *and poured out in prayer*
> *my heart's deepest anguish.*

Then from my laments
arose a cry so piteous
that it filled the air far and wide
with its vast reverberation.
I heard it echo far away
until it barely reached my ear;
then my eyelids closed
and I sank into a sweet sleep. . . .
Arrayed in shining armour
a knight was approaching.[17]

At first, Elsa's closed eyes hallucinate this knight, which is why he will soon appear on stage, just like Senta's Dutchman. And yet his presence—which, of course, coincides with the dramatic interaction as a whole—is the product of an acoustic hallucination. Elsa's pleas, laments, and moans have successfully commanded Lohengrin to appear from a distance of some four hundred miles, the distance between her duchy, Brabant, and his holy mountain, Monsalvat. An impossible achievement unless, already in Wagner, the medium is the message. But because Elsa passes over the contents of her laments, pleas, and moans—to mention only the fact of these sounds—McLuhan's theory becomes reality. As in Siegfried's listening to Brünnhilde, or in Kundry's speaking, which is but a "hoarse and broken" attempt "to regain speech," the discourse shrinks to its vocal-physiological modalities.[18] Hardly audible sounds, freed from the mouth and will of the one who utters them, swell to a "vast" or absolute "reverberation" that then travels through space and time as a "sound"[19] "echoing far away."

■ This acoustic effect could not have been implemented by either Elsa's medieval times or Wagner's nineteenth century. Our ears are the first to know it by heart: night after night, the public address systems of rock music (amplifiers and delay lines, equalizers and mixers) generate such vocal sounds, room noises, and reverberation effects.[20] In other words, the words of Jimi Hendrix: Wagner's Elsa is the first resident of Electric Ladyland.[21] What she describes with such incalculable precision as resonating, swelling, and reverberating has little to do with prayers or Christian belief. It simply anticipates the theory of positive feedback—and thus of oscillators.

■ Under the given technical conditions, Wagner could not implement the feedback of sound. Instead, he composed it, and even that was an innovation. Fantasies like Elsa's can be traced back to German Romanticism: to Schelling or Bettina Brentano.[22] But their realization had to wait until Wagner came along. What Elsa describes as the unending crescendo of her voice is in fact enacted by the orchestral background to her prayer and, even more so, by the Prelude to the whole music-drama. Breathing and its gradations (sighing, pleading, moaning) are thus only starting points for a second feedback, this time between vocal and instrumental effects. The orchestra and especially the brass have to take up Elsa's hardly audible laments in order to be able to amplify them, turning them into sound echoing in the distance.

■ Wagner's orchestra has the exact function of an amplifier. This is why his autobiography is repeatedly so fascinated with echoes and feedbacks, with fade effects and acoustic illusions.[23] This is also why Adorno, in his fidelity to European art and musical logic, was thwarted by Wagner. Amplifiers put philosophy out of commission. They cover up traditional musical values such as thematic workmanship or polyphonic style—all these fundamentally written data—and replace them with sound. Music, in Wagner, becomes a matter of pure dynamics and pure acoustics.

■ The proof of this is furnished—in both text and score—by *Tristan*. Of course, Wagner's most modern music-drama is also drawn from a medieval romance, but for a reason that is less well known. Its author, Gottfried von Strassburg, had woven acrostics and anagrams throughout the text of his *Tristan*, thus becoming the first writer in the vernacular to emphasize writtenness itself. It is no coincidence that he already bore the title of master, that is, expert writer. For Gottfried no longer addressed, as his many knightly predecessors had, a group of noble ear-witnesses; by making use of alphabet games that were necessarily lost on the ears, he instituted a new audience comprised of the literate, of . . . readers.[24]

■ Wagner's *Tristan* is the total revocation of this communication system as it had reigned from Gottfried via Gutenberg to Goethe; the revocation, then, of literature itself. In the courtly romance, Tristan and Isolde employed their initials "T" and "I" as a secret code to arrange illicit late-night rendezvous. The equally literate romance author could then also disperse this code as an acrostic throughout his text. In the music-drama, a sound appears at the exact place of this alphabet code. The second act opens with a whirring and ambiguous orchestral sound that Isolde's maidservant Brangaene hears only too correctly as King Mark's horn signal. On the other hand, the "wildness" of Isolde's "desire" for Tristan brings her "to interpret as" she "pleases"—the definition of an acoustic hallucination (*Tristan*, libretto, 57). Her maidservant answers Isolde: "No noise of horns sounds so sweet; the spring, with soft purling of waters runs so gaily along" (*Tristan*, libretto, 57). Thus, on an interpersonal level, Wagner's ambiguous orchestral tone becomes the theme itself, provoking an acoustic hallucination that literally removes the unloved one, Mark, and constructs Tristan's proximity through the natural sound of a spring. And since in Wagner text and score repeatedly motivate each other, the textual oscillation between natural sound and orchestral instrument, between random noise and hunting signal, is matched by two equally illiterate horns playing C major and F major at once.[25] This was a rather prohibited effect as long as music was subject to the domination of scores and while scores, in turn, were subject to the domination of writing. But Wagner's new medium, sound, breaks with 600 years of literality or literature.

■ Throughout *Tristan*, from beginning to end, acoustic effects replace the symbolic (i.e., written) structure of drama and music. This happens first of all to the voices and second to the instruments, because once again breathing becomes their common root. In a letter to Mathilde Wesendonk, his own Isolde, Wagner explained how the *Tristan* Prelude's dynamics were simply laid out in the composition and thus materialized "the Buddhist theory of the origin of the world." In the very beginning, before the first sound, there was endless silence or "nirvana" or "heavenly clarity." Then, "the heavenly clarity darkens" with the cello solo, which is explicitly labeled "a breath." Finally, the Tristan chord appears and the orchestra sound "begins to swell, becomes denser, and ultimately, the whole world in its impenetrable massiveness once again stands before me."[26] This is plain and simple; furthermore, as regards this massiveness, it is also a pure dynamic in the media-technical sense. From nirvana via an aboriginal breath up to the composed world, the orchestral Prelude to *Tristan* represents the first circuit of an acoustic feedback.

■ The second circuit, this time a vocal one, opens with the curtain. A "young seaman" sings, first of all, without the actor being visible, and second, a cappella, that is, without orchestra. He sings of the "wind that blows freshly homeward, " thus sending the ship and seaman farther and farther away from his "Irish child." Which is why the seaman, in his next breath, inquires of his distant love: "Are those the breezes of your sighs that fill the sails for me?" Distantly reverberating sighs, to use Elsa's term, should thus themselves create the distance they then bemoan: the paradox of a respiratory erotics. Thus wind and breathing, natural sound and the human voice become indistinguishable, even in the seaman's puns. For everything he says and sings simply exploits the nearly perfect homonym in the German words *weh* (meaning woe) and *wehen* (meaning to blow). His song ends with the dreamily sad verses: "Wehe, wehe du Wind! Weh, ach wehe, mein Kind!" ("Blow, blow, you wind; woe, oh woe, my child" [*Tristan*, libretto, 3; trans. modified]).

■ Human voices as winds, winds as human voices—only the linguistics of a Wagner or Siegfried in his disdain for meaning allow such equations that are, moreover, acoustic puns. Yet for music-drama they are essential: they alone can hook up voices and instruments, text and score. When the sailor, not by accident singing a cappella, reduces natural sounds to human voices, he already anticipates and motivates the following scene, where nonhuman, that is orchestral, sounds reenter. The seaman's song wanders to the strings in order to provide the background for an entrance that presents the real and only "Irish child" in the piece: Isolde. Thus a woman has the floor. And—as one would expect—she turns all the seaman's words around. Isolde, who suffers from Tristan's distance and his non-desire, herself desires straightforwardly: that all human voices should once again sink into noise or nirvana. Thus she wishes for the return of a magical power possessed and bequeathed by her mother:

Where now, O Mother,
have you given the power
to command the sea and the storm?
O feeble art
of the sorceress,
that now only brews balsam drinks!
Rouse in me again,
bold mastery;
come out from that bosom
wherein you hid yourself!
Hear my will,
trembling winds.
To arms, to breast
the elements' roar
and blustering tempest's
furious vortex!
Drive from its sleep
this dreaming sea,
stir up the deep
till it growls in its greed!
Show it the booty
which I now offer!
Demolish this insolent ship,
let it gobble up its shattered remnants!
And all that survives upon it,
the wafting breath,
I leave to you winds as your pay!
    (Tristan, libretto, 5, 7; trans. modified)

■ To this point, Isolde's magic had been reduced to an inwardness, and, not coincidentally, the whole magic of classic romantic poetry consisted in that openness. But as the music-drama begins, an older and external magic returns. Isolde's command is addressed to two sites at once: first to the winds and the woodwinds; second to nature and its correlative. With every word she sings, the orchestral dynamic swells. One human voice wants to drown in instrumental feedback together with all the other voices on the ship. It is therefore absolutely telling that the orchestral fortissimo behind the female voice pauses for one and only one measure. Unaccompanied, as if to recall the sailor's a cappella, Isolde sings the word "breath," that is, the semantic opposite of nonhuman sounds (*Tristan*, score, 37). So music-drama proceeds utterly precisely in hooking up textual and acoustic events.

■ Operas before Wagner were limited to a dynamic range where sound effects were simply not allowed to drown out human voices and human language. But this is precisely what happens when Isolde gives "the breath" of all living persons on board her ship "to the winds" as a reward. Which is to say, the physiology of voice is only a small part of acoustics in general. That is why Isolde's phantasmagorical wish provides a further definition of music-drama. That is also why, in the final scene, her wish comes true. Isolde's so-called *Liebestod* has no other function. It celebrates an acoustic power above and beyond all humanity under the exceedingly precise title World-Breath (*Weltatem*).[27]

■ Once again, the beginning is simple, gentle, and humane. Isolde remembers and sings an old "air" that is dubbed "so wonderful and quiet" because it stands, in terms of leitmotifs, for her dead lover. The air rises up from the wind instruments, followed by Isolde, after a delay of exactly one eighth note—it is composed with technical precision (*Tristan*, score, 994). But amid such a feedback between the orchestra and voice, everything quiet soon ends. In its place a literal crescendo begins: a "growing." Within the field of Isolde's hearing or hallucinations, Tristan's corpse begins to live again, to swell and to breathe.

> *Soft and quiet,*
> *how he smiles;*
> *how he opens*
> *his eyes sweetly,*
> *O friends, do you see it?*
> *don't you see it? . . .*
> *How from lips*
> *so joyful-mild*
> *sweet breath*
> *softly stirs—*
> *Friends! See!*
> *Don't you feel and see it?*
> *Is it only I who hear*
> *this air,*
> *so wondrous and quiet,*
> *sweetly lamenting,*
> *telling all,*
> *mildly reconciling,*
> *sounding from him,*
> *penetrating into me,*
> *rising upward,*
> *sweetly resounding,*
> *ringing round me?*
> *(Tristan,* libretto, 147,149; trans. modified)

■ A crescendo in both the text and the score thus enables a dead body or (in musical terms) a body no longer capable of breathing and singing to be brought back to life. Tristan's extinguished breath returns as orchestral melody: the sounds he emits penetrate the listener. But Isolde sings all this—from the crescendo to the sound effects. Her orchestrally amplified voice thus supplements the missing voice of her lover. The voice in Wagner is so unindividuated, his acoustics so ecstatic,[28] that to the ear of a woman singing, her own voice appears essentially as the voice of the other.[29] When Siegfried in *Götterdämmerung* forfeits breath and life, he celebrates the memory—until recently forgotten—of Brünnhilde like an artificial respiration, as if the "delicious waft" of her "breath" were greeting and bringing him, the singer, back to life, as if his death were thus the exact counterpart to Brünnhilde's previous reawakening (84).[30] Under such conditions, even the most hallucinatory and phantasmagorical claims come true, simply because they cannot be sung. "Friends! . . . Don't you feel and see it?" is a rhetorical question. Just like Jimi Hendrix's question "Have you ever been to Electric Ladyland?," it answers itself—by means of sound effects that it produces. In the orchestra, the dead Tristan experiences an acoustic erection. And because Isolde's friends, who are addressed here, already stand for the pre-programmed audience of the music-drama, the unthinkable does indeed become audible. Isolde and her auditors "drown," as she says (or recites), in the "highest," namely, "unconscious" "pleasure" of a "billowy surge," of a "sounding reverberation." Its name, "World-Breath"; its technology, the orchestral fortissimo.

■ Munich, 10 June 1865, the world premiere of *Tristan und Isolde* was the beginning of modern mass media. Wagner had good reason to fear that the "last Act" in a "completely *good* performance" would either be "banned" or "would have to drive people crazy."[31] Tristan's acoustic erection as the pillar of the orchestra's World-Breath nullifies all possibilities of traditional art. Only media can implement what Isolde—as much technically as erotically—labels billowy surge or sounding reverberation.

■ For once, Wagner was too modest when he described as "merely one of his plans" his intention to complete his discovery of the invisible orchestra with the additional discovery of invisible actors. In fact and in truth that is precisely what he did. Tristan, with his acoustic and thus invisible erection;[32] Alberich under his magic cap; the young seaman "audible from the heights, as if from the masthead";[33] the Rhine Maidens "in the valley below, invisible" beneath Walhalla[34]—these and all of Wagner's other leitmotifs inhabit a "total world of hearing," as Nietzsche recognized so clearly.[35]

■ And only when the total world of hearing is created with media-technical precision can its connection to a "world of seeing" step into the technical era.[36] A sound room that no longer needs the old-fashioned visibility of the bodies of actors, thanks to its positive feedbacks, allows for parallel connections with the new (namely, technical) visibility of film. As early as the premiere of the *Ring* in 1876, Bayreuth made use of the *laterna magica* in order to make it possible to hallucinate how the nine Walkyries ride—on the backs of their horses, i.e., on the sounds of the orchestra.[37] Finally in 1890, five years before the introduction of the feature film, Wagner's son-in-law suggested a "night-darkened" room in whose "background" moving "pictures fly by" accompanied by the sounds of a "sunken orchestra" à la father-in-law, and putting the entire audience in a state of "ecstasy."[38]

■ In the meantime precisely this ecstasy is produced as Hollywood film worldwide and in stereo. But at the time it merely delineated Wagner's technical innovations.

■ Music-drama is a machine that works on three levels or in three data fields: first, verbal information; second, the invisible Bayreuth orchestra; third, the scenic visuality with its tracking shots and spotlights *avant la lettre*. The text is fed into the throat of a singer, the output of this throat is fed into an amplifier named orchestra, the output of this orchestra is fed into a light show, and the whole thing, finally, is fed into the nervous system of the audience. At the very last, when the people are crazy, every last trace of alphabet is eradicated. Data, rather than being encoded in the alphabet of books and scores, are amplified by media, committed to memory, and recalled. (And, for Wagner, even scores, as if they were already phonographs, only had the function of precisely timing discourses or sound effects.[39]) Music-drama defeats all literature.

■ Thus World-Breath, Isolde's last word, is no metaphor. It is the orchestra's own and appropriate name. The orchestra—as drill, as power, and as instrumental unit—was also a creation of the great nineteenth century, just like the division, the fighting unit comprising three arms systems: infantry, cavalry, and artillery.[40] Wagner knew it and said so. Etymologically as well as in the tetralogy, his god Wotan, a god of armies and ecstasies, of initiation and of death, denotes the rage of a superhuman and prophetic voice. Correspondingly, the army of Wotan's nine Walkyrie daughters simply denotes storm. And all of this power, this noise, this roaring has its source in the Goddess Erda, which means, yet again, it has its source in the World-Breath. Wotan says to Erda, the mother of his storm-daughters or storm-troops: "Wherever life exists, your breath blows."[41]

■ The earth in its materiality—this precondition that is unthinkable for classical arts[42]—reigns over the music-drama as a whole. It reigns as breath out of the depth of graves or shafts that all circumscribe the bottomless depth of the body. And Wagner set just such graves on a level not only with the prophetic cave of Delphi but also with Bayreuth's orchestra pit. There is no difference between technological and psychedelic vapors.

■ Thus precisely and coherently, the name "World-Breath" holds all of Wagner's innovations together. The name demonstrates Wagner's statement that "music" is the "breath" of "language."[43]

■ Today, Wagner's media technology deserves a short epilogue.[44] I conclude, in every sense of the word, with *Apocalypse Now*. When the US Airborne Cavalry in Coppola's film started out on those famous operations christened "search and destroy" by General Westmoreland, seeking out towns suspected of being Viet Cong, they did so only with light music, with Muzak. Wagner's "Ride of the Walkyries," the pretty, old light show of 1876, droned in all the earphones of all the war helicopters. A feedback between music-drama and war technology transformed the Walkyries, Wotan's deadly daughters, into on-board MG-guards, their storm-horses into helicopters, and Bayreuth into Hollywood.

■ Thus the capitalist medium recalls above all its prehistory in Wagner. General staffs and stage or screen directors are more precise than critics. And yet, *Apocalypse Now*, this *post-histoire* of Wagner's riding Walkyries, itself has a prehistory in two world wars.

■ From 1941 to 1944 Major Ernst Jünger, staff officer *and* author for the German military, resided in Paris in the Hotel Raphael, one of the official German stations in the French occupied zone. And whenever night bombers of the Royal Air Force attacked the City of Lights from its bases in the south of England, Jünger would go up to the hotel rooftop terrace in order to enjoy the "great beauty" and "demonic power" of that multimedia "show." For precisely the *light rays* that his wartime diary merely promises in its title[45] were to be seen then, prepared by Field Marshal Harris with Lancasters and Blenheims over Paris, which was in flames. During which Jünger "held in his hand a glass of burgundy in which strawberries were swimming."[46]

■ French critics have recently attempted to deduce from this wine glass the nihilism and aestheticism of its drinker. That's how poorly informed critics are. For Jünger on his hotel terrace was only citing—another world war, another writer. Literary history knows that already in 1915 two residents of Paris stepped out onto a balcony in order to enjoy the light show between attacking German zeppelins and French defensive lighting installations. Bombing as world premiere . . . one of the two Frenchmen was Robert, Marquis de Saint-Loup, a brilliant young officer on leave from the trenches that would be his future grave. The other, less well known, was a certain Proust. And because neither world wars nor airborne attacks could cloud his love for Wagner and Germany, the Marquis explained to the author the beauty of the instances when the zeppelins "*make constellations*," as well as the even nicer moments when they crash, when they "*make apocalypse*." For then, Saint-Loup realized with his Wagner-ears, zeppelins become Walkyries and the sounds of sirens become the "Ride of the Walkyries."[47]

■ The tests of Wagner's media technology could not have turned out more empirically.

REFERENCE MATTER

Notes

Notes are of two kinds: original, and translator's or editor's notes. All notes are by the author unless they are enclosed in brackets and end with —*Trans.* or —*Ed.*

Introduction

1. Brecht was one of the first to perceive that opera served as a last bastion not only for the cultured bourgeoisie but for the very notion of a cultured bourgeoisie. Some of his most important writings on opera appear in Bertolt Brecht, *Writings on Theatre*, trans. and ed. John Willett (New York: Hill & Wang, 1964). For the notion of opera as "culinary," see "The Modern Theatre Is the Epic Theatre: Notes to the Opera *Aufstieg und Fall der Stadt Mahagonny*," in *Writings on Theatre*, 35.

2. An exception is Herbert Lindenberger's *Opera: The Extravagant Art* (Ithaca, N.Y.: Cornell University Press, 1984), a broad-based and far-reaching consideration of opera's long-standing association with hyperbole and excess.

3. I will examine some important exceptions to this tendency later in this Introduction. The founding of the *Cambridge Opera Journal*, edited by Roger Parker and Arthur Groos, finally provides a regular and sophisticated English-language forum for the commingling of literary criticism and opera. European literary and cultural theorists, especially in France, Germany, and Italy, have been much more inclined to take opera seriously than their counterparts in the United States; this also holds for discussions of opera productions in the European press, which have been much more nuanced in considering matters of staged interpretation than reviews in the American press. (For a more extensive characterization of the place of the libretto in European critical debates, see Arthur Groos, "Introduction," in Groos and Roger Parker, eds., *Reading*

Opera [Princeton, N.J.: Princeton University Press, 1988], 1–11.)

4. Paul Robinson, "A Deconstructive Postscript: Reading Libretti and Misreading Opera," in Groos and Parker, eds., *Reading Opera*, 328–46; quotation in text, 330.

5. Booth's claim refers to Shakespeare's sonnets. See his Introduction to Stephen Booth, ed., *Shakespeare's Sonnets* (New Haven, Conn.: Yale University Press, 1977), xiii.

6. The term "libretto bashing" is taken from Arthur Groos' Introduction to *Reading Opera*: "Libretto bashing has a distinguished tradition in the blood sport of opera" (2).

7. There are a number of theorists who have critiqued this escape plot. One of the most recent and most lively critiques can be found in Carolyn Abbate's provocative book *Unsung Voices: Opera and Musical Narrative in the Nineteenth Century* (Princeton, N.J.: Princeton University Press, 1991). On a couple of occasions, Abbate offers some skeptical comments on the notion of attempting to flee to music. Here is a typically elegant example: "Music, for many, is the sound over which one swoons once the thoughtful labors of the day are done—but if so music brings an ambiguous comfort. Far from being a refuge from worldly questions of meaning, it is the beast in the closet; seemingly without any discursive sense, it cries out the problems inherent in critical reading and in interpretation as unfaithful translation" (xv). Abbate is not just wary of attempts to claim music as a refuge from literary theory; she is also skeptical of any attempt to claim music as an outpost for it. Her interest in music's diegetic voices leads her to propose a sort of splendid isolation of music from language: "Insisting upon the voices in a musical work may be, then, an insistence that music is radically unlike language, that the *trope* of music as a language needs to be resisted. Music may thus escape philosophical critiques of language, perhaps even escape language entirely" (18).

8. "Opera," Abbate and Parker point out gently, "is not music alone; it lives in association with poetry and dramatic action, an association that has made it idiosyncratic and special." *Analyzing Opera: Verdi and Wagner* (Berkeley: University of California Press, 1989), 5; quotation in text, 4.

9. The term "interplay of systems," which has been appearing with increasing frequency in the critical literature on opera, is derived from Pierluigi Petrobelli's notion that "in opera, various systems work together, each according to its own nature and laws, and the result of the combination is much greater than the sum of the individual forces" (quoted in Abbate and Parker, eds., *Analyzing Opera*, 5). See Petrobelli, "Music in the Theatre (à propos of *Aida*, Act III)," in James Redmond, ed., *Themes in Drama 3: Drama, Dance and Music* (Cambridge, Eng.: Cambridge University Press, 1981), 129–42.

10. Herbert Lindenberger, for example, makes a very similar point in *Opera*: "To the extent that music and words belong to a different order of expression, music can use its interactions with words as a way of declaring at once its limitations and its ability to transcend, magnify, embellish, comment, or improvise upon (or whatever else composers conceive themselves to be doing) the texts that give it its starting point and even its authority" (125).

11. Although Jeremy Tambling, in *Opera, Ideology, and Film* (New York: St. Martin's Press, 1987), does not accept the primacy of music in the production of operatic meaning, Groos suggests that he and Roger Parker do (see *Reading Opera*, 1; I give a direct quote below). Lindenberger's position is less clear-cut, although I am uncomfortable with his readiness to assign words and music to their own discrete, secluded turf.

12. Roland Barthes, "The World of Wrestling," in *Mythologies*, ed. and trans. Annette Lavers (New York: Hill & Wang, 1972), 15.

13. Theodor Adorno, *In Search of Wagner*, trans. Rodney Livingstone (London: New Left Books, 1981), 146. This was originally published in 1952 as *Versuch über Wagner* and was reprinted in Volume 13 of Adorno's *Gesammelte Schriften*, ed. Rolf Tiedemann (Frankfurt am Main: Suhrkamp, 1970–86).

14. Barthes, "The World of Wrestling," 23.

15. See Adorno, "Bourgeois Opera," in this volume.

16. Tambling's *Opera, Ideology, and Film* is divided into two sections. The first seeks to "think [opera and film] together," primarily in terms of contemporary literary theory (Tambling refers extensively to Walter Benjamin's essay "The Work of Art in the Age of Mechanical Reproduction" as well as to the writings of Roland Barthes and Jacques Derrida). In the second, Tambling considers six examples of opera on film (or television), ranging from traditional large-scale productions, like Franco Zeffirelli's *La Traviata*, to more experimental works like Syberberg's *Parsifal* and Straub/Huillet's *Moses und Aron*.

17. Catherine Clément, *Opera, or the Undoing of Women*, trans. Betsy Wing (Minneapolis: University of Minnesota Press, 1988). Other recent books on opera include Peter Conrad, *A Song of Love and Death: The Meaning of Opera* (New York: Poseidon, 1987); Robert Donington, *Opera and Its Symbols: The Unity of Words, Music, and Staging* (New Haven, Conn.: Yale University Press, 1990); Peter Kivy, *Osmin's Rage: Philosophical Reflections on Opera, Drama, and Text* (Princeton, N.J.: Princeton University Press, 1988); Wayne Koestenbaum, *The Queen's Throat: Opera, Homosexuality, and the Mystery of Desire* (New York: Poseidon, 1993); and Ivan Nagel's *Autonomy and Mercy: On Mozart's Operas*, trans. Marion Faber and Ivan Nagel (Cambridge, Mass.: Harvard University Press, 1991).

18. Joseph Kerman, *Opera as Drama*, rev. ed. (Berkeley: University of California Press, 1988), 10.

19. According to Kittler (this volume), "In Wagner's music-dramas, music itself, whether vocal like the love song or instrumental like the horn and reed-pipe, is motivated and generated by the plot." In "Opera as Symphony, a Wagnerian Myth," Carolyn Abbate offers a detailed interrogation of the contradictory claims that Wagner made for his music and its relation to the text: "Music can be generated by poetry, and thereby transgress limits set upon instrumental (symphonic) music, and pass beyond what is comprehensible in the symphonic world. This is an image of music pulled awry by a text with which it cannot be at peace" (in Abbate and Parker, eds., *Analyzing Opera*, 95).

20. In English: "first comes the music, then the words."

21. In fact, in his essay in this volume, Philippe Lacoue-Labarthe takes Wagner to task for submitting all too readily to the claim of this phrase, accusing him of "too much credit accorded to the *prima la musica.*"

22. Adorno's major writings on opera that are available in English include *In Search of Wagner*; "Opera," Chapter 5 in *Introduction to the Sociology of Music* (New York: Seabury, 1976); and, most recently, "Fantasia sopra *Carmen*" and "Sacred Fragment: On Schoenberg's *Moses und Aron*," in *Quasi una Fantasia: Essays on Modern Music* (New York: Verso, 1992). His extensive writings on the form are dispersed throughout the *Musikalische Schriften*, Volumes 16–19 of the *Gesammelte Schriften*; they include his published reviews of performances at the Frankfurt Opera, dating from 1922 to 1934 (See *Gesammelte Schriften*, 19: 9–256), and various essays on specific works and composers, and on the social and historical situation as well as the aesthetics of the form.

23. For a review of the rancorous history of innovation in operatic production in pre-Hitler Germany, see Walter Panofsky, *Protest in der Oper* (Munich: Laokoon, 1966). The most innovative (and controversial) opera house in Weimar Germany was the Kroll Opera in Berlin, directed by Otto Klemperer from 1927 to 1931. The Kroll engaged some of the most celebrated avant-garde theater directors, set designers, and costume designers in an attempt to bring operatic production practices in line with the innovative spirit of theater and ballet production in the Weimar Republic. For a comprehensive treatment and documentation of the extraordinary innovations produced there, see Hans Curjel, *Experiment Krolloper: 1927–1931*, ed. Eigel

Kruttge, foreword by Ernst Bloch. Studien zur Kunst des neunzehnten Jahrhunderts, 7 (Munich: Prestel, 1975).

24. In fact, Chéreau's production stimulated a sizable and noteworthy body of critical literature beyond the storm of critical controversy that greeted it. Jean-Jacques Nattiez's *Tétralogies: Wagner, Boulez, Chéreau* (Paris: Christian Bourgeois, 1983) goes far beyond a detailed analysis of Chéreau's production to offer a series of informed, polemical readings of issues related to it (including, for example, readings of the *Ring*, of Wagner's conception of theater, of Chéreau's dramaturgical aesthetics, of Boulez's musical poetics). Nattiez's 1978 essay "La trahison de Chéreau" was translated into English by Thomas Repensek and appeared as "Chéreau's Treachery" in *October* 14 (Fall 1980): 71–100. Michel Foucault also wrote a brief review of this production, which appeared in English translation as "Nineteenth Century Imaginations," in *Semiotext(e): The German Issue* 4, no. 2 (1982): 182–90.

Bourgeois Opera

1. [The so-called Opern-Krise or opera crisis was hotly debated in the newspapers and journals of the Weimar Republic. There were two main points of contention in the crisis, which essentially resulted from opera's confrontation with modernity. The first involved the way operas were being staged: as of 1915, traditional operas were being radically reinterpreted by avant-garde directors and designers (most notably at Berlin's Kroll Opera house, which consistently presented controversial new interpretations of works by Mozart, Wagner, and Weber, among others). Here the debate concerned the proper form and function of opera, and Adorno came out strongly in favor of reform. A clear statement of his support for innovation in operatic production practices and specifically for the "Kroll experiment" appeared in the *Musikblätter des Anbruch* 11 (June 1929) under the title "Berliner Opernmemorial" (reprinted in Volume 19 of Adorno's *Gesammelte Schriften*, ed. Rolf Tiedemann and Klaus Schultz [Frankfurt am Main: Suhrkamp, 1984], 267–75). (Hereafter, references to Adorno's *Gesammelte Schriften* will be abbreviated as *G.S.*, with volume and page numbers.) The second component of the opera crisis involved the introduction of "contemporary" themes into new operatic works (such as Ernst Krenek's *Jonny Spielt Auf* [premiere: 1927], a jazz opera which chronicled the adventures of an African-American jazz saxophonist, or Brecht and Weill's *Rise and Fall of the City of Mahagonny* [premiere: 1930], whose premiere was interrupted by Nazi gangs; it is the allegorical tale of an Alabama town established by ex-cons where the only crime is lack of money). For a genealogical account of innovations on the operatic stage in Germany, see Walter Panofsky, *Protest in der Oper* (Munich: Laokoon, 1966). For an account of the new operas and the controversy that surrounded their introduction, see Susan C. Cook, *Opera for a New Republic: The "Zeitopern" of Krenek, Weill, and Hindemith* (Ann Arbor, Mich.: UMI Research Press, 1988). For an extraordinary account of the Kroll Opera and the various debates concerning its productions and its ultimate dissolution (including complete documentation of press responses, reviews, and polemics surrounding the institution), see Hans Curjel, *Experiment Kroll-oper: 1927–1931*, ed. Eigel Kruttge, foreword by Ernst Bloch, Studien zur Kunst des neunzehnten Jahrhunderts, 7 (Munich: Prestel, 1975). The book includes, for example, a dossier from the Berlin journal *Das Tagebuch*, entitled "Save the Kroll Opera," featuring short pieces by a cross-section of prominent figures in Weimar culture, including Thomas Mann, Kurt Weill, Igor Stravinsky, and Paul Hindemith. (See *Das Tagebuch* 11 [15 Nov. 1930], reprinted in Curjel, 485–87.) One gains a sense of the vociferous terms and popular reso-

nance of the debate by leafing through newspapers and music journals of the late 1920's and early 1930's. See, for example, the discussions in a special insert of the *Berliner Börsen-Courier*, 83 (19 Feb. 1929), 5, entitled "In Support of the Rejuvenation of Opera," where a series of prominent figures (Walter Gropius, Ernst Toller, Paul Hindemith, et al.) polemicize in favor of operatic innovations; or the debate "Is There an Opera Crisis?" published in the *Berliner Tageblatt* 58 (6 Mar. 1926), with contributions from Arnold Schönberg and Franz Schreker, among others, and partially reprinted in the *Musikblätter des Anbruch* 8 (May 1926): 209.—*Trans.*]

2. [English retained from the original.—*Trans.*]

3. [In *Opera: The Extravagant Art* (Ithaca, N.Y.: Cornell University Press, 1984), Herbert Lindenberger cites this passage in the course of a consideration of the parodic quality of arias. See Lindenberger, 80.—*Trans.*]

4. [*Der Freischütz* (premiere: 1821) is a three-act opera by Carl Maria von Weber, with a text by Friedrich Kind; it is known as an exemplar of German romantic opera. Mozart's *The Magic Flute* (*Die Zauberflöte*; premiere: 1791) is a two-act *Singspiel*; the text is by J. E. Schikaneder. Giuseppe Verdi's *Il Trovatore* premiered in 1853. It is a four-act opera with a text by Salvatore Cammarano.—*Trans.*]

5. [In sixteenth-century German lands, traveling theater troupes performed upon a green wagon.—*Trans.*]

6. [In this prelude to Goethe's *Faust* (Part One), the theater manager, the poet, and the comic character express their desires and expectations for the forthcoming drama. See *Faust*, Part One, trans. Peter Salm (New York: Bantam 1985), 4–15.—*Trans.*]

7. [*Simon Boccanegra* is an opera in three acts (with a prologue) by Giuseppe Verdi (text by Francesco Maria Piave) which premiered in 1857 and was revised in 1881. Adorno (who, incidentally, shares the name of an important character in the opera) found the piece particularly and indicatively inane. In a review of a new production of the opera in Frankfurt in 1930 he writes:

"As a novelty, Verdi's *Simon Boccanegra* was presented, an early work that Verdi later revised, with a political text that is not political, newly prepared [in German translation] by [Franz] Werfel. Musically, it does not compare to *La Forza del Destino*. No longer filled with the naive musical power of the *Trovatore* period, and not yet filled with the mature spirituality of *Aida*, and seldom compelling in its melodic ideas, it is nevertheless a Verdi, with some amazing ensemble passages. The whole thing could conceivably represent an enrichment of the repertoire if the libretto were not so confused and dumb—with a final revelation that reveals nothing: it does not fulfill even the most modest demands for a sensible operatic plot. Which is exactly why the infantile opera public seemed to be so utterly delighted with it." The review was originally published in *Die Musik* (Jan. 1931) and subsequently reprinted in *G.S.*, 19: 197.—*Trans.*]

8. [Literally: play-opera. The term applies to German nineteenth-century comic operas, including Albert Lortzing's *Der Wildschütz* (1842), Otto Nicolai's version of *The Merry Wives of Windsor* (1849), and Friedrich Flotow's *Martha* (1847).—*Trans.*]

9. [In Act I of Wagner's *Lohengrin* (premiere: 1850; text by the composer), the title character appears in a boat drawn by a swan.—*Trans.*]

10. [Act II, scene ii, of Weber's opera (see note 4 above) takes place in a wolf's glen, where apparitions, incantations, and lightning combine to create a quintessentially (and melodramatically) eerie romantic scene.—*Trans.*]

11. [French in the original.—*Trans.*]

12. [*Cavalleria Rusticana* and *I Pagliacci* are the two most famous works of the Italian style of *verismo*, a particularly torrid form of operatic realism that flourished in late nineteenth-century Italy. *Cavalleria Rusticana* is a one-act opera by Pietro Mascagni, with a libretto by Giovanni Targioni-Tozzetti and Guido Menasci; it premiered in 1890. *I Pagliacci*, with text and music by Ruggiero Leoncavallo, is in two acts (with a prologue); it premiered in 1892. Adorno wrote a brief article commemorating Mascagni's seven-

tieth birthday for the *Vossische Zeitung* in December 1933. See "Mascagnis Landschaft," *G.S.*, 18: 271–72.—*Trans.*]

13. [Arnold Schönberg's operatic output includes the monodrama *Erwartung* (1909), text by Marie Pappenheim; *Die glückliche Hand* (1913), text by Schönberg; the one-act *Von Heute auf Morgen* (1930), text by M. Blonda; and the incomplete three-act biblical opera *Moses und Aron* (1932), with a text by the composer. For an excellent analysis of Schönberg's operatic works and his relationship to opera, see Chapter 7, "Drama and Music in Arnold Schoenberg's Dodecaphonic Experience," in Luigi Rognoni, *The Second Vienna School*, trans. Robert W. Mann (London: Calder, 1977). For more on Adorno's view of Schönberg as an opera composer, see his "Sacred Fragment: Schoenberg's *Moses und Aron*," in *Quasi una Fantasia: Essays on Modern Music*, trans. Rodney Livingstone (New York: Verso, 1992). In "The Caesura of Religion" (in this volume), Philippe Lacoue-Labarthe analyzes Adorno's essay at some length. For Schönberg's sense of the relationship between music and text, see his 1911 essay "Das Verhältnis zum Text," in *Stil und Gedanke: Aufsätze zur Musik: Gesammelte Schriften*, ed. Ivan Vojtech (Frankfurt am Main: Fischer, 1976); English translation: "The Relationship to the Text," in *Style and Idea: Selected Writings of Arnold Schoenberg*, ed. Leonard Stein, trans. Leo Black (New York: St. Martin's Press, 1975), 141–45.—*Trans.*]

14. [Adorno is referring to Act I, scene ii, of Berg's opera, where Wozzeck, a soldier, and his friend Andres are cutting sticks in a field. Wozzeck, who is subject to hallucinatory delusions, yells to his friend: "Quiet, Andres, it was the Freemasons! That's it! The Freemasons! Quiet! Quiet!" A few moments later, as the sun sets, Wozzeck cries: "A fire! A fire there! Rising from the earth to the sky, and a crashing noise coming down, like trumpets!" (See the excellent English translation in George Perle, *The Operas of Alban Berg*, vol. I, "Wozzeck" [Berkeley: University of California Press, 1980]. Quoted material appears on 49–50; translation slightly modified.) The three-act opera, which premiered in 1925, is

based on Georg Büchner's *Woyzeck*, an extraordinarily avant-garde dramatic fragment published in 1879, forty-two years after the author's death. Berg's opera has played a profoundly important role in the development of twentieth-century opera. Adorno, who had studied composition under Berg in the 1920's, wrote an impassioned review of the world premiere of the opera: see "Zur Uraufführung des *Wozzeck*," *Musikblätter des Anbruch* 7 (Dec. 1925): 531–37; reprinted in *G.S.*, 18: 456–68. In a review of the premiere of *Wozzeck* at the Frankfurt Opera in 1931, Adorno writes: "*Wozzeck* is a work with a validity unto itself, a work which is not merely an intermediate step upon a route whose destination no one can know in advance. Even today, *Wozzeck* is the most important document of those works of new music for which one does no favor when one plays them, but instead to which one owes thanks for being allowed to play them" (*G.S.*, 19: 204). For a translation of Adorno's extremely cogent analysis of the work, see "On the Characteristics of 'Wozzeck'" in Alban Berg, *Wozzeck*, Opera Guide 42 (New York: Riverrun Press, 1990), 37–40. Berg's own extensive writings on *Wozzeck* include "A Word about *Wozzeck*" and "A Lecture on *Wozzeck*," both reprinted in Douglas Jarman, ed., *Alban Berg: "Wozzeck,"* Cambridge Opera Handbooks (New York: Cambridge University Press, 1989), 152–53, 154–70. An English translation of Berg's "The Preparation and Staging of *Wozzeck*" is reprinted as an Appendix to Perle's *The Operas of Alban Berg*, 203–6.—*Trans.*]

15. [*Lulu*, Berg's second and final opera, remained incomplete upon the composer's death in 1935. The incomplete two-act version premiered in 1937 with a text by the composer, based on two dramas by Frank Wedekind; a complete version of the opera, based upon Friedrich Cerha's orchestration of the third act, premiered in 1979. For a fuller account of Berg's work and Adorno's sense of its significance, see the English translation of Adorno's "A Talk on *Lulu*" (1960) published in the text accompanying a 1968 Deutsche Grammophon recording of the opera (two-act version) conducted by Karl Böhm (DGG 139273-75). Parts of the "Talk" were

incorporated into Adorno's monograph on Berg, recently published in English translation. See "Experiences with *Lulu*," in *Alban Berg: Master of the Smallest Link*, trans., intro., and ann. Juliane Brand and Christopher Hailey (New York: Cambridge University Press, 1991), 120–35.—*Trans.*]

16. [Igor Stravinsky's *Renard* is a one-act stage piece which premiered in Paris in 1922; the text is by the composer. As Adorno suggests (and Stravinsky himself claimed), *L'Histoire du Soldat* is not an opera per se (there is no singing, and a narrator narrates the action); according to the work's title page, *L'Histoire du Soldat* was "to be read, played and danced." The text is by C. F. Ramuz; it premiered in Switzerland in 1918. See Stravinsky, *Chroniques de ma vie* (Paris: Denoel & Steele, 1935); English translation: *An Autobiography* (New York: M. & J. Steuer, 1958 [1936]). —*Trans.*]

17. [Max Brand's *Maschinist Hopkins* (text by the composer) was a sensational success when it premiered in Duisburg, Germany, in 1929, although it has hardly been performed since the 1930's. The piece was labeled a "milieu opera," thanks to its clearly contemporary setting and trappings, including jazz bars, machines, labor unrest, etc. Adorno detested the piece and wrote a blistering review in *Die Musik* in January 1930. Adorno directed many of the same criticisms at George Antheil's *Transatlantic*. His (English-language) review was published in *Modern Music* in 1930; it is reprinted in *G.S.*, 19: 182–84. For Brand's vision of operatic innovation, see his "'Mechanische Musik' und das Problem der Oper," *Musikblätter des Anbruch* 7 (1926): 356–59.—*Trans.*]

18. [Opera in three acts by Paul Hindemith with a libretto by Ferdinand Lion, based on E. T. A. Hoffmann's "Das Fräulein von Scuderi." The original version premiered in 1926; a revised version premiered in 1952. A 1928 review by Adorno can be found in *G.S.*, 19: 128–31.—*Trans.*]

19. [Comic opera in eight scenes with a prologue; Brecht wrote the pointedly political libretto, Weill composed the music (including the famous "Ballad of Mack the Knife"). The work is a free adaptation of John Gay's *Beggar's Opera*

(1728); it premiered in Berlin in 1928 and had a run of more than four thousand performances in more than a hundred German theaters. For a very polemical and illuminating statement of Brecht's program of operatic innovation, see his essay "The Modern Theatre Is the Epic Theatre: Notes to the Opera *The Rise and Fall of the City of Mahagonny*," in Brecht, *Writings on Theater*, trans. and ed. John Willett (New York: Hill & Wang, 1964), 33–42. Brecht's "The Literalization of the Theater: Notes to *The Threepenny Opera*" is also included in Willett's collection (43–47). A selection of Weill's extensive writings on opera appears in Kurt Weill, *Ausgewählte Schriften*, ed. David Drew (Frankfurt am Main: Suhrkamp, 1975); a companion volume of writings *on* Weill was also published by Suhrkamp in 1975. See *Über Kurt Weill*, ed. David Drew (Frankfurt am Main: Suhrkamp, 1975), which includes a number of Adorno's essays on Weill's operatic works. —*Trans.*]

20. [See Max Horkheimer's 1936 essay "Egoismus und Freiheitsbewegung," in *Kritische Theorie*, 2 vols. (Frankfurt am Main: Fischer, 1968), 2: 161ff. For an English translation (with an introduction by Martin Jay), see "Egoism and the Freedom Movement," trans. David J. Parent, *Telos* 54 (Winter 1982–83): 10–60.—*Trans.*]

21. [French in the original.—*Trans.*]

22. [Comte Joseph de Maistre (1754–1821) was a passionate traditionalist and royalist, and an ardent theorist of both views. According to George Boas, de Maistre was the first philosopher of the counterrevolution in France. Selections from his works, including *Considérations sur la France* (1796), *Soirées de Saint-Petersbourg* (1821), and *Du Pape* (1817), have been published in *The Works of Joseph de Maistre*, ed. and trans. Jack Lively (New York: Schocken Books, 1971 [1965]).—*Trans.*]

23. [Volker and Hagen are figures in the medieval German epic *The Nibelungenlied*: both are feudal lords and vassals of the Burgundian kings. Volker, lord of Alzey, is the Burgundian minstrel and fiddler; Hagen, lord of Troneck, is the principal (and utterly ruthless) strategist of the Burgundian court and Siegfried's unrepentant assassin.—*Trans.*]

24. [Adorno is referring to Hanns Gutman's article "Literaten haben die Oper erfunden!" in *Musikblätter des Anbruch* 11 (June 1929): 256–60. The "Florentine circle" referred to here is generally known as the "Camerata," a group that formed in the last decade of the sixteenth century. The Camerata was led by the noblemen Giovanni Bardi and Jacopo Corsi and included the poet Ottavio Rinuccini (librettist for many of the earliest operas) and the composers Vincenzo Galilei (father of the astronomer) and Jacopo Peri (whose *Dafne* [1597] is often cited as the first opera).—*Trans.*]

25. [Because the first public opera house opened in Venice in 1637, some writers, including the preeminent opera historian Donald Grout, would assign the beginnings of opera to Venice. Claudio Monteverdi (1567–1643)—composer of *L'Orfeo* (1606) and *L'Incoronazione di Poppea* (1642) among many others—was appointed music director of St. Mark's Cathedral in Venice in 1613; his student and successor at St. Mark's was Francesco Cavalli (1602–1676), who wrote more than forty operas (including the first piece designated an *opera* rather than *dramma per musica*). Marc'Antonio Cesti (1623–1669) wrote eight operas, including *Il Pomo d'Oro* (1667).—*Trans.*]

26. [Reinhard Keiser (1674–1739) is reputed to have composed as many as one hundred operas—some of them in German—of which only twenty-five have been preserved. The Bürgeroper in Hamburg was founded in 1678, and Keiser served as its managing director from 1694 until his death.—*Trans.*]

27. [The Neapolitan school was founded around 1685 and predominated in Italy until the middle of the seventeenth century.—*Trans.*]

28. [The forerunner of comic opera, the intermezzo offered comic relief between the acts of more elevated (indeed, usually tragic) operatic works. Two of the most famous intermezzi are Jean-Jacques Rousseau's *Le Devin du village* (1752), the tale of Colette, a village girl, who consults a soothsayer in order to regain her lost sweetheart Colin; and Giovanni Battista Pergolesi's *La Serva*

padrona (1733; text by G. A. Federico), a two-act piece in which the maid Serpina enlists the aid of the valet Vespone in order to become the wife of Uberto, their bachelor employer.—*Trans.*]

29. [Adorno made a very similar point in his monograph on Wagner (published in English as *In Search of Wagner*, trans. Rodney Livingstone [London: New Left Books, 1981]): "Thus we see that the evolution of opera, and in particular the emergence of the autonomous sovereignty of the artist, is intertwined with the origins of the culture industry. Nietzsche, in his youthful enthusiasm, failed to recognize the artwork of the future in which we witness the birth of film out of the spirit of music" (107).—*Trans.*]

30. [Adorno is referring to Giacomo Meyerbeer's (1791–1864) grandiose five-act operas *Les Huguenots* (premiere: 1836), *Le Prophète* (premiere: 1849), and *L'Africaine* (premiere: 1865). *Les Huguenots* (text by Eugène Scribe and Emile Deschamps) is based on the French religious wars of the late sixteenth century, culminating, as Adorno notes, in a depiction of the St. Bartholomew's Day massacre. (Adorno wrote a brief review of a performance of *Les Huguenots* in April 1925; it can be found in *G.S.*, 19: 51–52.) *Le Prophète* (text by Scribe) is based on the career of John of Leyden, leader of the sixteenth-century uprising of the Anabaptists in Holland. *L'Africaine* (text by Scribe again) takes place in early sixteenth-century Lisbon and Madagascar; it is based on the career of Vasco da Gama.—*Trans.*]

31. [The several phrases in this sentence which appear within quotation marks are English in the original.—*Trans.*]

32. [Engelbert Humperdinck (1854–1921) is best known as the composer of *Hänsel und Gretel* (premiere: 1893; text by Adelhaid Wette, the composer's sister, based on Jakob Grimm's fairy tale). Earlier, Humperdinck had assisted Wagner in preparing the premiere of *Parsifal*.—*Trans.*]

33. [Claudio Monteverdi's *L'Orfeo* (text by Alessandro Striggio) premiered in Mantua in 1607. *Orfeo ed Euridice* (premiere: 1762 in Vienna; text by Raniero da Calzabigi) was Christoph Willibald Gluck's first attempt to move

opera from the pomp and artifice of the Italian tradition to a new, simpler, more credible form. —*Trans.*]

34. [In Act II, scene vii, of *The Magic Flute*, Tamino plays his magic flute for protection as he leads Pamina through two caverns, one of fire and one of water.—*Trans.*]

35. [The last two scenes of *The Magic Flute* mark the literal collapse of the discredited realm of Pamina's mother, the Queen of the Night (scene ix) and the ascendancy of Sarastro's Temple of the Sun (scene x). (According to the stage directions, the Queen, her three ladies, and the "moor" Monostatos "all sink into the earth.") —*Trans.*]

36. [The high priest Sarastro supposedly knows no revenge; his aria (#15) in Act II, scene xii, begins: "These halls know no revenge. If a man should stray from the true path, love leads him back to his duty." See "The Magic Flute," in *Mozart's Librettos*, trans. Robert Pack and Marjorie Lelash (Cleveland, Ohio: World, 1965), 451.—*Trans.*]

37. [The trumpet fanfare in Beethoven's *Fidelio* (premiere: 1805; text by Josef Sonnleithner and Georg Treitschke) marks the opera's climactic moment, the arrival of Don Fernando (Act II, scene i). Don Fernando orders the release of the prisoners from jail, the arrest of the evil prison warden Pizarro, and the release of Florestan, whom Pizarro had wrongfully imprisoned. —*Trans.*]

38. [Verdi's *La Forza del Destino* (text by Francesco Piave and Antonio Ghislanzoni) is a four-act opera that premiered in 1862. Both *Il Trovatore* (see note 4 above) and *La Forza del Destino* involve improbable and ultimately tragic tales of twisted familial fate. In a 1928 review of a performance of *La Forza del Destino*, Adorno writes, "Every possible complaint can be lodged against the *Forza* text, with its 'destiny mania.' Its romanticism is so thoroughly worn that the text can only really be judged with recourse to puppet-theater dramaturgy" (*G.S.*, 19: 120).—*Trans.*]

39. [Adorno is referring to the celebrated and celebratory union of brother and sister (Siegmund and Sieglinde) in *Die Walküre*, the second

piece in the tetralogy *Der Ring des Nibelungen.* —*Trans.*]

40. [*Die Entführung aus dem Serail* (1782) is a *Singspiel* in three acts. The Turkish pasha Selim has purchased Constanze and her maid Blonde from the pirates who abducted them; he soon captures Constanze's lover Belmonte, who has come to rescue his sweetheart. Despite the couple's foiled attempt at escape and the revelation that Belmonte is the son of the Pasha's worst enemy, the Pasha (a speaking role) renounces revenge and frees the lovers.—*Trans.*]

41. [Jacques Fromental Halévy's five-act opera (text by Eugène Scribe) premiered in Paris in 1835. Act V begins with an absolutely astonishing chorus where the crowd eagerly awaits the execution of Eléazar, a Jewish goldsmith, and his daughter Rachel, the title character. Rachel is to be executed for having made love to the (Christian) Prince: she and her father are to be boiled in oil, and the crowd celebrates: "Quel plaisir, quelle joie!" As Rachel is thrown into the caldron, Eléazar reveals that she is neither his biological daughter nor a Jew, but the daughter of his nemesis, the Cardinal.—*Trans.*]

42. [For Meyerbeer's opera, see note 30 above. Selika, an African queen, is taken to Portugal as a slave by the explorer Vasco da Gama. By Act IV, Vasco and Selika are back in her native land of Madagascar and are in love. But with the arrival of Vasco's earlier (and Portuguese) beloved Inez, the intercultural and interracial relationship is broken up. As Vasco and Inez sail back to Portugal, Selika and her beloved slave Nelusko fatally poison themselves.—*Trans.*]

43. [Verdi's *La Traviata* is a three-act opera based on Alexandre Dumas' play. The text was written by Francesco Maria Piave; it premiered in 1853.—*Trans.*]

44. [Verdi's *Aida* is in three acts. The text is by Francesco Maria Piave; it premiered in 1871. Aida is an Ethiopian princess who has been captured and now serves as a slave to the Princess of Egypt. Both women are in love with the same man, Radames, leader of the Egyptian army, who in turn loves the presumed slave Aida. The love between army hero and slave, Egyptian and Ethi-

opian, is doomed. In the end, Radames is sentenced to be buried alive for divulging state secrets to the Ethiopian enemy; Aida joins him in the tomb.—*Trans.*]

45. [Léo Delibes' *Lakmé* is an opéra-comique in three acts with a text by Edmond Gondinet and Philippe Gille; it premiered in Paris in 1883. The piece is set in India in the mid-nineteenth century. Lakmé is the daughter of a Brahman priest; she falls in love with Gerald, an Englishman who has desecrated the Indian temple. As Gerald is about to return to his regiment, and as Lakmé's father is about to have him killed, Lakmé commits suicide.—*Trans.*]

46. [Georges Bizet's four-act opera (text by Henri Meilhac and Ludovic Halévy) is based on the story by Prosper Mérimée; it premiered in 1875. The tale involves a gypsy femme fatale who ensnares the unwitting (and dim-witted) soldier Don José only to dump him for another (and/or for no one). Don José's jealousy is boundless and he kills her.—*Trans.*]

47. [See *Siegfried*, Act II, scene i. Wotan's words "alles ist nach seiner Art" (which he actually speaks in disguise as The Wanderer) are difficult to translate. William Mann offers: "everything happens according to its kind" (*Siegfried*, libretto, English and German, trans. William Mann [London: Friends of Covent Garden, 1964], 53), and Andrew Porter proposes "all things go their appointed way" (*The Ring of the Nibelung*, libretto, English and German, trans. Andrew Porter [New York: Norton, 1976], 197).—*Trans.*]

48. [Here, as above (see the formulation "in Wagner," in the preceding sentence), the German phrase *bei dem* carries a number of simultaneous meanings. Much like the French term *chez*, *bei dem* suggests a combination of "for [Wagner]," "in whom," as well as "in whose works" and "in whose mind."—*Trans.*]

49. [Giacomo Puccini's *Madama Butterfly* (text by Luigi Illica and Giuseppe Giacosa) is based on a play by David Belasco; it premiered in 1904. The geisha Cio-Cio-San (Madame Butterfly) is deeply in love with and marries B. F. Pinkerton, a lieutenant in the U.S. Navy stationed in Nagasaki.

Having severed familial, religious, and cultural ties in Japan, Butterfly bears Pinkerton's child and awaits his return from the U.S. When the lieutenant finally does return, he is accompanied by his new American wife Kate: they have come to retrieve Pinkerton's child. When Pinkerton arrives at Butterfly's house to pick up his child, he finds the boy next to his mother who has committed suicide.—*Trans.*]

50. [For Berg's opera, see note 15 above. —*Trans.*]

51. [The reference is to Bizet's *Carmen*. See note 46 above.—*Trans.*]

52. [One of the sharpest formulations of this contradiction—one which Adorno may well have had in mind here—can be found in Bertolt Brecht's "Notes on the Opera *The Rise and Fall of the City of Mahagonny*." According to Brecht, "The irrationality of opera lies in the fact that rational elements are employed, solid reality is aimed at, but at the same time it is all washed out by the music. A dying man is real. If at the same time we are translated to the sphere of the irrational. (If the audience sang at the sight of him the case would be different.)" See Brecht, *Writings on Theatre*, 35–36.—*Trans.*]

53. [The compositional practice of the Florentine Camerata (see note 24 above) involved a single voice accompanied by supporting chords rather than the elaborate choral polyphony of the popular (and contested) madrigal style. —*Trans.*]

54. [On Gluck's reforms, see note 33 above. —*Trans.*]

55. [Literally: speech-song. The term should be understood in juxtaposition to the related practice of *Sprechstimme*, or speech-voice, championed by Schönberg. *Sprechgesang* designates singing inflected as speech, whereas *Sprechstimme* is speech inflected as singing.—*Trans.*]

56. [In the first two published versions of this essay, Adorno formulated this sentence much more polemically: "In the process one is reminded of the definition which Lukács offered forty years ago in a piece which established his reputation as a philosopher and through which his

influence lives on even today, although he has long since recanted the piece in deference to the Russian cultural authorities." (See "Theater-Oper-Bürgertum," in *Theater*, 130, and *Der Monat*, 536.)—*Trans.*]

57. [See Gyorgy Lukács, *The Theory of the Novel: A Historico-Philosophical Essay on the Forms of Great Epic Literature*, trans. Anna Bostock (Cambridge, Mass.: M.I.T. Press, 1971). —*Trans.*]

58. [In *Siegfried*, Act II, scene ii (conclusion) and scene iii. Upon slaying the dragon and unwittingly tasting its blood, Siegfried is able to understand the bird's song.—*Trans.*]

59. [See note 58 above.—*Trans.*]

60. [For more on *Lulu*, see note 15 above. In the first published version of this essay, Adorno formulated the beginning of this paragraph as follows: "Nor did this work—whose instrumentation Berg could not complete—help resolve the opera crisis. Incidentally, the special application of the term 'crisis' to innumerable little areas is at once naive and pompous in the face of the one crisis shaking everything—the crisis of bourgeois society itself" (*Theater*, 132; see also *Der Monat*, 537).—*Trans.*]

The Caesura of Religion

1. In *The Birth of Tragedy*, trans. Walter Kaufmann (New York: Random House, 1967), "culture of opera" or "civilization of opera" designates the "Socratic civilization," insofar as it is responsible for the (false) "renaissance" of tragedy in modern Europe from the sixteenth century at least until the neoclassicism of the end of the eighteenth century, itself impregnated with Rousseauism. What is incriminated here is the renaissance of a belated and inauthentic antiquity, a Hellenistic, or—what is worse—Roman antiquity. Elsewhere I have attempted to show the immense political stakes of this dispute. See Lacoue-Labarthe, *L'imitation des modernes* (Paris: Galilée, 1986), and *Heidegger, Art, and Politics: The Fiction of the Political*, trans. Chris Turner (Oxford: Blackwell, 1990).

2. [Richard Wagner, quoted in Adorno, *In Search of Wagner*, trans. Rodney Livingstone (London: New Left Books, 1981), 99. For the two passages quoted here, Adorno cites Richard Wagner, *Gesammelte Schriften und Dichtungen*, 2d ed., 10 vols. (Leipzig: E. W. Fritzsch, 1888), 4: 127, 103. English translation: *Richard Wagner's Prose Works*, trans. W. A. Ellis, 8 vols. (London: Routledge & Kegan Paul, 1892–99; New York: Broude Brothers, 1966), 2: 265, 236. I have slightly modified the published translation to accord more

closely with the original. Oddly, the entire clause set off by dashes in the second quotation is missing from Ellis' published English translation of Wagner's works and from Livingstone's translation of Adorno's book.—*Ed.*]

3. ["Sakrales Fragment: Über Schönberg's *Moses und Aron*" was first published in *Quasi una fantasia* (Frankfurt am Main: Suhrkamp, 1963); subsequently, it appeared in *Musikalische Schriften*, 454–75, volume 16 of *Gesammelte Schriften* (Frankfurt am Main: Suhrkamp, 1978). English translation: "Sacred Fragment: On Schoenberg's *Moses und Aron*," in *Quasi Una Fantasia: Essays on Modern Music*, trans. Rodney Livingstone (New York: Verso, 1992), 225–48. Hereafter, references to this work will appear in parentheses in the text and will refer to the English translation.—*Ed.*] The intention of "saving" [*retten*] the work is a critical motif that is already present in Benjamin's work, particularly in *The Origin of German Tragic Drama*. The *Rettung* consists in "mortifying" works in order to extract a second beauty from their ruins, a beauty that is an "object of knowledge." To save, in this sense, is to accede to the *Wahrheitsgehalt* of artworks. Adorno applies this concept to "problematic" works, that is, to works that are the successful expressions of "false consciousness." See Benja-

min, *The Origin of German Tragic Drama*, trans. John Osborne (London: New Left Books, 1977); and Jean-Louis Leleu, "Présentation," an essay included in the French translation of Adorno's *Quasi una fantasia* (Paris: Gallimard, 1982), vii, ix.

4. [Here Lacoue-Labarthe refers to a French translation of the first version of Heidegger's essay, which has not yet appeared in English translation. See *De l'origine de l'oeuvre d'art*, trans. E. Martineau (Paris: Authentica, 1987). Parenthetical page references are to this French translation of Heidegger's lecture.—*Trans.*]

5. See Jean-Joseph Goux, *Les iconoclastes* (Paris: Seuil, 1978). On this and many other points I have allowed myself to be guided by the analyses contained in Goux's book.

6. [The translated passages of Rilke's poetry are taken from Rainer Maria Rilke, *Book of Hours*, trans. A. L. Peck (London: Hogarth Press, 1961), 98.—*Trans.*]

7. [The translated passage is taken from *Moses and Aaron*, libretto accompanying a phonograph recording, trans. Allen Forte (Mainz: B. Schotts Söhne, 1974). Recording cond. Michael Gielen, chorus and orchestra of the Austrian Radio, Philips, 6700-084, 1974.—*Trans.*]

8. This is not at all the case in the *Aesthetic Theory*. See *Aesthetische Theorie*, ed. Gretel Adorno and Rolf Tiedemann (Frankfurt am Main: Suhrkamp, 1970). A controversial English translation was published by Routledge & Kegan Paul in 1984. See *Aesthetic Theory*, trans. C. Lenhardt (Boston: Routledge & Kegan Paul, 1984).

9. See Hegel's *Lectures on the Philosophy of Religion*, ed. and trans. Peter Hodgson (Berkeley: University of California Press, 1987), esp. sec. II-2.

10. Already in Longinus, the biblical pronouncement (as it happens, the *Fiat lux* of Genesis) is a major example of a sublime utterance. On this subject, and on the subject of Kant, see my essay "La vérité sublime," in *Du sublime* (Paris: Belin, 1988). A translation, entitled "Sublime Truth," appeared in two parts in *Cultural Critique*. Part one appeared in vol. 18 (Spring 1991): 5–31; part two in vol 20. (Winter 1992): 207–29.

11. I will do this on the basis of what I have tried to show in "Sublime Truth."

12. It is true that Adorno thinks that Kant's error is to have reserved the sublime for nature. See Adorno, *Aesthetische Theorie*, 496.

13. Immanuel Kant, *The Critique of Judgment* (Oxford: Clarendon Press, 1928).

14. This formula is taken up once again textually by Heidegger in "The Origin of the Work of Art."

15. See "Sacred Fragment": "When Schönberg was once asked about a piece that had not yet been performed, 'So you haven't heard it yourself?', he replied, 'Yes, I have. When I wrote it.' In such a process of the imagination, the sensuous is directly spiritualized without losing any of its concrete specificity. What was realized in the imagination thereby became an objective unity. It is as if Schönberg's musical mind recapitulated that movement from the tribal gods to monotheism, the story of which is encapsulated in *Moses und Aron*. If our epoch refuses to vouchsafe to us a sacred work of art, it does at its close give birth to the possibility of something under whose gaze the bourgeois age was ushered in" (248).

16. On this motif, which reappears often in Adorno's work (especially as regards Mahler), but which Adorno does not make explicit for himself, see Olivier Revault d'Allonnes, *Musical Variations on Jewish Thought*, trans. Judith L. Greenberg (New York: Braziller, 1984).

17. See Section 1 of Hölderlin's "Anmerkungen zum Oedipus," in Friedrich Hölderlin, *Werke und Briefe*, ed. Friedrich Beißner and Jochen Schmidt, 2 vols. (Frankfurt am Main: Insel, 1969), 2: 729–31. In Benjamin's essay on Goethe, the caesura intervenes to justify the category of the "expressionless" [*das Ausdruckslose*], which Adorno never ceases referring to: "The 'expressionless' is the critical power which, although it is not capable of distinguishing appearance from essence in art, nonetheless prevents them from commingling. It has this power in its capacity as moral word. In the expressionless, the sublime power of the true appears, just as it determines the language of the real world according to the laws of

the moral world. It, namely, destroys the last remnants of inherited chaos in all beautiful appearance: the false, mistaken totality—the absolute totality. It completes the work, which it smashes into a patchwork, into a fragment of the true world, into a torso of a symbol. A category of language and art, not of the work or of genres, the expressionless cannot be more stringently defined than Hölderlin defined it. . . . The 'Hesperian, Junonic sobriety' . . . is just another term for that caesura in which, along with harmony, every expression places itself in order to give space to an expressionless power within every artistic means." See "Goethes Wahlverwandschaften," in Walter Benjamin, *Gesammelte Schriften*, Werkausgabe in 12 vols. (Frankfurt am Main: Suhrkamp, 1980), 1: 123–201. The passage cited here appears on 181–82. Benjamin situates the caesura of Goethe's *Elective Affinities*, understood in this sense, in one phrase, the one that "interrupts all the action": "Hope passed over their heads as a star which falls from the sky." In Goethe's novel, this phrase, in fact, seals the des-

tiny of the heroes, Eduard and Ottilie, and all the more so because "they do not see it pass" (200).

18. For more on this topic, see *Heidegger, Art and Politics*, Chapter 5.

19. See Sigmund Freud, *Moses and Monotheism*, trans. James Strachey, vol. 23 of *Standard Edition*, ed. James Strachey (London: Hogarth Press, 1964), as well as Philippe Lacoue-Labarthe and Jean-Luc Nancy, "Le peuple juif ne rêve pas," in *La psychoanalyse est-elle une histoire juive?* (Paris: Seuil, 1981).

20. Adorno, "Fragment über Musik und Sprache," *Musikalische Schriften*, 251–56, vol. 16 of *Gesammelte Schriften* (Frankfurt am Main: Suhrkamp, 1978), 252. Adorno first published this piece in 1956. English translation: "Music and Language: A Fragment" in *Quasi una Fantasia*, 1–6 (quote on p. 2).

21. See Walter Benjamin, "On Language as Such and on the Language of Man," in *Reflections*, trans. Edmund Jephcott, ed. Peter Demetz (New York: Schocken Books, 1978), 314–32.

22. See Lacoue-Labarthe, "Sublime Truth."

The Replay's the Thing

1. "The Work of Art in the Age of Mechanical Reproduction," in *Illuminations*, ed. Hannah Arendt, trans. Harry Zohn (New York: Schocken Books, 1969), 228–29.

2. "Opera on a Grand Scale," *New York Times Magazine*, 11 Oct. 1987.

3. David Sawyer, quoted in E. J. Dionne, Jr., "China Lets World Hear But Not See," *New York Times*, 21 May 1989.

4. See in particular *Vitesse et politique* (Paris: Galilée, 1977) and *La machine de la vision* (Paris: Galilée, 1988).

5. Jonathan Lieberson, "Nixon in Brooklyn," *New York Review of Books*, 21 Jan. 1988, 35.

6. Michael Walsh, "Stagecraft as Soulcraft," *Time*, 9 Nov. 1987, 110.

7. *Le Monde*, 11–12 June 1989.

Taking Place

1. Theodor Adorno, "Opera," in *Introduction to the Sociology of Music*, trans. E. B. Ashton (New York: Seabury, 1976), 71–84.

2. In the three decades that have passed since Adorno wrote, contemporary music has increasingly sought to problematize such notions of

autonomy (John Cage being the best-known instance), and this may explain a renewed interest shown by composers for the operatic form.

3. "Opera," 81, trans. modified.

4. Ibid, 81–82, trans. modified.

5. Ibid, 81, trans. modified.

6. This tendency toward the homogenization and pasteurization of opera is particularly evident in countries like the United States, where the dramatic aspect often survives only as the brief plot résumé provided in the program and where the libretto itself is usually linguistically incomprehensible.

7. The appreciative cries of "bravo" constitute an effort on the part of the audience to respond in kind, i.e., by overcoming its collective anonymity and giving voice to its individuality.

8. A later version had been published in 1977 by Jean Humbert, in the *Revue de Musicologie* 63, no. 1 (1977), but the earlier text was printed for the first time, together with Humbert's commentary, in the remarkable program notes that accompany the Frankfurt staging.

9. See Klaus Zehelein, "Death of Opera, Death in Opera," in *enclitic* 8, nos. 1–2 (Spring/Fall 1984), 116–23.

10. See S. Weber, "Tertium datur," in Friedrich Kittler et al., *Die Austreibung des Geistes aus den Geisteswissenschaften* (Schöningen: Paderborn, 1980), 201–21; English translation: in my *Institution and Interpretation* (Minneapolis: University of Minnesota Press, 1987).

11. One such category I have sought to develop is that of *Auseinandersetzung*, a German term that may be rendered in English as "setting apart." Later on in this discussion I shall try to demonstrate this category at work. Cf. S. Weber, *The Legend of Freud* (Minneapolis: University of Minnesota Press, 1982), 1–62.

12. Freud's phrase, of course, is: "Wo es war, soll ich werden." In this context his discussion of the joke structure should be recalled, in which one only becomes a "first person"—a joke-teller—*after* one has been a "third person," a listener.

13. See, for instance, his book *Opera and*

Drama (1850–51) in *Richard Wagner's Prose Works*, trans. W. A. Ellis, 8 vols. (London: Routledge & Kegan Paul, 1899; New York: Broude Brothers, 1966).

14. A. Boucourechliev, "Écouter Wagner aujourd'hui" (Listening to Wagner Today), *L'Avant-Scène Opéra*, Special Wagner Issue, "L'Or du Rhin" (Nov. 1976): 56.

15. "Über die Benennung 'Musikdrama,'" in R. Wagner, *Dichtungen und Schriften* (Frankfurt am Main: Insel, 1983), 9: 276.

16. Here, as throughout, the translations of Wagner are my own.

17. Such an assumption—that of an untroubled, unproblematically "natural," prelapsarian state of innocence here at the beginning—has governed most of the interpretations of *Das Rheingold*, with the recent and notable exception of Chéreau, Boulez, and Pedruzzi. Whatever one may think of their hydroelectrified Rhine, it has the undeniable virtue of stressing what should be, but has not been, obvious: that the most "unnatural" conflicts of desire and relations of power are *dammed up* in this initial and initiating scene.

18. Wagner's German deserves to be cited in its entirety: "Der ganze Boden ist in ein wildes Zackengewirr zerspalten, so dass er nirgends vollkommen eben ist und nach allen Seiten hin in dichtester Finsternis tiefere Schluchten annehmen lässt." The stage description thus ends in a double assumption: the audience is assumed to assume the proliferating gorges.

19. For a more elaborate discussion of this position as it is at work in the theory of W. Iser, see my article, "Caught in the Act of Reading," *Demarcating the Disciplines*, Glyph Textual Studies 1 (Minneapolis: University of Minnesota Press, 1986), 181–214.

20. S. Freud, *The Interpretation of Dreams*, trans. James Strachey, *Standard Edition*, 5: 530, translation altered (emphasis added). See S. Weber, *Legend of Freud*, 75ff., for a more extended reading of this passage.

21. Weber, *Legend of Freud*.

22. Here, too, one can discern something like an allegory of the Freudian unconscious, in which the position of the spectator is revealed both as

specious and as unavoidable. The dreamer appears to be a mere observer of the dream, but this is merely part of the dream's structure as *Entstellung*. The perspective of the spectator is ineluctable—it is the vantage point of the conscious Ego—but it remains inscribed in a spectacle that no glance can ever oversee.

23. The difficulty of dealing with the ring as a stage property is directly related to the problem of the *Ring* itself, as the effort to stage this self-destructive and ambivalent desire for appropriation. The "power" of the ring is, and must be, in direct proportion to its physical smallness and "unobtrusiveness." The contradiction between its phenomenal reality and its theatrical importance provides an exemplary instance of the figuration of disfigurement, which is the formative—or, rather, deformative—principle of the tetralogy. Another instance, which I shall discuss shortly, is that of Loge.

24. The prominence of recapitulative narration in the *Ring*, as later in *Parsifal* (where Gurnemanz is forever retelling what should be common knowledge), should be interpreted in this context as a kind of "secondary revision" aimed at reinforcing the semblance of a sequential, diachronic, causal continuity, where one event follows as the result of a previous one. Theatrically, however, such narratives only confirm the nonlinear character of the conflicts at work: the decisive tensions and struggles in the *Ring* play themselves out not in sequence, as the relation of one self-contained event (or subject) to another, but simultaneously, and this is why the real drama of this spectacle is inseparable from the scene it is constantly setting and unsettling, locating and dislocating.

25. In psychoanalytical terms, Wotan's refusal of alterity is tantamount to what Freud calls "disavowal" (*Verleugnung*) and what Lacan has described as "forclusion." Rather than merely supplanting one representation by another, as is the case in repression, disavowal entails the effort to foreclose the representation as such, rejecting its status as signifier and thereby implicitly redefining it as "reality." Walhalla itself would be the most symptomatic manifestation of such foreclosure, in the double sense of the word. Intended to provide a perfectly secure and self-enclosed space from which Wotan can pursue his conquests with impunity and in which he can conserve his property (family and heroes), Walhalla is also the object of foreclosure on the part of the Giants. Wotan can afford neither to repay them nor even—and above all—to acknowledge his indebtedness to them. What is of interest, of course, is not merely to confirm what is more or less obvious—the paranoic aspect of the *Ring*, but rather to understand just why and how such paranoia should be able to enthrall a largely nonpsychotic audience. And it is here that the notion of *narcissism*, with the repudiation of alterity it entails, can help to establish a link between the more familiar, "neurotic" processes by which identity is established and maintained, and their more psychotic manifestations.

26. In this respect, Wotan recalls Freud's remark about the narcissism of "His Majesty, the Baby"; the desire for power is in inverse proportion to the extent of dependence.

27. In one respect, Loge could be compared to a psychoanalyst without a therapeutic goal: his game is simply to allow "resistances" to play themselves out, without worrying about "working them through."

28. R. Wagner, "Das Bühnenweihfestpielhaus zu Bayreuth," in *Dichtungen und Schriften*, 10: 37.

29. Ibid.

30. The passion with which he condemns "the impudent advance of the stage into the orchestra" suggests that he was not insensitive to the seductive force of such "advances."

Monteverdi's 'L'Orfeo'

1. Richard Alewyn, *Das grosse Welttheater* (Reinbeck: Rowohlt, 1959), 9.

2. [In "Bourgeois Opera," which appears in its first English translation in this volume, Adorno

describes *L'Orfeo* as "the first authentic opera."
—*Trans.*]

3. English translation from the libretto accompanying the Harnoncourt recording of the opera. See Claudio Monteverdi and Alessandro Striggio, *L'Orfeo*, cond. Nikolaus Harnoncourt, Capella Antiqua Concentus Musicus Wien. Telefunken, 1969. The text of the libretto accompanying the recording is trilingual: Italian, German, English.

4. See Norbert Elias, *The Court Society*, trans. Edmund Jephcott (Oxford: Blackwell, 1983); Rudolf Zur Lippe, *Naturbeherrschung am Menschen* (Frankfurt am Main: Suhrkamp, 1974); Theweleit, *Male Fantasies*, vol. 1, trans. Stephan Conway with Erica Carter and Chris Turner (Minneapolis: University of Minnesota Press, 1987), 315–31.

5. [This Zurich production of Monteverdi/Striggio's *L'Orfeo* was directed by Ponelle and conducted by Nikolaus Harnoncourt for television broadcast on German television in December 1975. It has since been released on videotape (Unitel ORF, Wien-Film-Gesellschaft in 1978; distributed in the U.S. by HRE Recordings, Kew Gardens, N.Y.); more recently, the production has been released on laserdisc (London: 071 203-1).—*Trans.*]

6. Aristaeus, who chases Eurydice through the fields, is a son of Apollo. In this triangle, the one who is more powerful—the god with the lyre (Apollo)—takes away the wife of the half-god with the lyre (Orpheus). She is an invention of Vergil. Vergil (who writes his *Georgics* in honor of the Emperor Augustus) introduces Aristaeus to represent the Roman Empire's victory over Antony and Cleopatra. Here, "Orpheus" and "Eurydice" are Antony and Cleopatra; Aristaeus, who pursues Eurydice, is Octavian/Caesar/Augustus himself. The "serpent" that bites Eurydice/Cleopatra in the "heel" does so at the sea battle of Actium. Vergil is the only author who has Eurydice die not simply from a serpent (*serpens*) but from a sea serpent. The serpent that the Romans ultimately forced upon Cleopatra is well known (albeit no suicide, but Roman orders). Ovid rejected Vergil's figure of the Emperor/

Apollo's son, who doesn't appear in his version; he had other things in mind. Nor does Aristaeus appear elsewhere in the Roman authors. He was specially made for Augustus. Ovid's version prevails. I do not know why Poliziano goes back to Vergil in his *Favola di Orfeo* (1471), written for the Mantuan court. In any case, he starts out with Aristaeus (probably in order to give his piece some sting against the "wild and uncontrolled" element mentioned in the Prelude). The absence of Aristaeus in the Striggio/Monteverdi version shows that it is based on Ovid rather than on Poliziano.

7. [Earlier in the book from which this essay is excerpted, Theweleit examines Elias Canetti's *Crowds and Power* in order to explore the role of the survivor, which he variously labels the "S" pole, function, or position. For Canetti's argument, see the chapter entitled "The Survivor," in *Crowds and Power*, trans. Carol Stewart (New York: Viking, 1962), 227–78; for Theweleit's discussion of Canetti's position, see the section "Überleben und Aufschreiben," in *Buch der Könige*, vol. 1, *Orpheus und Eurydike* (Frankfurt am Main: Stroemfeld/Roter Stern, 1988), 204–13. —*Trans.*]

8. [The notion plays on a German saying: "Sohn macht die Faxen, aber Vater die Gesetze."—*Trans.*]

9. [The German term *Schattenreich* translates literally as "realm of shadows"—which underscores her sense of "losing the sun."—*Trans.*]

10. [Emphasis added by the author.—*Trans.*]

11. [English in the original.—*Trans.*]

12. [Emphasis added by the author.—*Trans.*]

13. Edgar Wind, "Orpheus in Praise of Blind Love," in *Pagan Mysteries in the Renaissance* (New Haven, Conn.: Yale University Press, 1958), 57–78. [Hereafter, references to this work will appear in parentheses in the text.—*Trans.*]

14. Erwin Panofsky, *Studies in Iconology* (New York: Harper & Row, 1939).

15. There is an extensive discussion of "blind" and "not-blind" Amor in Panofsky's *Studies in Iconology*. See "Blind Cupid" in *Studies in Iconology*, 95–128. In incessantly seeking "to see" the woman, Monteverdi's Orpheus violates the form

of "the highest love"—of the divine principle of loving. In this case he in fact wants her sexually . . . he wants to see her . . . the sparkle of her eyes . . . but won't let go of his lyre . . . sings his love songs to his lyre . . . it is as if he is violating both—heavenly as well as worldly love . . . his love flows wholly into his instrument. In this way, he is the singer neither of "blind" nor of "seeing" Amor . . . instead, he is one who loves his self-extension in his gadget . . . his amplifier . . . (drugged for love).

16. According to Edgar Wind, there are no unambiguous gods in the Orphic system of the Renaissance; they are always multifaceted, multi-functional, mixed gods (just as later in psycho-analysis disentangled emotions are seen as destructive and compound emotions are seen as differentiated). See Wind, 161–63. Here Orpheus is busy disentangling.

17. [A member of the reed organ family of instruments. According to the *Oxford Companion to Music*, the regal was a tiny portable one-manual organ with reed pipes whch came into use in the fifteenth century and remained popular through the sixteenth and into the seventeenth. —*Trans.*]

18. [The term "Old Amor" appears in English in the original.—*Trans.*]

19. When someone claims that a work is based on Ovid, it means that the work is based on one of the various (Christianized or Neoplatonized) forms of Ovid then in circulation. This had already begun in the third and fourth centuries. For Orpheus as "*Logos*-carrier" symbolizing Christ, see Gabriele Brackling-Gersuny, *Orpheus, der Logos-Träger: Eine Untersuchung zum Nachleben des antiken Mythos in der französischen Literatur des 16. Jahrhunderts*, Freiburger Schriften zur romanischen Philologie, 13 (Munich: Fink, 1975). On Orpheus as a Christian-pagan "King" of redemption through art, see John Block Friedman, *Orpheus in the Middle Ages* (Cambridge, Mass.: Harvard University Press, 1970). For seventeenth-century Jesuit selection and distribution, see Ann Moss, *Ovid in Renaissance France: A Survey of Latin Editions of Ovid and Commentaries Printed in France Before 1600* (London: Warburg

Institute, University of London, 1982). In Italy in the sixteenth century, commentaries on Ovid outnumbered those on Vergil. As for France, Moss writes that "Ovid's fabulous world of erotic fantasy and changing forms" experienced a peak of publication between 1550 and 1560. Martin Langbein suggests that the Italians and French crooned Orpheus-Ovid fantasies to themselves and each other at will, just like the English and Americans with Bob Dylan's songs in 1965—something binding across the oceans; Maria de' Medici as "Eurydice." Indeed, to send a surviving Eurydice to France as the wife of the king was thus a bit of antiquitarian-Jesuit late-Renaissance pop culture. "Queen Mary, she's my friend," sings Bob Dylan ("Just Like a Woman"). "She wears an Egyptian ring, / It sparkles before she speaks"— Cleopatra's ring is on the finger of the woman he loves and "She's got everything she needs / She's an artist, she don't look back!" ("She Belongs to Me") . . . this doesn't mean she's not interested in the past, it means she doesn't turn around (on the steps), walking in front of him. It all belongs to him. (It has often occurred to me that the Americans' use of antiquity and of "European History" is very similar to the Renaissance use of antiquity.)

20. [For an explanation of this abbreviation, see note 7 above.—*Trans.*]

21. [Emphasis added by the author.—*Trans.*]

22. Marshall McLuhan, *Understanding Media: The Extensions of Man* (New York: McGraw Hill, 1964).

23. "In 1839 Johannes Müller, the 'great Rheinland physiologist' and Goethe's personal conversation partner, had removed a number of larynxes from corpses—whose acquisition usually involved quite an adventure—in order to study the concrete circumstances of the production of specific vocal sounds. As Müller blew into one larynx, it sounded 'like a county-fair whistle with a rubber membrane.'" (See Johannes Müller, "Über die Kompensation der physischen Kräfte am menschlichen Stimmorgan" (Koblenz, 1839), cited in Wolfgang Scherer, "Klaviaturen, Visible Speech und Phonographie," *Diskursanalysen 1: Medien* (Wiesbaden: n.p., 1986), 49. Six hundred years

earlier, the Hohenstaufen Emperor Frederick II had made similar use of his knowledge of the origin of sound. In his pamphlet "On the Art of Hunting with Birds," there is a report on the use of the body parts of birds in order to produce mating calls. The breast-cage of dead cranes—with the lung and larynx attached—was surgically removed. The lung was inflated; if one allowed the air to escape through the larynx, the dead bird cried its crane call. The first *machine* to reproduce technically the voice of a bird was built from the bird itself.

24. Samuel Beckett's first poem is called "Echo's Bones." Here too we find a voice that is inflamed by the remains of transformed women. (Thus the reproductive devices, the recording devices are women before they are machines.)

25. "La mémoire et le phonographe," *Revue philosophique de le France et de l'étranger* 5: 319–22. Translated into German as "Gedächtnis und Phonograph" (1880) in Friedrich Kittler, *Grammophon, Film, Typewriter* (Berlin: Brinkmann & Bose, 1986), 52.

26. "Without a doubt, this game with the echo certainly offered a most appropriate opportunity for musical games," writes Silke Leopold, blinded by the realization that the "echo" was also a literary topos of pastoral literature of the time. For her, "Orpheus' echo scene is part of a long tradition stemming from the pastoral drama and leading into opera. The game with the reverberation in which the scenery becomes an active part of the action, fits perfectly into the conception of that dream-like world. For Echo was an Arcadian nymph and had withered into a disembodied voice out of pain over a scorned love. Out of the simple pleasure in echoes, poetry soon developed a game of question and answer." See Silke Leopold, *Claudio Monteverdi und seine Zeit* (Laaber: Laaber, 1982), 123. Leopold's book recently appeared in English translation. See *Monteverdi: Music in Transition*, trans. Anne Smith (New York: Oxford University Press, 1991). Strange, how the formulaic recognition of a "tradition" immediately turns into the characteristic blindness of scholarship in the humanities, which claims that there is nothing here, nothing but rote musical exercises—. Monteverdi veers away from the echo exercise . . . damns the echo . . . scorns it as inadequate . . . he wants to have the "whole lament" recorded . . . that is to say, one cannot see a relationship to the "nymph Echo" . . . or an *exit* from Narcissus' stupor through recording. One cannot see this, if one thinks that the mere recognition of a "tradition" already constitutes a recognition.

27. In the Zurich production, Ponelle has the court prince Vincenzo Gonzaga appear as Apollo.

28. [Italian retained from the original.—*Trans.*]

29. Now we also know why as early as Act I the stars are called "the many eyes of heaven."

30. [Abbreviations retained from the original.—*Trans.*]

"The Wound is Healed"

1. We follow here Ivan Nagel's path-breaking study of Mozart's operas *Autonomy and Mercy*, trans. Marion Faber and Ivan Nagel (Cambridge, Mass.: Harvard University Press, 1991).

2. As to this symbolic exchange, see Mladen Dolar, "Filozofija v operi," *Razpol* 7 (Ljubljana, 1992); the present text owes a lot of instigations to Dolar's essay.

3. Such a reading of the Orpheus myth is proposed by Klaus Theweleit in his essay "Monte-verdi's *L'Orfeo*: The Technology of Reconstruction," in this volume.

4. The very words of this aria attest to its aim of eliciting an answer of the real: "O Dio, rispondi! [O God, answer!]."

5. On the relationship between the two versions of Orpheus, see Chapter 2 of Joseph Kerman's *Opera as Drama* (Berkeley: University of California Press, 1988).

6. The standard "deconstructionist" version of

Don Giovanni is that of a subject "not bound by words," i.e., systematically violating the commitments imposed on him by the performative (illocutionary) dimension of his speech (cf., for example, Shoshana Felman, *Le scandale du corps parlant* [Paris: Seuil, 1978]). However, its reverse is that Don Giovanni complies with the rules of etiquette even after it becomes obvious that, by way of assuming a symbolic commitment, he got more than he asked for. Don Giovanni's dinner invitation to the statue in the graveyard, for example, was undoubtedly meant as an empty gesture, as a blasphemous act of defiance. Yet when "the real answers," when the dead follows the invitation and actually appears at Don Giovanni's home as the Stone Guest, Don Giovanni, in spite of his visible astonishment, *keeps to the form* and asks the guest to take his place at the table.

7. Ivan Nagel, *Autonomy and Mercy*, 26. This codependence of the subject's autonomy and the Other's grace is further exemplified by the well-known paradox of predestination: the very belief that everything is decided in advance by God's inscrutable grace, far more than the Catholic conviction that our deliverance depends on our good deeds, charges the subject with incessant frenetic activity. Cf. Chapter 6 of Slavoj Žižek, *The Sublime Object of Ideology* (London: Verso Books, 1989).

8. See Jon Elster, *Sour Grapes* (Cambridge, Eng.: Cambridge University Press, 1982).

9. See Claude Lefort, *Democracy and Political Theory* (Minneapolis: University of Minnesota Press, 1988).

10. As we shall see later, the ultimate proof of the constitutive character of the dependence on the Other is precisely so-called totalitarianism: in its philosophical foundation, "totalitarianism" designates an attempt on the part of the subject to surmount this dependence by taking upon himself the performative act of grace. Yet the price to be paid for it is the subject's perverse self-objectivization, i.e., his transmutation into the object-instrument of the Other's inscrutable Will.

11. G. W. F. Hegel, *Phenomenology of Spirit* (Oxford: Oxford University Press, 1977), 476.

12. This simultaneity of positioning and withholding finds perhaps its purest expression in Kant's theory of the Beautiful with its four consecutive crossings-out of what was first posited as the fundamental feature: finality *without* end, etc.

13. Jacob Rogozinski (in "Kant et le régicide," *Rue Descartes* 4 [Paris: Albin Michel, 1992], 99–120) pointed out how, in Kant's political philosophy, this simultaneity of positioning and withholding the object assumes the form of the "antinomy of political reason": on the one hand, power belongs to the People (the totality of its subjects), nobody is allowed to appropriate it, any pretender to the place of power (the king, for example) is by definition a tyrant; on the other hand, every attempt, on the part of the People, to assert itself immediately as the actual, positively given sovereign necessarily reverts into its opposite and ends in the radical Evil of Terror. This is the reason for Kant's ambiguous views on the French Revolution, simultaneously an object of sublime enthusiasm (the affirmation of the sovereignty of the People as the sole legitimate bearer of power) and the point of unthinkable, diabolical Evil (the Jacobin reign of terror).

14. See Bernard Baas, "Le désir pur," in *Ornicar?* 43 (Paris: Navarin, 1987).

15. This mediating role of *Fidelio* can be established even at the biographical level. As is well known, it was the profound impression made on the young Wagner by the great soprano Wilhelmine Schröder-Devrient in the role of Beethoven's Fidelio which inspired him to become a composer for the theater. The role of Senta in the *Dutchman* was written expressly for Schröder-Devrient.

16. It is safe to surmise that what takes place behind the fallen curtain, in this intermediate time between the duet "Namenlose Freude [Nameless joy]" and the finale, filled out by the orchestral music, is the "Big Bang", the long overdue sexual act between Florestan and Leonora. With reference to the dialectical tension

between private and public, *Fidelio* marks the utopian moment when the affirmation of the conjugal couple's "private" love possesses the weight of the public act of asserting one's allegiance to political freedom.

17. Theodor Adorno, *In Search of Wagner* (London: Verso Books, 1991), 88. Let us bear in mind that a spectral fantasy is at work again at the very end of *Lohengrin* when Elsa's allegedly dead brother appears as an "answer of the real" to Lohengrin's fervent prayer.

18. Do we not encounter this logic of the spectral fantasy already in *Fidelio*, in the famous aria of Florestan which opens up Act II, where Leonora emerges as Florestan's vision? Is therefore her later emergence "in reality" not again a kind of "answer of the real" to his spectral desire? The place of the spectral fantasy par excellence in Wagner, of course, is the locus of incestuous enjoyment: from Venusberg in *Tannhäuser* to Klingsor's Flower Garden in *Parsifal*: in both cases, its spell is broken, the place disintegrates, the moment the (male) hero "purifies his desire" and gains distance from it.

19. Quoted from Robert Donington, *Wagner's 'Ring' and Its Symbols* (London: Faber & Faber, 1990), 265.

20. In *Tannhäuser*, for example, the woman is split into self-sacrificing redemptress (Elisabeth) and pernicious seductress (Venus), the cause of the hero's damnation; the truth concealed here is that they are ultimately one and the same, since "the wound is healed only by the spear that smote you" (this truth is finally realized in *Parsifal*, which reunites both aspects in Kundry). *Lohengrin*, on the other hand, brings about the opposite to the subject condemned to eternal suffering: the pure object-instrument of the Other's will, i.e., the tool of God's intervention in the world.

21. A desire for death ("Lasciate mi morir") is of course at work in the subject's entreaty from the very beginning, yet prior to Wagner, it follows the simple logic of despair at life's calamities ("better to die than to endure this misery"), whereas the Wagnerian subject already dwells in the domain "between the two deaths."

22. Quoted in Lucy Beckett, *Parsifal* (Cam-

bridge, Eng.: Cambridge University Press, 1981), 119.

23. Klingsor's further essential feature is his self-castration—the proof of his being unable to dominate the sexual urge. This violent abnegation of one's sexuality confirms Schelling's thesis according to which the true, demonic Evil is far more "spiritual," hostile to sensuality, than the Good: Klingsor's spiritual domination over Kundry, his insensibility to her charms, is the very proof of his ultimate evilness.

24. There are two exceptions to this (Parsifal's killing of the swan; his slaying of the knights who guard Klingsor's castle), yet, significantly, both take place offstage, and we see only the effects (the dead swan who falls on the stage; Klingsor's description of the battle).

25. It is at this precise moment that Parsifal becomes aware of the innocent beauty of nature absolved from sin (the "magic of Good Friday"): this "innocent" nature is by no means simply nature "as such," "in itself"—it appears as "innocent" only when the subject assumes the appropriate attitude toward it. Or, to put it even more pointedly: nature becomes innocent only through Parsifal's assuming the symbolic mandate of the King. Far from registering the subject's "inner purification" enabling him finally to perceive nature in its innocence, Parsifal's performative act absolves nature itself from sin.

26. Ernest Newman, *Wagner Nights* (London: Bodley Head, 1988), 221.

27. Ellipses in original.

28. Jacques Lacan, *The Four Fundamental Concepts of Psycho-Analysis* (New York: Norton, 1979), 197–98.

29. It is precisely this physical, tangible impact of "lamella" which gets lost in *Aliens* II, which is why this sequel is infinitely inferior to *Alien*.

30. As a general introduction to Wagner's *Parsifal*, see Lucy Beckett, *Parsifal*.

31. Jacques Chailley, *Parsifal de Richard Wagner. Opéra initiatique* (Paris: Editions Buchet/Chastel, 1986), 44–45.

32. Sigmund Freud, *Introductory Lectures on Psychoanalysis* (Harmondsworth: Penguin Books, 1975), 300–301.

33. This myth of the curious woman asking the forbidden question (or, according to the Bluebeard myth, entering the only forbidden room in the house—cf. its different versions up to Hitchcock's *Notorious* and Fritz Lang's *Secret Beyond the Door*) is usually interpreted as the woman's readiness to confront the secret of her own (feminine) sexuality: *Pandora's Box* ultimately stands for female genitals. Perhaps it would be more productive to reverse the perspective by conceiving the mystery which has to remain hidden as the impotence, the imposture, of the Master: the true "secret beyond the (forbidden) door" is that the phallus is a semblance—not only woman, but man himself is also already "castrated." It is almost superfluous to point out the key role of the figure of the humiliated master in Wagner. Suffice it to mention Alberich from *Der Ring des Nibelungen* (not only Alberich's curse after he is forced to cede the ring to Wotan, but even prior to it his utter humiliation when his slaves, the Nibelungs, see him as the helpless prisoner of gods to whom he is forced to deliver all his gold).

34. When Lacan says that the "secret of psychoanalysis" consists in the fact that "there is no sexual act, whereas there is sexuality," the act is to be conceived precisely as the performative assumption, by the subject, of his symbolic mandate. Consider the passage in *Hamlet*, where the moment when finally—too late—Hamlet is able to act is signaled by his expression "I, Hamlet the Dane": this is what is not possible in the order of sexuality, as soon as the man proclaims his mandate, saying, "I, . . . [Lohengrin, Batman, Superman]," he excludes himself from the domain of sexuality.

35. The first thing that strikes the eye here, of course, is how this opposition coincides with sexual difference: in *Lohengrin* the woman asks the forbidden question, whereas in *Parsifal* the man abstains from asking the required question.

36. According to Lacan, the symptom always includes its addressee (every symptom that the analysand produces during his/her analysis includes the transferential relationship to the analyst as the subject supposed to "know," that is to

say: to detain its meaning). This is what Parsifal fails to grasp when he witnesses the strange Grail ritual: the fact that *this ritual is staged for his gaze*, that *he is its addressee* (as in Kafka's *Trial* where the man from the country fails to see how the door of the Law is meant for him only).

37. It is here that the insufficiency of the Jungian interpretation which centers on Parsifal's "inner development" becomes manifest: by conceiving Parsifal's ability to ask the required question as the sign of his spiritual maturity (the capacity of compassion for the other's suffering), this approach fails to take notice of the true enigma which concerns not Parsifal but the other side, the Grail community: how can the simple act of asking a question possess the tremendous healing power of restoring the health of the King and thereby of the entire community held together by the King's body? The reading of *Parsifal* as an allegorical staging of the hero's "inner journey" totally misses the crucial point that Parsifal functions as an "empty integer" without depth, without "psychology": the overlap of innocence and unheard-of monstrosity—not really a "person" at all but rather a kind of logical operator which renders possible the healing of the community. The entire "psychology" is on the side of Amfortas and Kundry, these two suffering souls who wander in the domain "between the two deaths."

38. *Lohengrin*, for example, would remain a standard romantic opera, if it were not for the "psychological" intricacies of Act II.

39. Jacques Lacan, "Logical Time and the Assertion of Anticipated Certainty," *Newsletter of the Freudian Field* 2, no. 2 (Columbia: University of Missouri, 1988).

40. This change also accounts for leaving out the display of the bleeding sword: this display again presupposes the big Other as its addressee.

41. This difference between the refusal of the woman in *The Magic Flute* and in *Parsifal* can be pinned down in a very precise way. In Act II of *Parsifal*, Kundry at first manipulates—she tries to seduce Parsifal by reminding him of his guilt toward his mother, who died of grief after he left her, and then offers her love as simultaneously

maternal and sexual ("a last token of a mother's blessing, the first kiss of love"). After Parsifal's refusal, however, her manipulative seduction changes into true love's desperate attempt to reach the partner—it is only now that she starts really to appreciate him and desperately looks to him for a support that would enable her to escape her damnation. At the level of *The Magic Flute*, this would suffice: Parsifal would now be allowed to accept Kundry's "mature" love which has integrated the loss, i.e., his initial refusal—yet Parsifal *again* refuses even her "mature" love.

42. Otto Weininger, *Geschlecht und Charakter* (Munich: Matthes & Seitz, 1980). This work was originally published in Vienna in 1903.

43. As to this notion of the "non-all" feminine *jouissance*, see Jacques Lacan, *Le Séminaire, livre XX: Encore* (Paris: Seuil, 1975); the two key chapters are translated in *Feminine Sexuality: Jacques Lacan and the école freudienne*, ed. Juliet Mitchell and Jacqueline Rose, trans. Jacqueline Rose (New York: Norton, 1982).

44. Frank Wedekind was well aware of this dimension of the figure of Parsifal in his two Lulu-dramas, *Earth Spirit* and *Pandora's Box*, which later served as the basis for Alban Berg's unfinished *Lulu*, the work whose claim to the title "the last opera" is perhaps most fully justified. The parallel drawn by Wedekind is not, as one would expect, between Lulu and Kundry, but between Lulu and Parsifal. This scandalous equation, worthy of the Hegelian infinite judgment "Spirit is a bone," between Parsifal's elevated spirituality and Lulu's total apathy in which the ultimate Evil coincides with irresponsible childish innocence without any traces of hysteria, can be detected in the scene where Lulu answers the questions of the painter Schwarz concerning "higher spiritual matters" (God, soul, love) with a six-time "Ich weiss es nicht" ("I don't know"), an obvious allusion to the scene in *Parsifal* where Parsifal also answers repeatedly with "Das weiss ich nicht" when Gurnemanz questions him about killing the sacred swan. See Constantin Floros, "Studien zur 'Parsifal'-Rezeption," in *Musik-Konzepte* 25: Richard Wagner *Parsifal* (Munich: edition text + kritik, 1982), 53–57.

45. This shrinking back also accounts for the above-mentioned exceptional status of *Parsifal* among Wagner's operas: the sudden reversal into fairytale bliss and, accompanying it, the initiatory dimension. The shift occurs at the precise moment when the inherent logic of development would bring about the figure of the non-hystericized woman, i.e., of the woman beyond phallic enjoyment. Upon approaching this borderline, Wagner "changes the register."

46. This point was already made by Michel Chion in his *La voix au cinéma* (Paris: Cahiers du Cinéma, 1982).

47. Unfortunately, Syberberg himself falls prey to eclectic confusion and gives way to the ideology of hermaphroditism, which takes the edge off his subversive gesture: at the opera's end, following the final reconciliation, both Parsifals (male and female) are brought *face to face*, looking into each other's eyes, and thus constitute a complementary, harmonious couple. This, however, is precisely what *never can happen*: for structural reasons, the subject can never confront face to face its own objective surplus correlative, since its very existence qua $ hinges upon the object's occultation (in topological terms, $ is the object's reverse, $ and *a* are on opposite sides of the Möbius band).

48. Let us not forget that in *Fidelio* we also come upon the disguise which trespasses sexual difference: in order to be able to serve as "Fidelio," the jailer's assistant, Leonora dresses up as a man.

49. Claude Lefort, *Democracy and Political Theory*.

50. Michael Tanner, "The Total Work of Art," in *The Wagner Companion*, ed. P. Burbidge and R. Suton (London: Faber & Faber, 1979), 215.

51. In other words, nature is dying (cf. the "ecological" undertones of the third act with the desolate landscape around Monsalvat) because of the King's wound, because of this surplus of indestructible life which perturbs the "normal" circuit of generation and dissolution.

52. Insofar as the traditional authority is Oedipal, i.e., the authority of the dead father who reigns as his Name, Parsifal can be conceived as a

case of anti-Oedipus. In his "De Chrétien de Troyes à Richard Wagner" (*L'Avant-Scène Opéra 38–39: Parsifal* [Paris, 1982], 8–15), Claude Lévi-Strauss proposes a detailed structural analysis of the opposition of Parsifal and the Oedipus myth: the "Oedipal" element in *Parsifal* is the antipode to the Grail temple, Klingsor's magic castle (the place of potential incest under the rule of the castrated father figure).

53. As to this *voix acousmatique*, see Michel Chion, *La voix au cinéma*.

54. However, if one is not to miss the point altogether, one has to conceive the notion of ritual in *Parsifal* in an appropriately broad way which exceeds by far the ritualistic enactment of the sacred enjoyment (the Grail's disclosure): the very failure to perform the ritual properly is part of the ritual. Amfortas' lamentation, for example, is by no means a spontaneous outburst of an unbearable suffering, but a thoroughly *ritualized*, "formalized" performance—the proof of its "non-psychological" character is the finale of Act I. After Titurel's super-ego voice repeats the command "Disclose the Grail!" the unbearable pain miraculously passes and Amfortas is able to perform the required motions with no trouble at all. Far from being an exception, this reflective shift from the failed ritual to the ritualistic performance of a failure offers the key to the very notion of the ritual: "ritual" is originally, constitutively, the formalized repetition of a failure.

55. Ivan Nagel, *Autonomy and Mercy*, 147–48.

56. In this respect, Kant's God therefore *does* act like Descartes' Evil Spirit: he does deceive the human subject intentionally, i.e., in order to render possible his moral activity.

57. On another level, Martin Scorsese's *Last Temptation of Christ* proposes the same thesis: Jesus himself ordered Judas to betray him, so that he was able to fulfill his destiny as the Savior. Judas was thus a kind of forerunner of the Stalinist traitor who commits the supreme crime against the Cause in the interest of the Cause. For a reading of it, see Chapter 3 of Slavoj Žižek, *The Sublime Object of Ideology*.

World-Breath

1. For a systematic development of this argument, see Rudolf Arnheim, *Kritiken und Aufsätze zum Film*, ed. H. H. Dieterichs (Munich: Hanser, 1977), 27.

2. "The Artwork of the Future," *Richard Wagner's Prose Works*, trans. W. A. Ellis, 8 vols. (London: Routledge & Kegan Paul, 1899; New York: Broude Brothers, 1966), 1:67–213.

3. On the categories of classical aesthetics as rewritings of a new and perfect alphabetization, see my *Aufschreibesysteme 1800/1900* (Munich: Fink, 1985), 115–36; English translation: *Discourse Networks*, trans. Michael Metteer with Chris Cullens (Stanford, Calif.: Stanford University Press, 1990). On inherited arts becoming obsolete, see Nietzsche's "Richard Wagner in Bayreuth," *Unmodern Observations*, gen. ed. William Arrowsmith, intro. and trans. Gary Brown (New Haven, Conn.: Yale University Press, 1990), 227–304: "For if anything at all distinguishes [Wagner's] art from all art of the modern age, it is this: it no longer speaks the language of caste culture, and in general no longer recognizes the difference between cultivated and uncultivated. It thereby stands in opposition to all Renaissance culture which has until now enveloped us moderns in its light and shadow" (299). A century after Nietzsche, we allow ourselves to substitute for some of the terms of his exceedingly precise definition of a modern medium: thus we can replace "Renaissance" with Gutenberg, and "light and shadow" with paper and printer's ink.

4. According to Georg Gustav Wiessner, "In Bayreuth the darkened room was the aim. At the time, this too was a surprising stylistic means. 'The deepest night was created in the audito-

rium, such that one could not even recognize one's neighbor,' writes Wagner's nephew, Clemens Brockhaus, on the occasion of the Emperor's visit to Bayreuth in 1876. 'And out of the depths the wonderful orchestra began!' "(*Richard Wagner der Theaterreformer: Vom Werden des deutschen Nationaltheaters im Geiste des Jahres 1848* [Emstetten: Lechte, 1951], 115). Thus, with even emperors and kings now in darkness—those who had until that point been guaranteed a representative visibility by the architectonics of the old European theater—the new era for art's audience arrived. In 1913, barely four decades later, a cinema in Mannheim employed the following advertising slogan: "Come right on in! We have the darkest cinema in town!" Quoted in Silvio Vietta, *Expressionistische Literatur und Film: Einige Thesen zum wechselseitigen Einfluss ihrer Darstellung und Wirkung*, Mannheimer Berichte 10 (Mannheim: n.p., 1975), 295.

5. According to André Glucksmann, "Behind the theft of the Ring is Wotan's enterprise. Behind the phantasm of capital is the question of power. The gods with long teeth have need of final battles. If Valhalla, power, the Forbidden City, the palace of the Central Committee burn, then everything burns" (*The Master Thinkers*, trans. Brian Pearce [New York: Harper & Row, 1980], 261).

6. Elsewhere, I have described the stereophonic effects to which the producers John Culshaw and Georg Solti were inspired by the scene in *Rheingold* in which Mime wrestles with his invisible brother. See "Der Gott der Ohren," *Das Schwinden der Sinne*, ed. Dietmar Kamper and Christoph Wulf (Frankfurt am Main: n.p., 1984), 145.

7. A statistical analysis concluded that in the *Ring* alone the stage directions offer 220 acoustic and 190 optic data. This already relativizes the study's conclusion that Wagner preferred optical to acoustic data "because the musical treatment does justice to the auditory needs of its own accord." See Karl Gross, "Die Sinnesdaten im *Ring des Nibelungen*: Optisches und Akustisches Material," *Archiv für die gesamte Psychologie* 22 (1912): 401–22.

8. *Siegfried*, trans. William Mann (London: Friends of Covent Garden, 1964), 91; translation modified. [Hereafter, references to this work will appear in parentheses in the text. When appropriate, as in this instance, I have modified the published translation to accord more closely with the original. Hereafter, such modifications will be indicated in parenthetical references by the abbreviation "trans. modified."—*Trans.*]

9. See Wolfgang Scherer, "Klaviaturen, Visible Speech und Phonographie," *Diskursanalysen 1: Medien* (Wiesbaden: n.p., 1986), 37–54.

10. [English retained from the original.—*Trans.*]

11. On the "erotogeneity of breathing," see Jacques Lacan, "The Subversion of the Subject and the Dialectic of Desire in the Freudian Unconscious," *Écrits: A Selection*, trans. Alan Sheridan (New York: Norton, 1977), 292–325. The concept of a partial object voice as it is set up here derives solely from Lacan.

12. Already this symmetry between the two lovers in *Die Walküre* suggests that music-drama as a whole—as is demonstrated here only with reference to *Tristan und Isolde*—could be analyzed as the curve of a single, large breath. The orchestral Prelude begins with the superhuman breath of precisely the storm that leads to Siegmund's breathlessness and powerlessness at the outset of the piece. After Sieglinde has (in song) returned life and breath to the refugee, their mutual love grows to the natural "breath" of "Easter" that virtually orders them to engage in sibling incest. (See also the "Easter," its "resonance," its crescendo, and its feedback through love in *Die Meistersinger* [Wagner, *Musikdramen* {Munich: Deutscher Taschenbuch, 1978}, 422f].) When, on the other hand, Wotan's intervention destroys the possibility of this love, breathlessness and a fainting spell befall Sieglinde. Which is why the third act resumes the triumph of that superhuman storm-breath that is designated as much by the "Hojotoho!" of the Walkyries as by Wotan's "Thunderstorm." *Die Walküre*, trans. William Mann (London: Friends of Covent Garden, 1964), 61–68.

13. *Tristan and Isolde*, libretto, trans. Stewart Robb (New York: Dutton, 1965). Quotations in

text, 107, trans. modified; 139. [Hereafter, references to this work will appear in parentheses in the text.—*Trans.*]

14. [English retained from the original.—*Trans.*]

15. *Götterdämmerung,* trans. William Mann (London: Friends of Covent Garden, 1964), 44. [Hereafter, references to this work will appear in parentheses in the text.—*Trans.*]

16. *The Flying Dutchman,* trans. David Pountney, Opera Guide 12 (New York: Riverrun Press, 1982), 58, 65.

17. *Lohengrin,* trans. Lionel Salter, libretto accompanying a phonograph recording of the opera, cond. Rafael Kubelik, Bavarian Radio Symphony Orchestra (Deutsche Grammophon Gesellschaft 2713 005, 1971), 8–9.

18. Wagner, *Parsifal,* trans. Andrew Porter, Opera Guide 34 (New York: Riverrun Press, 1986), 101. All of Kundry's speaking could be analyzed as a hysterical speech disorder in the technical sense of psychoanalysis, i.e., as a separation of head and body, as the throat runs between them (see Lucien Israël, *Die unerhörte Botschaft der Hysterie* [Munich/Basel, n.p., 1983]). Thus, Gurnemanz too—therapist *avant la lettre*—listens with such concentration to Kundry's "dull groaning," which, as always in Wagner, signals non-death. See *Parsifal,* 118.

19. [English retained from the original.—*Trans.*]

20. See my essay "Der Gott der Ohren," in *Das Schwinden der Sinne.*

21. Jimi Hendrix, *Electric Ladyland,* Polydor LP 2335 204, side A.

22. Compare, for example, Bettina Brentano's "Goethes Briefwechsel mit einem Kinde": "The stars set in a sea of colors, flowers blossomed, they grew into the heights; distant golden shadows shielded them from a higher white light, and thus in this inner world one apparition followed another; in the process, my ears felt a fine, silvery tone, gradually it turned into an echo that grew greater and more powerful the more closely I listened to it; I was happy, for it strengthened me, it strengthened my spirit, to harbor this great tone in my ear." In *Werke,* ed. Gustav Konrad, 5 vols. (Frechen: Bartmann, 1959–61), 2: 51–52.

For Schelling, one would consult the opening of the dialogue "Bruno."

23. For references to all of this, see Wagner, *My Life* (New York: Dodd, Mead, 1911), 361 (on echo), 369–70, 401–2 (feedback), 436, 648–49 (fading). The well-known legend of how Wagner supposedly hit upon the *Rheingold* Prelude in his sleep amounts to an acoustic hallucination (603). In the end, Echo triggers the sibling incest between Siegmund and Sieglinde (see *Die Walküre,* 27).

24. For a detailed analysis of literality or sound in the two versions of *Tristan,* see Norbert W. Bolz, "*Tristan und Isolde*—Richard Wagner als Leser Gottfrieds," *Mittelalter Rezeption: Gesammelte Vorträge des Salzburger Symposions,* ed. J. Kühnel, H.-D. Mück, and U. Müller (Göppingen: Kummerle, 1979), 279–84.

25. Wagner, *Tristan,* score (London: n.p., n.d.), 323, 328. [Hereafter, references to this work will appear in parentheses in the text.—*Trans.*]

26. Letter of 3 March 1860, in *Richard Wagner und Mathilde und Otto Wesendonk: Tagebuchblätter und Briefe,* ed. Julius Kapp (Leipzig: Hesse & Becker, 1915), 293.

27. [Stewart Robb translates *Weltatem* as "World Spirit"; "World-Breath" represents a more literal (if less elegant and less rhythmically compatible) translation of Isolde's and Wagner's neologism.—*Trans.*]

28. An acoustics that—and this would require more precise definition—is strictly opposed to the philosophical phantasm of hearing oneself speak as a substratum of all theorems of consciousness. See Jacques Derrida, *Of Grammatology,* trans. Gayatri Chakravorty Spivak (Baltimore: Johns Hopkins University Press, 1976), 240.

29. This (and not so much so-called intellectual history) would offer a starting point for reading Wagner with Lacan. See Jochen Hörisch, "Wagner mit Homer: Zur Dialektik von Wunsch und Wissen in Wagners Musikdrama," *Der Wunderblock: Zeitschrift für Psychoanalyse* 3 (1979): 20–32.

30. On Siegfried's last words, see also my essay "Forgetting," *Discourse* 3 (1981): 113.

31. Wagner, letter of April 1859, in *Wesendonk*, 185.

32. The exclusion of visuality at the conclusion of *Tristan* is, at the same time, an expurgated phallocentrism. Wagner's draft for the *Tristan* text included five lines with an explicitly phallic meaning: "How it shines, / how it lovingly, / ever stronger, / surrounded by shining stars / rises." In the final composition, the two middle lines with their key words "lovingly" and "ever stronger" were dropped.

33. *Tristan*, libretto, 3; trans. modified.

34. *Das Rheingold*, trans. William Mann (London: Friends of Covent Garden, 1964), 84.

35. Nietzsche, "Richard Wagner in Bayreuth," 289.

36. Ibid.

37. See Werner Wahle, *Richard Wagners szenische Visionen und ihre Ausführung im Bühnenbild: Ein Beitrag zur Problematik des Wagnerstils* (Zeulenroda: B. Sporn, 1937), 93n77. One of Wagner's demands upon his architect Semper was "to invent new scenic visions and their realization." See Wagner, "A Music School for Munich," *Prose Works*, 4: 171–224; quotation on 179.

38. Paul Pretzsch, ed., *Cosima Wagner und Houston Stewart Chamberlain im Briefwechsel 1888 bis 1908* (Leipzig: Reclam, 1914), 146. Adorno's commentary on the passage, namely, that "Nietzsche, in his youthful enthusiasm, failed to recognize the artwork of the future in which we witness the birth of film out of the spirit of music," only shows, all its perspicuity notwithstanding, how Adorno misunderstood Nietzsche's enthusiasms and writings. See *In Search of Wagner*, trans. Rodney Livingstone (London: New Left Books, 1981), 107. The characterization of Attic tragedy as "a bright image projected on a dark wall" is certainly filmic, but appears in *The Birth of Tragedy* (1871). See *The Birth of Tragedy*,

trans. Walter Kaufmann (New York: Random House, 1967), 67.

39. See Wagner, "The Destiny of Opera," *Prose Works*, 5: 127–56.

40. For the history of music, see Paul Bekker, *The Story of the Orchestra* (New York: Norton, 1936); for the military history, see Hansjürgen Usczeck, *Scharnhorst: Theoretiker, Reformer, Patriot* ([East] Berlin: Militärverlag, 1974), 31–35. The historical parallels between music and strategy remain to be drawn. Initially, commands such as Isolde's to the winds or Elsa's to Lohengrin are the clearest evidence.

41. *Siegfried*, 78. [The German original reads: "Wo Wesen sind, wehet dein Atem."—*Trans.*]

42. Gilles Deleuze and Félix Guattari develop this argument in *Mille plateaux: Capitalisme et schizophrénie* (Paris: Minuit, 1980), 338–42. English translation: *A Thousand Plateaus: Capitalism and Schizophrenia*, trans. and foreword, Brian Massumi (Minneapolis: University of Minnesota Press, 1987).

43. Wagner, *Opera and Drama*, in *Prose Works*, 2: 265.

44. [This epilogue was added in 1985.—*Trans.*]

45. [The title of Jünger's wartime diary can be roughly translated as "light rays."—*Trans.*]

46. Ernst Jünger, *Strahlungen*, 2 vols. (Stuttgart: E. Klett, 1963), 2: 159f, 281.

47. See Proust, *A la recherche du temps perdu*, ed. Pierre Clarac and André Ferré (Paris: Gallimard, 1954), 3: 758. On Wagner, Proust, Jünger, and Coppola, see Norbert W. Bolz, "Vorschule der profanen Erleuchtung," in *Walter Benjamin: Profane Erleuchtung und rettende Kritik*, ed. Norbert W. Bolz and Richard Faber, 2d ed. (Würzburg: Königshausen & Neumann, 1985), 219ff. On Proust's description of the air war, consult—yet again—Felix P. Ingold, *Literatur und Aviatik: Europäische Flugdichtung 1909–1927* (Frankfurt am Main: Birkhauser, 1980), 259–61.

Index

Index

Index